"Many factors are propelling the populist wave rolling through political systems around the world. This compelling, erudite, and accessible volume clarifies them in comparative context and sets the stage for urgently needed responses. Drache and Froese provide a passionate and convincing warning of the dangers immediately ahead for all of us. If you only read one book this year on the turbulent politics of our time, this should be it."

— Louis W. Pauly, J. Stefan Dupré Distinguished Professor of Political Economy, Munk School of Global Affairs and Public Policy, University of Toronto

"*Has Populism Won? The War on Liberal Democracy* is brilliantly lucid in its account of the global upsurge of right-wing populism. Here, the fate of liberal democracy is analysed against a gathering storm of powerful right-wing populist movements, all motivated by the politics of grievance, all moving from country to country, continent to continent at the speed of (digital) light, and all bent on undermining, discrediting, and eliminating democratic discourse. In explicit detail and with great lucidity, *Has Populism Won?* explores the many different varieties of contemporary populism, their entanglements, and their likely political trajectories. A must-read for understanding twenty-first century politics."

— Arthur Kroker, Professor Emeritus, University of Victoria

"Daniel Drache and Marc Froese have written an essential primer on modern populist authoritarianism. They unpack its origins, its internal dynamics, and its likely evolution, demonstrating why it poses a mortal threat to liberal democracy. We can't defend the freedoms and institutions we treasure if we don't accurately understand why they're in danger. This book is a vital contribution to that defence."

— Thomas Homer-Dixon, Director of the Cascade Institute, Royal Roads University, Victoria, British Columbia

"A fascinating and necessary look at 'the anti-system vote' around the world and what it means for the future of democracy. Populism, and the Ur-fascism it so often falls into, isn't done with us yet."

— Stephen Marche, author of *The Next Civil War*

HAS POPULISM WON?

THE WAR ON LIBERAL DEMOCRACY

DANIEL DRACHE
MARC D. FROESE

This book is also available as a Global Certified Accessible™ (GCA) ebook. ECW Press's ebooks are screen reader friendly and are built to meet the needs of those who are unable to read standard print due to blindness, low vision, dyslexia, or a physical disability.

Purchase the print edition and receive the ebook free!* For details, go to ecwpress.com/ebook.

Published by ECW Press
665 Gerrard Street East
Toronto, Ontario, Canada M4M 1Y2
416-694-3348 / info@ecwpress.com

Editor for the Press: Susan Renouf
Cover Designer: Jessica Albert

LIBRARY AND ARCHIVES CANADA CATALOGUING IN PUBLICATION

Title: Has populism won? : the war on liberal democracy / Daniel Drache and Marc D. Froese.

Names: Drache, Daniel, 1941- author. | Froese, Marc D., author.

Identifiers: Canadiana (print) 2022022899X | Canadiana (ebook) 20220229007

ISBN 978-1-77041-705-2 (softcover)
ISBN 978-1-78520-56-3 (ePub)
ISBN 978-1-78520-57-0 (PDF)
ISBN 978-1-78520-58-7 (Kindle)

Subjects: LCSH: Populism. | LCSH: World politics—21st century.

Classification: LCC JC423 .D73 2022 | DDC 320.56/62—dc23

This book is funded in part by the Government of Canada. *Ce livre est financé en partie par le gouvernement du Canada.* We acknowledge the support of the Canada Council for the Arts. *Nous remercions le Conseil des arts du Canada de son soutien.* We acknowledge the support of the Ontario Arts Council (OAC), an agency of the Government of Ontario, which last year funded 1,965 individual artists and 1,152 organizations in 197 communities across Ontario for a total of $51.9 million. We acknowledge the support of the Government of Ontario through Ontario Creates.

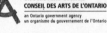

PRINTED AND BOUND IN CANADA

PRINTING: MARQUIS 5 4 3 2 1

CONTENTS

LIST OF FIGURES AND TABLES   VII

INTRODUCTION: A Warning   XI

PART I: The Big Lie   I

Chapter 1: Welcome to the Revolution   3
Chapter 2: The Big Lie   27
Chapter 3: Charismatic Big Men and the *Volk*   55

PART II: The Insurgency   81

Chapter 4: The Sovereignty Project   83
Chapter 5: The Post-Liberal Order   101
Chapter 6: Pandemic Nationalism   118
Chapter 7: Darkness at Noon   139

APPENDIX I: The Anti-System Vote in Thirty-Six Countries,   163
     Including Far-Right Opposition Parties, 2015–2021

APPENDIX II: The Reelection Prospects of a Cross-Section   166
     of Populist Governments and Far-Right
     Opposition Parties

FURTHER READING: Our Top Recommendations   180

ENDNOTES   182

ACKNOWLEDGMENTS   220

INDEX   222

LIST OF FIGURES AND TABLES

FIGURE 1: The Ascendance of Authoritarian Populist Governments Globally, 1990–2018   18

FIGURE 2: The Authoritarians   28

FIGURE 3: The Dangerous Upsurge in Extreme Speech around the World, 1990–2016   39

FIGURE 4: The Archetypes of Populist Leadership   56

FIGURE 5: The Global Vaccine Divide: The Advanced Economies versus "the Rest"   133

APPENDIX I: The Anti-System Vote in Thirty-Six Countries, Including Far-Right Opposition Parties, 2015–2021   163

APPENDIX II: The Reelection Prospects of a Cross-Section of Populist Governments and Far-Right Opposition Parties   166

For Marilyn and Charlotte, and Gina and Arabel,
who have been immensely patient and always encouraging.
Their constant support makes our work possible.

Those who can make you believe absurdities,
can make you commit atrocities.

Voltaire, *Questions sur les miracles*

Only the mob and the elite can be attracted by the momentum of
totalitarianism itself. The masses have to be won by propaganda.

Hannah Arendt, *The Origins of Totalitarianism*

There is no sovereignty in solitude.

Mario Draghi, on becoming Italian prime minister in 2021

INTRODUCTION

A Warning

Tasting Victory

It didn't start with Donald Trump and it certainly won't end with him. But he gave the global populist movement a blast of dark energy and launched it into the popular consciousness of people everywhere. While Trump didn't invent conservative populism, he certainly grabbed onto a rising movement and rode it to electoral victory in 2016. He showed seventy million angry Americans how to win elections by being outrageous with a constant barrage of hate speech and lies designed to divide an already polarized electorate.

Undeniably, we have been here before.[1] When the old order runs out of steam, waiting in the wings of every society are the tarnished stars who crave a turn in the big chair. Today, populism is a worldwide phenomenon, growing, metastasizing, and reaching into every corner of modern politics. Our research shows that authoritarian opposition to world order today is a global movement of grievance and anger and must be understood as coming from many directions at once. There is no one-size-fits-all template for how authoritarian populists win and hold on to power.[2]

A good example to recall is Silvio Berlusconi, an early avatar of the dark arts of hypocrisy and three-time Italian prime minister between 1994 and 2011. He was often ridiculed for his vanity, corruption, sex scandals, and blatantly authoritarian style of leadership. With his larger-than-life personality, he dominated Italian politics even when he was not prime minister.

During his prime, Berlusconi controlled six out of the seven main television channels in Italy. In a country where fewer than 10 percent of people buy newspapers, he maintained an iron grip on Italy's political discourse, shaping his public image as an everyman who climbed the social pyramid on his own, and apologized to nobody for his enormous appetite for wine, women, power, and money. His main supporters, like those of Trump, were working-class people who considered themselves to be apolitical, but who admired his riches, chest thumping, and talent for puncturing the aristocratic pretensions of Italy's upper classes.[3]

So the conventional explanation of populism leaves much to be desired. For one thing, we can't pin all the blame for populism on a few self-interested cynical fat cats. We need to think about populism as the progeny of three forms of political action. Angry voters choose political leaders who paint simple solutions to complex problems. Celebrity-seeking social media activists celebrate voters' anger with images of revenge and score-settling. Opportunistic leaders jump in to stir division, raise the temperature, and profit from all the lies and accusations. After Putin's murderous invasion of Ukraine, will the populist movement continue to gain steam, or will vociferous publics turn against the insurgency now that Putin has shown his true colours as one more megalomaniac with delusions of imperial grandeur?

The Russian invasion of Ukraine drives home the point that global populism is not a singular movement, but rather a broad front of many movements, events, victories, and setbacks. Even when the pro-democracy populist Volodymyr Zelensky defends his country against the worst, Vladimir Putin, we gain little clarity about the future. Win, lose, or stalemate, populism is relentless. Many will turn against Putin, at least in the short term, saying that they admired his traditionalism but oppose his militarism. Then they double down on their own movements, building the new tomorrow for their tribe. There is a political magnetism and psychological appeal to populism that many experts don't understand.

Right at the outset we need to clarify four key concepts: populism, authoritarianism, nationalism, and nativism. We will examine them more closely later, but we should introduce them right now. People often use the terms populism, authoritarianism, nationalism, and nativism interchangably, but they are very different concepts. Populism is a way of speaking about politics that sets up a moral dichotomy and creates a conflict between the "true people," who are honest and good, and the "elite," who are evil and corrupt. Authoritarianism demands obedience to state authority at the expense of freedom. As a form of government it rejects pluralism in favour of centralization around a charismatic leader and hand-picked loyalists. The populist leader is an authoritarian who believes that centralizing his own power requires undermining democracy. The solution he offers is a mix of nationalism and nativism. Nationalism is the love of one's country to the exclusion of others. Nationalists want their country to always win, even if that means others must always lose. Nativism is a fear of foreigners and a belief that ethnicity is part of what makes a country great. The populist system smashers use racism and xenophobia to demand a new social contract based on skin color and cultural domination, protecting the privileges of the plurality at the expense of the rest.

The common denominator among each of these key concepts is the perception that big dogs are gobbling up society's pie, and the honest, hardworking people are getting cheated out of their fair share. And the prescription is always the same: an authoritarian leader promises to save the people from the evil elites and foreigners. The authoritarian bargain is one in which obedience to power will supposedly free the people from the clutches of their enemies.[4]

Academics make careful distinctions between different flavors of populism, but authoritarian leaders do not.[5] The enemies of the people are found among political refugees, corporate managers, foreign oligarchs, domestic media outlets, and even a nation's own political leadership. This big tent approach is at least one of the principal reasons why the big lie, extreme speech, and disdain for foreigners have converged to create a single network of hatred with many national characteristics.

While we discuss many varieties of populism, each is a product of a unique set of circumstances. For example, Brexit is the result of long-festering political resentment. Britain used to be the center of an empire. Now it is not even indispensable to the European Union. Brazil's populist president is a consequence of Brazil's long history of corruption and its earlier dictatorship, not to mention massive poverty and the collapse of an economic supercycle that drove up commodity prices.

The recent victories of India's Narendra Modi were also victories for Hindu fundamentalism, a backlash against the corruption of the Nehru dynasty, and the logical outcome of dozens of broken promises by India's political class. India's corporate and media elite put their money on Modi and dug deep in their pockets to bankroll his win. At a minimum, these diverging narratives tell us this: Insurgencies spring from the populist playbook, but each will survive or fail for reasons unique to its national context. Some movements will die and be replaced by moderate democratic governments; others will surge and change the direction of democracy in their country for many years. Still others will fly beneath our radar and impact the future in unforeseen ways. We are in the thick of it, where authoritarians battle democrats. The fog of war makes it difficult to get our bearings.

The Populist Story: Three Unsolved Puzzles

Three puzzles complicate our understanding of modern populism. The first is the ubiquitous dog whistle. A dog whistle is a form of coded racist messaging that can't be heard by people who are not listening for it. To some it sounds like a slip of the tongue; to others it is a call to arms. When Trump spoke of the Charlottesville riot, saying, "There are very fine people on both sides," his followers knew he was speaking to them. When in a presidential debate he told the Proud Boys to "stand back and stand by," they knew he was ordering them to stand ready to rally for their leader. Racist dog whistles such as these used to be confined to extreme corners of the public sphere. Today they have become a mainstay of retail politics across the globe, from India to Hungary, Turkey, and the Philippines. Racism used to be at the margins of political discourse, but now it has moved decisively into the mainstream as a weapon to be used consistently against pluralism.

The second puzzle is the hyper-individualism of modern identity politics. Activists used to stress that "we are all in this together," because conventional wisdom believed that building a big tent of many different political tribes required cooperation and tolerance. But now the center and the extremes are pitted against each other. In the United Kingdom, the United States, Poland, Hungary, Brazil, India, Turkey, and the Philippines, populists are radicalizing their base by using the courts and legal institutions against the democratic state. When elected to high office, populists are prepared to subvert the law where they can, threatening judges and putting independent courts under their thumb by appointing jurists who are loyal to the leader not the law.[6] They imperil the rule of law where they can't bend it to their own purposes. Donald Trump and Jair Bolsonaro were willing to endanger the national rule of law if the system did not deliver an electoral victory. This is what makes populism today so dangerous. It purposefully tramples the law every time judges and state officials oppose the leader's corruption. Even if we have been here before, this time it's different.

The authoritarian populist movement believes that tolerance is a fool's errand. Their leading lights, such as American alt-right architect of Trumpism Steve Bannon and British Vote Leave campaign chief strategist Dominic Cummings, disdain the rules of parliamentary democracy. They prefer confrontation and brinksmanship in the name of absolute freedom over compromise and cooperative achievement.[7]

The third puzzle concerns the rise of post-truth politics, defined by conspiracy theories and dark predictions in which enemies of the people must be destroyed in the name of freedom. It used to be that motivating voters required the use of narratives and messages that spoke to a promising future. Since 9/11 and the near collapse of the global economy in 2008, in many countries across the globe there is no longer a shared left/right consensus over core values in the spheres that define who we are—be they economic, cultural, or political. The post-truth politician must therefore be a leading figure in the tribe, participating in conspiracy theorizing on social media and weaving a narrative of super-heroic action against the shadowy web of the elite. These are dark narratives about immigrants and minorities meant to drive voters with fear, not attract them with promise. And that is the crux of this final puzzle. How can we maintain democracy when it caters to the basest impulses of society? Most evidence points to a tipping point for liberal democracy burdened by the trifecta of systemic racism, hyper-individualism, and a post-truth social media environment.[8]

All of these factors force us to analyze the manipulative tactics used to create and maintain populist movements around the world. Because they play such a pivotal role in our narrative, we identify the lies, manipulation, hypocrisy, and hate speech that embody authoritarian populism today. These are the divisive tools available to every activist and leader from New Delhi to Warsaw.

In a secret meeting in 2021, Marine Le Pen, the longtime leader of Rassemblement National, the French far-right party, tried to convince Éric Zemmour, her far-right political rival, not to run in the upcoming presidential election. He was stealing her thunder. Zemmour, who is a firebrand personality on CNews ("France's Fox News"), spoke bluntly about the populist playbook: "If you want to win, be radical, even outrageous . . . people expect firmness and conviction, even radicalism."[9] For Zemmour, Le Pen was not radical enough to satisfy the bloodlust of the angry French voter. It is not inconceivable that the authoritarian right could become more extremist and politically powerful in the United States, France, Hungary, Poland, India, and Brazil. There are blinking red lights all over the map that warn us of the global crisis ahead.

Turbulence Ahead

This book is written as a warning about the startling momentum of authoritarian populism's assault on liberal democracy everywhere. To that end, we will show how populist movements around the world operate seemingly independently while building a loose network of like-minded voters, activists, and autocratic leaders with unprecedented impact and reach. The individualistic projects pursued by authoritarians at home such as Orban of Hungary and

Morawiecki of Poland merge with a collective call for more sovereignty. Their ideas need to be closely interrogated because these projects for less democracy and fewer rules have already deeply scarred our admittedly flawed liberal capitalist societies.

Writing the story of the global authoritarian populist movement relies on a broad range of empirical sources and expert analysis. The true believer poses a huge challenge to researchers of all stripes. As political scientists, we cannot only make sense of political behavior by tracking votes or following dollars. We must also pay attention to the narratives that people use to make sense of their world at a time in which so many ordinary people feel swept up into the current of history.[10] The in-depth look at electoral results of populist victories we have developed ourselves. In other places we have relied upon the expertise of the Pew Research Center, the International Monetary Fund, and other non-partisan organizations that analyze political and economic trends. Such a multifaceted story requires that we draw our evidence from many places, from academic experts in the traditional social sciences of history, economics, psychology, and political science, and also from philosophers, novelists, essayists, and civil society activists.

Our research highlights the connection between rising inequality and the mass psychology of resentment that has fueled the populist insurgency to win election after election. Populist voters are angry about the loss of jobs due to hyper-globalization and the decline in social standing as they are pressed by billionaires from above and immigrants from below. Rising levels of economic inequality, corruption, and social polarization are all symptoms of political decay.[11] But the populist leader, like a mob boss, is never part of the solution. He is a symptom of social anxiety; he's part of the problem. The comparison with organized crime is apt because authoritarian populists, just like the Italian Mafia, prey upon the anxious and vulnerable. In Poland, Hungary, and most certainly Brazil, the alpha leader has provided economic support for the poor to shore up his religious and cultural base. In Russia, Putin branded himself as the champion of the people, bankrolled by six oligarchs. They preferred him to the communists, whom they feared would "hang them from the nearest lamppost."[12]

Populism is always two things. On the surface it is a social movement that is organized by angry, alienated voters and controlled by the big men and rich donors. But beneath the memes, and hate speech, and endless posturing, there is a deeper logic at work. It is a timeless way of outmaneuvering dominant political narratives by undermining the political identity of your rivals. To that end, the populist method pits people against each other and divides them into two groups: the "true people" who are good, versus the evil elite.

But is that all there is, a story about scrappy underdogs and sneering fat cats? Hardly. There are three core actors driving modern populism: frustrated people who feel they are losing something, activists who peddle conspiracies and lies, and the opportunistic leaders who stoke grievance for personal gain. When these three come together, the result is broken institutions, the degradation of law, oligarchic leadership, and less democracy. If democracy dies, millions of us will have had a hand in it.

Italian novelist and public intellectual Umberto Eco has argued that modern democratic societies live under a constant threat from populist authoritarianism, whether we acknowledge it or not. He called this potential for democratic backsliding "Ur-Fascism." He located this "ur," or eternal fascist impulse, in political cultures that nurture grievance, in extreme speech that advocates violence, and in wrathful movements sustained by "a beehive of contradictions."[13] This last point is really important. A highly polarized and belligerent group identity is formed in the crucible of misinformation and hammered into shape by the hierarchy of authority.

We intend to make sense of the beehive of modern populism by examining first the big lie and the rising populist threat to democracy, and analyzing the rise of authoritarian movements with a focus on voters, activists, and leaders. Second, we intend to show how the populists have placed the dismantling of the postwar order at the center of their project for more national sovereignty. Sovereignty is a mainstay of the modern world, but populists are intent on weakening human rights and undermining international law around climate collapse, refugees, international security, and trade. They want more sovereignty for their own countries, and less for everyone else. As we will learn, populists have smashed more of the postwar order than most insiders in Washington, London, and New Delhi care to admit. Beyond liberal internationalism lies a different kind of emerging international order that is dangerously state-centric, minimizing multilateral cooperation, and where every country is for itself.

So this is our warning: authoritarianism is radicalizing the true believer, and the populist insurgency is growing more brazen and dangerous. The more extreme the tone of politics inside a growing number of states, the more worried we should be that something is going terribly wrong globally. Will agents of misinformation paralyze our democracies, or will we turn away from the cursed attraction of simple answers to wicked problems? There is no immediate answer to how our societies should address these primal challenges. But they are going to be with us for the next decade. It is going to be a dangerous time as extreme elements in leading states fight for influence and tear at the global order that constrains their darkest desires. We have entered a long transition following the end of the American Century. We hope this book will be valuable for everyone who has been watching the populist insurgency with growing anxiety. Defending democracy starts with unmasking those who would destroy it.

Daniel Drache and Marc D. Froese
May 2022

PART I
THE BIG LIE

CHAPTER 1

Welcome to the Revolution

Populist Agency

When Arthur Miller's *Death of a Salesman* opened on Broadway in 1949, the titular salesman, Willy Loman, was instantly recognizable as the archetypal everyman of the postwar period. The character was so appealing to the theater-going public because he represented the ordinary individual beaten down by a capitalist system that treated him like an expendable cog in the profit machine. Today, the same is true of Walter White in TV's *Breaking Bad*, another loser at rock bottom.[1] Like Willy Loman, he was bullied and betrayed by the liberal order. He can't catch a break. But where Willy accepted defeat, Walter fought back, taking his piece of the American dream by hook or by crook. Today, the people who have been knocked around won't be denied. If they have to break the system to get what they believe they're owed, then so be it.

The ethos of populist politics is one in which flawed characters have the moxie to beat the system and the drive to win the affection of the rest of us. We weep for Willy and cheer for Walter because we fear the same impersonal economic forces that drove them to such lengths will also steamroll us. Voters cheer for populist leaders because they represent the average person going up against the system, like Sarah Connor in *Terminator* or Frank Castle in *The Punisher*. The goal is to beat the rigged system or die trying, like Bonnie and Clyde. Of course, the fact that all of these tragic figures are brought down by their own flaws tells you a lot about the narcissistic logic of identity politics in which populist strongmen masquerade as competent leaders because appearance matters more than substance and character.

We need to ask one very essential question: If these leaders are so flawed, incapable, and corrupt, how have populist movements convinced so many people to rally around their cause? Populist activists tell a good story about how the system has been brought low by the unscrupulous elite. The populist leader responds by portraying himself as the opposite of those supposedly corrupt leaders. He wears the guise of the everyman, who is reviled by his betters but loved by underdogs everywhere. The thing about a good lie is that it contains a kernel of truth. And this is particularly true of the everyman persona. Most populist leaders are the sort of people who really believe themselves to have the common touch, like India's Narendra Modi or Mexico's Andrés Manuel López Obrador, and for the most part they do. Like-minded voters are seduced by their charisma and charm. Those who like them idolize them, and those who dislike them revile them. But there is no such thing as bad publicity. Even hatred has its uses in identity politics.

When Donald Trump descended a golden escalator to announce his candidacy in the Republican presidential primaries in 2015, nobody in America was taking populism very seriously. Populist politicians were most famous for being entertainers. They were clownish and out of their depth, and so many were clearly pursuing political power for all the wrong reasons. Who could take a man like Donald Trump seriously? Certainly not the power brokers at the top of the

Republican Party. For them, Trump was an interloper—good for ratings, but not a serious man. He flew into regional airports aboard his personal Boeing 757, complete with gilded bathroom fixtures and seat buckles, to tell blue-collar Middle Americans that he was one with their struggles. Trump portrayed himself as a scrappy billionaire; the elite laughed, but the voters paid attention. The everyman narrative is a potent device in modern electoral politics, the secret sauce of the insurgency movement.

Other populists use the everyman narrative to disrupt politics as usual. Jair Bolsonaro portrays himself as an ordinary Brazilian who makes his own coffee and doesn't want servants to wait on him hand and foot in the presidential palace. In Ukraine, Volodymyr Zelensky was a comedian and actor who became famous playing an everyman on his hit television show, *Servant of the People*. When Russia invaded Ukraine he became a national hero and wartime president of Churchillian stature. Art imitates life and Zelensky the actor finally became Vasily Petrovych Goloborodko, the ordinary man thrust into extraordinary circumstances that he played on TV.

In India and the Philippines, Narendra Modi and Rodrigo Duterte have successfully adopted stylings of the simple, regular man whose conscience and common sense tells him what his country needs. Each of these men plays the role of the regular guy, the homespun father, the rough-and-ready man willing to roll up his sleeves and get dirty in the cause of radical reform. These are compelling stories that play well in the media, but they are far from the truth.

Here, at the beginning of our story, let's not put all of the agency on the shoulders of the big-chested leaders. They would like to think of themselves as engines of history, but they are nothing without the anger of voters and the energy of activists. True believers are voters who not only watch them on television, but also follow on social media, a world of echo chambers, memes, and misinformation. They work hard to diffuse the narratives devised by high-profile activists. The goal: to "red pill" their friends and neighbors. The red pill refers to the moment in the film *The Matrix* when the main character takes a pill that allows him to experience the world as it really is. In right-wing activist communities, "taking the red pill" refers to the "aha moment" when the contradictions in your world make sense and you realize the wild conspiracies were right all along.

Post-truth activists have invented a narrative in which the world is a dark place of corruption and criminal intent. Their goal is to push voters toward the party of law and order. But they do much more than that. They create a world in which truth is partisan, subjective, and open to constant reinterpretation depending on the needs of the party or movement. In this socially constructed environment of extreme moral relativism, the authoritarian leader is an inveterate opportunist and egoist who takes the anger, energy, and compelling narratives of grievance and reshapes them as agents of political change.[2] He is the only person to lead the people because he perfectly embodies their struggle against the evil elite.

Digging into Nationalism and Nativism

In the popular lexicon, the terms "nationalist" and "nativist" are frequently deployed interchangeably by journalists because they describe a worldview of generalized opposition to the foreigner, the refugee, and the practitioners of a minority religion among us.[3] But we should take a moment to identify their differences.

Nationalists from Bucharest to Mexico City privilege state power as their foremost lens. The national interest and national primacy are of central importance to them. In the academic literature, nationalism is a foundational idea that aims to build the nation bigger, stronger, mightier, and more united and secure. As an ideology and instrument of statecraft, nationalism is usually concerned with the protection of state sovereignty from external threat, and is therefore opposed to any policy or law that reduces the capacity of the state to protect itself and advance its core interests.

More than anything else nationalism has enormous attraction as a philosophy of political action that places the nation first in all things. The national interest, national power, national prestige, and the strength of the state in comparison with other states are the concerns of nationalists.

We need to make a careful distinction between nationalism and patriotism. Patriotism describes my feelings about my country. Most people would describe themselves as patriots, at least on certain holidays, or during the Olympic games when they cheer for their country's athletes. French president Charles de Gaulle captured the essential differences between patriotism and nationalism elegantly: "Patriotism is when love of your own people comes first; nationalism, when hate for people other than your own comes first." Nationalism is a negative image of patriotic love. It is a dislike of other "shithole countries,"[4] a bellicose form of identity, and a competitiveness that places others second.

Singer Bruce Springsteen, whose album *Born in the USA* is one of the highest-selling records ever, is often cited as the cultural figure who best embodies American patriotism. He loves the ideals his country claims to uphold. But he is willing to speak out when he believes that his country does not live up to its own ideals. A patriot strives to make their country better; a nationalist believes their country is the best because everywhere else is worse.

Nationalists don't speak out when their country misses the mark, because for them, it is always "my country, right or wrong," like Boris "Damn the Consequences" Johnson leading Britain out of the EU or supporters of the extreme right French presidential candidate Éric Zemmour, who was convicted of hate speech in January 2022.[5] Certainly, one can be a patriot without being a nationalist. But all nationalists declare themselves as patriots because they conflate love of their home with its supremacy. We will leave you to judge for yourself whether nationalism is really the best way to love your country.

Nativists are nationalists with an ethnocentric understanding of home and country. They believe that nations ought to be understood as homelands, in which (at least in the former European colonies) white settlers are constructed as the rightful inheritors of the space and place. Nativists everywhere have a dysfunctional relationship to their country, in which only *their* connection to the land is legitimate. People of color are understood as foreigners even if they are the original inhabitants, like the Indigenous people of Australia, New Zealand, and the Americas. Nativism in the hands of authoritarian populists like Marjorie Taylor Greene, Georgia's representative for the 14th Congressional District, is even more toxic than nationalism because it argues that the nation is a special place for only one group of people in which culture, blood, and environment come together to create a spiritual bond between people and land. The connection between culture, ethnicity, language, and territory is sacred, as far as nativists are concerned. And their extreme politics leads inevitably to violence and conspiracy, as did the American ultra-conservative John Birch Society in the mid-20th century.[6]

Hungary's populist prime minister Viktor Orbán takes the racist elements of nativism further by arguing that the "native-born" have a privileged connection to the land and to each other that an immigrant can never have. He does not think that there is any historical precedent for the successful integration of immigrants into Hungarian society.[7] A little farther to the east, Putin has taken his nativism into the realm of foreign policy and used it to justify military invasion of neighboring countries. In an essay he published on the Kremlin's website in July 2021, he defended Russia's occupation of Crimea by arguing that Ukraine is unified with Russia by not only bonds of religion and culture, but also by "essentially the same historical and spiritual space."[8] In February 2022 he launched a massive assault from the air, sea, and land to decapitate the government in Kyiv. His final goal: to recreate the Russian empire from which to oversee the decline of the West.

For nativists at the far-right end of the political spectrum, the idea that outsiders cannot understand the mystical connection that binds people and land has important policy implications. If people come as immigrants, they should meekly accept their second-tier status. If they are outside experts or foreign governments, they ought to recognize that they have no standing and no right to criticize the decisions of the native-born. The comingling of blood and soil is particularly worrying for many social scientists today because nativism was the foundation of fascism in Italy and Nazism in Germany in the 1920s.[9]

Weaponizing Populism

Ernesto Laclau, a noted Marxist scholar, has theorized populism as a way of thinking politically about the individual in a hostile world.[10] Populism's most basic political goal is to wrest the nation from the clutches of the elite and restore it to the people, and by doing so provide some meaning for people whose lives have been undermined by the last thirty years of market fundamentalism. Populism is a way of speaking about politics that places resentment and nostalgia at the center of a project. It is also a method for organizing political action to ignite an explosive confrontation between today's true believers and the establishment on a range of issues such as rights for refugees, open borders for trade and investment, equal rights for women, addressing climate collapse, and even wearing masks to prevent spreading COVID-19. We call this menacing global movement a populist post-truth insurgency.

From Manilla to Brasilia, populists deploy ideas of declining national greatness and multicultural swamping for their political agenda. They also offer nationalists and nativists an enemy against which to direct their fury.[11] Of primary importance for the angry populists is their opposition to the governments that presided over the past four decades of growing interdependence, and they locate the authority behind those governments in the urban, educated elites. The putative problems of national decline and multicultural friction can be reduced to easy moralistic generalizations about evil elites who stymy the will of the people. And the populist leaders oblige, providing a constantly growing list of enemies to fuel the fire. Clearly, this phenomenon of populism has many dimensions. It is not one thing but many ways of expressing anger against an array of targets.[12]

Cultural Populism

As an ideal type, cultural populism is the most virulent form of the anti-system virus. In all of the thirty-six countries we studied, cultural populism attacks immigrants and political refugees, some of the most defenseless members of the body politic. (See Appendix One: *The Anti-System Vote in Thirty-Six Countries, Including Far-Right Opposition Parties, 2015–2021*.) It seeks to deny them a seat at the table and to strip them of legal rights. It also uses the shared tropes of racism and xenophobia to argue that the so-called legitimate inhabitants of a nation are swamped and beset by immigrants, ethnic minorities, and the elite, all of whom are framed as criminals acting against the interests of the true people.[13]

Starting in 2015, the Syrian refugee crisis overwhelmed German, Italian, and Greek authorities with hundreds of thousands of political refugees seeking sanctuary. Meanwhile, European countries have steadily shifted to the right on migration. Hungary's Viktor Orbán and Austria's disgraced former chancellor Sebastian Kurz were once on the margins of refugee policy, but their xenophobia is now normalized as mainstream. This is not because they are becoming less extreme, but rather because their brand of extremism is shifting the discourse. Commenting in March 2020 on Greece's decision to temporarily suspend asylum applications, Gerald Knaus, chair of the European Stability Initiative, a nongovernmental organization, said, "This could be the year that the EU's support for the UN Convention on Refugees dies."[14] Cultural populists confront the challenge of refugee migration by pulling up the drawbridge to keep the "undesirables" out and to remind voters that they have a protected position inside the castle.

Cultural populists are resentful and angry about jobs lost to immigrants, privilege eroded by multiculturalism, and influence eroded by globalization. In this sense, resentment is a "poison in the human soul," according to Max Scheler, an early twentieth-century German philosopher.[15] But Jan-Werner Müller, an authority on populism, reminds us that to reduce cultural populism to the quintessence of resentment is to forego an important opportunity to think about the reasons behind the bitterness and anger.[16] There may be a simple and racist basis for cultural populism, but it might also be rooted in hyper-globalization that has been poorly managed by national governments and their institutions. In the twenty-first century, resentment politics are driven by both subjective definitions of identity and the dismal failure of governments to redistribute the gains from a strong surge in economic growth in many countries after the 2008 global financial meltdown.

Hating outsiders is nothing new in liberal societies. Xenophobic nationalists maintain a long list of enemies, including Jews, Muslims, African Americans, and the LGBTQIA2+ community. We will show that populism is not simply the latest chapter in a story of backwards yokels and greedy capitalists. Sometimes journalists prefer a simple story of white hats and black hats. And sometimes scholars complicate things by standing above the fray and acting as arbiters between left and right. We don't want to do either. Choosing good guys and bad guys and playing the referee are not useful to developing a thorough understanding of how populism functions.[17] That said, we see something very dangerous in modern right-wing authoritarian populism.

According to Umberto Eco, Ur-Fascism, or "Eternal Fascism," is a constantly evolving movement that exploits and exacerbates this contemporary "fear of difference." It appeals to an increasingly precarious segment of the less-credentialed middle class.[18] Eco explains: "To people who feel deprived of a clear social identity, Ur-Fascism says that their only privilege is the most common one, to be born in the same country."[19] He argues that the audience for this tempting message is always the "old proletarians," industrial workers who are trying to keep their noses above the rising tide of inevitable change. This is indeed the case in the United States where Tucker Carlson of Fox News inveighs against the evils of immigration five nights a week. The people who watch *Tucker Carlson Tonight* are older, white, blue-collar workers without a university degree.

The industrial working class used to be the backbone of socialist and social democratic parties. Deindustrialization in the advanced capitalist economies has decimated their communities, but many have nowhere else to go. As their industries die, they decline in importance, sidelined by the growth of an economy based on professional services. They have been replaced in the national conversation by a new working class, populated by educated workers who form the reserve army of workers in this vast, new gig economy. In response, the old industrial proletarians have voted with their feet, abandoning labor parties of the left. In looking for parties to support them, they have embraced the identity politics on the right in North America, Western Europe, the former communist states, and parts of Latin America.

These de-skilled workers have sought refuge in evangelical churches in their search for community and fellowship, especially in Brazil and the United States. Global markets have cost them good jobs and they worry that their children will face a declining standard of living. They are a constituency waiting for a strong charismatic leader with a social media megaphone. Turning the clock back is impossible, but someone is always willing to sell the dream of simpler times. The story hasn't changed much since the golden age of liberalism after World War II. The working class is always on the brink of losing out. Just when these proletarians get comfortable with a set of industrial tools, the tech revolution reshapes the landscape of work, and their government abandons them to the fate that awaits everyone who fails the test of market competition.[20]

Socioeconomic Populism

Then there is socioeconomic populism, which identifies the true people as members of the working class. This is the populism of revolutionary Cuba in the mid-twentieth century, or Chile today, where a mass movement of radical student and working-class laborers protested for more than a year. Socioeconomic populism has not always been aligned with the right. In fact, it is very often aligned with the left in Latin America. In North America too, there has been a deep historical vein of progressive populism in which poor farmers and factory workers advocated for a bigger return on their investment in the nation, especially after the sacrifices of the war.[21] This culminated in the postwar liberal consensus on progressive taxation, employment insurance, public health care, and social security legislation.[22] Worker populism against predatory capitalism is usually associated with higher levels of social protection and more frequent government spending deficits.[23] Most recently, socioeconomic populism has been responsible for the policies of the leftist populist parties Syriza in Greece that opposed the fiscal austerity demanded by German banks. These parties held anti-austerity, anti-corruption, and antiestablishment views of the political class.

The "enemies of the people" in this narrative are wealthier economic classes or business professionals. Left populism often uses a narrative of the working class beset by parasitic capitalists. Left-wing populism regularly makes an appearance around elections in liberal market economies. Bernie Sanders in the United States has consistently come in second in the Democratic primaries with a populist message of power to the people, health care for all, and tax increases for billionaires. Hugo Chávez in Venezuela also relied on a powerful socioeconomic populist approach to rally his voting base of the urban poor. Socioeconomic populism has been a key feature of Bolivarian reforms throughout Latin America for much of the past two centuries.

Economic resentment born of systemic oppression is a common theme on both the right and the left. More than a hundred years ago, in one of the early dystopian novels, Jack London called the oligarchic exploitation of labor an "iron heel . . . descending on and crushing mankind."[24] Of course, the economic establishment today flat out rejects the idea that they are the bad guys. They see themselves as risk-takers who turn opportunity into wealth, and they are quick to point out that in a market slump they feel the pain first.

Lloyd Blankfein, former CEO of Goldman Sachs, sat down for a steak lunch with the *Financial Times*. Everyone loves to blame the bankers, for both the strength of the economy and its shortcomings, he theorized. "We drive the risk, people lavish praise on us, then it blows up on your watch. What are people supposed to think of you?"[25] Well, for starters, they think you're the guy who has been found at the scene of the crime. Whether or not the bankers are guilty, they make fat targets for socioeconomic populists of all stripes.

It is not only the poor and dispossessed who embrace socioeconomic populism. Business leaders in Wall Street's banks cheer from the sidelines when populist governmental leaders weight the scales in favor of their own nation's firms or weaken the positions of foreign competitors. But the same actors are alarmed by the schemes of populists that threaten supply chains, in-bound investment flows, and access to foreign markets. Many of the same people who fly business class and supported the Democrats also saw a significant upside to supporting Trump's Republican candidacy in 2016 because it was thought to be an effective way to neutralize the instinctual appeal of left populism.[26] They decided that Bernie would be bad for the markets.

Bernie Sanders has a lot of ideas on how to redistribute the enormous wealth that flows from the American financial system. He has proposed a tax on transactions of stocks, bonds, and derivatives. He wants to use the $2.4 trillion raised to shore up the American social safety net, including making tuition free for students at public colleges. Such an audacious plan would only take a tiny percentage of Wall Street's earnings, but many financiers were apoplectic at the idea that their trading strategies should be disrupted by a tax. For them, Donald Trump's rhetorical authoritarianism was easier to swallow because he reduced the rate of corporate taxation.

Antiestablishment Populism

And finally, there is antiestablishment populism, which pits the people against "the establishment." The best examples are the Anonymous hacker collective that protests the corruption of conventional elite morality, and the Occupy Wall Street movement, which protested rising inequality in America. In 2011 Occupy's chant of "We are the 99 percent" entered our popular consciousness. Establishment elite are defined as those in a position to make and enforce rules and regulations. Antiestablishment populism paints with a broad brush, understanding "the people" as an assemblage of farmers, students, retailers, auto workers, hamburger flippers, jobless millennials, caregivers, the poor, racialized minorities, stay-at-home moms, and small-business owners, who are all victims of crony capitalism and corrupt regulation.

How is antiestablishment populism different from other forms?[27] Whereas cultural populism locates the "elite" in high-prestige occupations and socioeconomic populism locates them in business and finance, antiestablishment populism targets the elite in positions of societal power and influence. Politicians, judges, civil servants, and those who set the rules of the game are the elite. For the insurgents of the Arab Spring in Egypt, Tunisia, and Syria, for example, the authoritarian, corrupt political class was identified as the root of society's evils. In the eyes of the antiestablishment populists, the enemy was their lawmakers who had become rich and corrupt in office, making rules that benefited themselves and their friends.

The diagnosis for what ails society is therefore different for each of these groups. Cultural populists argue that society needs to protect the true people as a special ethnic or cultural group. Socioeconomic populists argue that society needs to protect workers from the wealthy and those who wield financial influence. The purest expression of socioeconomic populism we have heard in recent history is Bernie Sanders's 2019 tweet: "Billionaires should not exist."[28] Antiestablishment populism argues that society needs to thoroughly repudiate its political elites. In Trump's words, we need to "drain the swamp."

Putin expressed a generalized populist sentiment most plainly when he said in 2019:

> Has anyone ever given a thought to who actually benefited . . . from globalisation? China has made use of globalisation to pull millions of Chinese out of poverty. What happened in the US? In the US, the leading companies—their managers, shareholders, and partners—made use of these benefits. Large sections of the downwardly mobile middle class have not benefited; they were left out when the pie was divided up.[29]

The people versus an elite group of managers, partners, and assorted big shots: what a perfectly crafted populist message against the global liberal order.

The Populist Club

If there is any place the populists are generous it is in laying blame. And it's an electoral tactic that has proved to win elections. Since 2000, conservative populist governments have been winning far more than they lose, and their victories are not concentrated in one continent, but are spread across the globe. (See fig. 1.) In the early 2000s, Venezuela, Argentina, and Italy were the only major economies with populist leaders. But membership in the populist club began to blow up between 2006 and 2009. By our count, another thirty populist governments and oppositions were elected in the next decade.

Figure 1: The Ascendance of Authoritarian Populist Governments Globally, 1990–2018

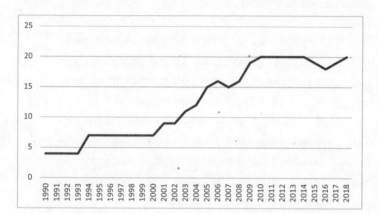

Source: Jordan Kyle and Limor Gultchin, "Populists in Power around the World," Tony Blair Institute for Global Change, November 7, 2018, institute.global/policy/populists -power-around-world.

Even in elections where populists failed to gain power, support for populist opposition parties grew in leaps and bounds. In 2021, Sweden, the home of European social democracy, was flipped into the populist camp when its government was defeated by a coalition of the ex-communist left party and the Sweden Democrats, a right-wing populist party making common cause with its natural enemy, the Marxists.[30] The social democrats had their worst electoral showing in 110 years. Most estimates show populist administrations as having increased by a factor of four around the world. (See fig. 1.)

We have identified thirty-six high-profile, mostly conservative, and always populist chieftains. Ours is a story that is both global and regional. Every region in the world has been touched by populism in the past decade, but some are more affected than others. The United States, Latin America, Europe, the subcontinent of India, and parts of Southeast Asia figure prominently. In Korea, Japan, and China, conservative populism has been a harder sell because of a long history of left activism (in Japan), enormous postwar growth across the entire region, and effective poverty reduction programs in all three countries. But we still see the shadow of populism across the region.

The left-populism of South Korea's Moon Jae-in is a prime example.[31] President Moon defeated Park Geun-hye on an anti-corruption platform in 2017. President Park was impeached for corruption after a scandal in which an off-the-books aide solicited funds from Korea's chaebol (family-controlled mega-corporations) for a foundation controlled by the president herself.[32] Mr. Moon ran on a platform of left-populist reform, promising a government of law and order. But he has faced his own scandals, appointing a justice minister whose wife had been recently indicted on forgery charges.[33]

In Japan, national politics is stolid and institutionally conservative. Japan lacks the political polarization that we see in the United States and Europe. It has less poverty, less conspicuous consumption of wealth, less immigration, and, in fact, is facing a demographically driven labor shortage. All of this means lower levels of populism. But surprisingly, populism still exists in Japan. It was left-populism in the postwar era of the 1960s and 1970s that had an outsized role domestically, before the powerful railway labor union was gutted in the early 1980s. Since that time, populist politicians on the right have risen occasionally but were all but extinguished at the national level by the premiership of Shinzo Abe. Today, conservative populism drives some big city mayors and regional governors.

For example, Tōru Hashimoto, governor of Osaka and then mayor from 2008 to 2015, celebrated his humble beginnings and lashed out at his enemies in the national bureaucracy, labor unions, and the Japanese Communist Party. But according to Charles Weathers, professor at Osaka City University, "compared to what you are seeing in some Western countries—people like Trump—really threatening or violating democratic norms, he didn't go nearly that far, because Japan has simply not been that polarised."[34]

All of this makes China's hard-nosed nationalism and institutionalization of populism by the Chinese Communist Party a notable development in the region. President Xi Jinping favors an approach to politics that is rooted in nationalism, authoritarianism, and traditionalism, and he is not a populist—at least not in a conventional sense. China's political culture is organized around one-party rule, Han dominance, and the cult of the supreme leader.

Xi is an authoritarian in the mold of Mao Tse-Tung. His immediate predecessors produced highly unpopular outcomes, like rising wealth inequality, a homegrown billionaire class, and a housing crisis in major urban centers. With his anti-corruption campaign and common prosperity promise to eradicate poverty, he is not averse to populist politics. But it is quite different from populism in North America and Europe. It's populism with Chinese characteristics. There is a broad populist streak running through recent reforms that rein in China's billionaire class and attempt to reassert governmental control over Chinese culture. In 2021, the three wealthiest billionaire entrepreneurs, Jack Ma, Ma Huateng, and Zhong Shanshan, were worth more than $175 billion and had been placed under judicial Party review of different kinds.[35] They make for fat targets in a country where an increasingly urban workforce demands sustained prosperity, affordable housing, and less corruption.

Xi may be late to the dance, but he moves to the populist music. Just prior to the 2022 winter Olympic games, Xi and Putin signed a "no limits" partnership to deepen cooperation and support each other internationally. Furthermore, there are populist currents that circulate on Chinese social media in which racists and nationalists peddle an exclusionary, anti-Muslim vision for national belonging.[36] But while China will be a main beneficiary of the populist surge, by and large, Chinese leadership works to tamp down Western-style antiestablishment populism because it is too unpredictably explosive.

Iconic Left Populism

There is a modern-day assumption that authoritarian populism is a solely conservative phenomenon, but that's not true. Historically, authoritarianism has thrived on the left and right. In Africa, populism has been grafted onto postcolonial independence politics. Jacob Zuma in South Africa and Robert Mugabe in Zimbabwe represented left and right variants of a similar style of rule, even if the men themselves and the countries they governed were very different. Populism became the weapon of choice for marginalizing enemies and looting state coffers.

Fidel Castro was the biggest name in Latin American *el jefe*-style populism during the Cold War, but Che Guevara was the global rock star of left dissent.[37] Forever young, a martyr to the cause, true believer, and romantic, his cigar and beret were then, and remain today, synonymous with socialist revolution. His photo is still everywhere: on album covers, spray-painted on the walls of tenements, on the iconic T-shirts of Generation X. Guevara was the archetypal freedom fighter, photogenic, poised, aware of his place at the fulcrum of history, and a global symbol for generations of anti-capitalist activists after him.[38]

More than fifty years after his death at the hands of the CIA, he remains a ubiquitous figure, but only in pop culture because we no longer see this brand of magnetic and alluring left-populism in global politics today. As a hero of the working class and man of the people, Guevara represented the romance of revolution without borders.[39] Today, the authoritarians offer a counterrevolution within borders—smaller, angrier, and without a vision for sharing the planet. When we compare the present moment with the world of only five decades ago, we can see how far we have tilted toward the conservative vision.

Che Guevara and the other Cold War Bolivarian freedom fighters left an enormous imprint on Latin America. Evo Morales in Bolivia and Hugo Chávez in Venezuela (when he was alive) fit the description of socialist, anti-elite populism. Like his compatriots in Nicaragua, Bolivia, Colombia, and Peru, Chávez was a staunch anti-imperialist in defense of socialism and Bolivarian independence movements.

The contrast is stark; today, populism has swung decidedly to the right. Even the populist big men of Latin America who claim to be left-leaning, such as Andrés Manuel López Obrador (AMLO in the popular Mexican press), have adopted a decidedly nationalist form of social solidarity that leaves behind the radicalism of the Cold War socialist project for a pro-poor reformist agenda.[40]

López Obrador is an important case study in the contradictions of modern populism. He is pro-poor and has enacted social programs that have benefited twenty million Mexicans.[41] At a time when half the country lives in poverty, he raised the minimum wage by 60 percent, an unprecedented pay hike.[42] For good reasons, López Obrador remains steadfastly popular among his electoral base. But he also followed the populist line on the pandemic, continuing rallies and playing down the severity of the virus, especially during the first critical months, when his government could have done much more to stock Mexican hospitals with oxygen and other essential supplies.

Even so, he is not in the same mold as Fidel Castro or Hugo Chávez, or even Evo Morales, who were doctrinaire socialists. Nevertheless, his critics charge that he wants to remain in power beyond his constitutionally mandated single six-year term, a claim that has more to do with fear of his genuine popularity than any evidence of corruption. In fact, he has been as tough on institutional corruption in Mexico City as he has been ineffective on the narco gangs that control portions of Northern Mexico. Most populists use the rhetoric of reform as a cover for personalized authoritarian retrenchment, but López Obrador uses populism to simultaneously bolster reform efforts while boosting his own popularity. He is challenging international oil markets to strengthen Pemex, Mexico's state-owned enterprise.[43] López Obrador is very consistent in his reliance on Pemex, the traditional champion of the Mexican economy, as both an anchor for diversification and a tool to increase Mexico's energy independence. He is an atypical, individualistic, narcissistic, left-leaning populist leader, and in his contradictions, we can see his likeness to other populists in our group.

All of the system disrupters as we know them today are culturally conservative, López Obrador included. Whether they identify with radical or reactionary traditions, they traffic in the tropes of twenty-first-century populism as we've come to know them: the charismatic leader, misogynistic paternalism, the big lie, and a jagged-edged nationalism. The current upsurge in populism is unique in that it is rooted in a particular form of conservative identity politics where the personal is political, and the political is reactionary.

A Profile of the Angry Populist Voter

What matters most are the voters who choose strongmen. The cliché is that they are the people who don't often vote, who hold fringe views, who talk a lot of garbage on social media. Hannah Arendt, world-renowned critical theorist, referred to them, as a group, as the people who mainstream political parties ignore because they are "too apathetic or too stupid for their attention."[44] But is it really the case that populist leaders are maintained by such apolitical and apathetic voters? Certainly, they are helped by elections with low turnout, but the populist voter is, despite the appearance, highly motivated and politically active. Donald Trump and Steve Bannon in the United States, Dominic Cummings in the UK, and Narendra Modi in India saw in these people a potential for rage and thereby a path to power.

Looking more closely, it's the over-sixty crowd in Southern England who are filled with nostalgia for empire and a time when the high street was more than Walmart and Amazon.[45] It's the grade eleven dropout in Spain. It's small-business owners in France who have been put against the wall by cheap imports from Brazil and India. It's former communists and socialists in Italy, and mainstream conservatives in Poland angered by politicians' broken promises and the secular creep of postmodern society. It's also the rich and powerful who bankroll campaigns and for whom national mythologies are secondary to the economics of tax cuts and cheap labor.

The populist insurgency is harvesting the anger and alienation that flow from the structural dynamics of hyper-globalization. People are angry that the benefits of trade seem to flow to the billionaire class, and nothing much trickles down. The often-repeated response is that people in the Global North live better than ever, awash in cheap credit, fast fashion, and "life-changing" gadgets. If you can imagine it, there's an app for it. But given a choice, people don't want more credit; they want job security, a bigger paycheck. They want their kids to get a good education that doesn't cost a fortune and they want social protection in retirement. Right across the spectrum, governments have failed to recognize that populism is a consequence of the failure of liberalism to spread the benefits of globalization more equally. Markets have produced enormous wealth, but governments have dropped the ball on redistribution.[46]

So what's the answer? How do we rid ourselves of populism? Is there an easy cure, or must we do the heavy work of rebuilding our national communities? German political scientists Armin Schäfer and Michael Zürn have shown that the decay of political institutions has left our societies defenseless against viruses like populism. Parliaments are less responsive today, and there is a smaller space at the national level for substantive political decision-making.[47] Less room for meaningful political debate and less responsive government are enormous challenges, but they aren't the only broken things.

Taxes for corporations and high-worth individuals are lower than ever. Postsecondary tuition fees have been deregulated in most high-income countries, making university a more expensive path to social mobility. In labor markets, employment insurance and the other benefits of the social safety net have been slashed in many jurisdictions. The decay of postwar social protection means that the compromise we made with liberalism after World War II is not worth much anymore, and citizens have noticed. They are once more turning to the extremes to vent their frustration and voting for populist authoritarians in record numbers, abandoning old party loyalties.

With their enormous financial resources and well-oiled election machinery, populist challengers have successfully captured long-established mainstream and predominantly conservative political parties in the US, the UK, India, Brazil, and Central Europe. So populists have won twice: once at the polls and then again by institutionally embedding themselves in command of the heartland of liberal democracy. Jan-Werner Müller, an expert on American populism, says that the key to resetting our democracies is to make populism less attractive by reinvigorating political parties and the mass media, the so-called intermediary institutions of liberal democracy.[48] Certainly, our societies would be better off with an accountable media, healthier electoral systems, and renovated institutions. We would have fewer populist headaches if globalization were fairer and if we could crack the code of persistent socio-legal exclusion of minority groups.

We don't see an easy fix for the populist malaise, and that does not bode well for the future of democracy. It will be very hard to roll back the worst features of the neoliberal state that protects businesses and exposes citizens to the temperature extremes of globalization. How badly do we want our societies to be healthy? Are we willing to put in the hard work to make it happen? This is a generational struggle, and it won't be fixed in one or two elections, or even in a decade of activism. Populism has irrevocably scarred our societies, and its extremism has shifted the developmental arc of our democracies for the next generation or even longer.

CHAPTER 2

The Big Lie

Rallying the Tribe

Modern authoritarian populism promises to slash the state's regulatory authority over "little" people while still somehow reaping the rewards of globalization. It doesn't matter that populist leaders don't have a real plan; it is enough that millions believe in them. We have already showed that populism today is different from other popular reform movements of previous decades because activists and leaders don't seek to build upon earlier democratic projects. Rather, they are cultural disrupters who say one thing and do another. They advertise their movements as giving power back to the people while simultaneously building political machines that give more power and authority to the leader themselves. At the level of the state, leaders like Jair Bolsonaro and Narendra Modi leverage their enormous power to shape the national narrative on social media. Their goal is to steamroll any overzealous judge or high-minded bureaucrat who is intent on stopping the populist machine.[1]

At the global level, they want to strip international organizations of their legal authority and reassert the power of the state.

They want more power and fewer rules, and they are willing to dissemble, lie, and misrepresent the problems facing their societies to achieve this dystopic vision. In this way, right-wing populism shares with fascism an impulse to twist the national narrative, rallying the tribe behind a big lie.

Figure 2: The Authoritarian Leaders

Source: Authors' original dataset, 2021

In broad strokes, the big lie is this: You aren't getting ahead because somebody else is stealing your share. Or, you are being replaced in your own country. Or, you are being robbed of your income, culture, and place at the table. The big lie creates a list of scapegoats and enemies. In each country, the big lie is framed differently, and the existence of an enemies list reflects that. But all of the national variants of the big lie have one thing in common: they are always organized around the idea of fraud. Every big lie maintained by authoritarian populism claims that the people are cheated and ripped off by the governmental, corporate, and scientific elite, who exploit their position in authority for their own gain. The populist insurgency operates, then, as a truth serum (the ubiquitous red pill!), exposing the elite's crimes against the people and promising a way for the people to take back their power.

In Republican America, the populist big lie asserts that illegal immigrants are the root of America's problems and the elite are lying to the people about the massive holes in America's immigration system. These holes are exploited, so the argument goes, by liberals and manipulative migrants who fraudulently misuse American generosity. Populist activists and leaders repeat the smear that refugees bring crime, guns, poverty, and inequality. In short, they blame immigrants and refugees for the low wages of blue-collar Americans. Notably, they don't fault the policies of business owners. The monied elite in Washington and New York, so the story goes, don't care that Latin American immigration is "causing" misery in the rural heartland. Corporate America turns a blind eye to the suffering because they profit from cheap labor, outsourcing jobs, and open borders. A maverick in the Oval Office exposed their wickedness, and the swamp monsters in Washington fought back. They found a way to steal the election! So one big lie builds on another. In 2020 the people were robbed of their powerful protector. The solution is more truth serum, more radicalization, fight like hell![2]

In the UK, the big lie works in comparable ways. Washington insiders are replaced by Brussels bureaucrats, and Mexican workers with Polish ones. In 2016, the Vote Leave campaign falsely— but successfully—argued that Britain paid much more into the European Union than it got in exchange.[3] The cost savings of leaving the EU would be so substantial that it would revitalize the National Health Service and thereby provide better value than EU membership.

What's more, they argued, opportunists from central and Eastern Europe exploited the EU rules and thereby lowered salaries for hardworking British laborers. If that wasn't bad enough, Vote Leave campaign propaganda argued that EU standards raised the cost of doing business in Britain, locking the UK into a cycle of trade and investment that benefits Europe.

Yet none of it was true. Britain was a net beneficiary of EU funding. Workers from Europe took jobs that many in Britain didn't want, driving trucks and stocking shelves. And Britain traded much more with its European neighbors than it did with overseas former colonies. Harmonizing standards guaranteed far more trade than it denied. British people were sold a bum deal.[4]

In Putin's Russia, the big lie is that the people ought to fear the modernizing ambitions of governments such as Finland, Latvia, Ukraine and Georgia. These peoples of the old Russian empire are a threat to Russian security today. Putin is convinced that Washington, NATO, and Europe are a structural security threat determined to deny Russia its place in the world as a global superpower. The Russian people can reverse their nation's decline with a strong leader backed by the might of the Russian military, which will put things right by knocking back Western-oriented democrats and returning Russia to the bosom of the Church and orthodox morality.

In Israel, the big lie is that the Palestinians exploit the forbearance of the Jewish people to cause chaos, support militants, and oppose a just peace. They claim Israeli citizenship but are actually loyal to Hamas (a Palestinian Sunni-Islamic fundamentalist, militant, and nationalistic organization), whose stated aim is the destruction of Israel. Such a manipulative people are an existential threat that must be suppressed by any means necessary. The illegal settlements are therefore actually justified because hardline Israeli governments recognize the higher truth that Palestinians can never be trusted to negotiate in good faith.

In Hungary and Poland, the lie is that the true people are beset by evil atheists, Africans, Jews, and EU bureaucrats who threaten to destroy the Christian values of a proud people.[5] The people are cheated of their cultural patrimony by groups who care nothing about their endangered status as a "Christian culture."[6] The Hungarians and Poles have been held back by the EU's democratic norms and rules, which are arbitrarily used against them for political ends. But their call to arms is that they, the people, will resist, protect their culture, and stand tall once more.

In relation to the COVID-19 pandemic, populists in the United States and Europe forwarded a series of big lies about the public response to the fast-moving virus: You can't trust the government because they exaggerate the deadliness of COVID-19. Populists attack mask mandates with Orwellian claims that name-less bureaucrats are dictating how you should run your life. They use lockdowns to punish churches that stand up for freedom of conscience! Ron DeSantis, the Republican governor of Florida, pushes this big lie by arguing, "We can either have a free society or we can have a biomedical security state," a false dichotomy that sounds truthy when paired with a rousing call for greater freedom of choice around masks and vaccines. But the big lie is not only about government manipulation. What's in these vaccines? Are they a fraudulent strategy for using people like guinea pigs? Will they harm a woman's fertility or magnetize her body? Do they contain a computer chip? Big Pharma ought not to be trusted either because big business is a willing participant in conspiracy.

Why do voters believe big lies? It seems ridiculous to think that migrant workers or Polish plumbers living in the UK are at the root of big national problems in industrialized states. But the big lie is palatable to a large plurality of voters because it flatters the people's intelligence and psychological courage. They may have been defrauded in the past, but they are savvy and have seen through the lies of the elite. The people's courage is needed now like never before. Take the red pill.[7] Resisting mask mandates and forwarding wild narratives on social media are promoted as patriotic acts of resistance.

Populism's Outsized Confidence

But voting for extreme nationalist parties always gives voters more than they bargained for. In a significant study of seventy Western European elections across thirteen countries between 1987 and 2017, researchers found that "accommodating radical views . . . led to greater gains for more radical parties."[8] Voters can't choose extremist candidates to send an anti-system warning to their governments without the risk of those politicians, once inside, shifting the electoral balance toward the extreme right. The cost of courting extreme politics is a more extreme political system.

The populists are trying to accomplish a major electoral realignment when a new conventional wisdom takes hold across multiple national jurisdictions. When such a shift occurs, national parties realign to capture the moment and reorganize the national consensus on how to understand major issues of public importance, such as employment, public finance, the climate crisis, and the role of trade and investment in economic development. The populists want to lurch the entire political consensus to the right, but not toward a small-state form of government preferred by conservatives in the postwar period. Rather, they want to create a new consensus for a security-obsessed state, with a small public sphere, hungry national champions prowling global markets like sharks, and big governments with imperial ambitions and grandiose schemes. From creating a Space Force to swallowing Crimea, the armored imperial state would obey the logic that says that the best defense of national sovereignty is a ferocious offence.

What also needs to be confronted is that earth-shaking electoral realignments are rare hinge moments.[9] Seismic shifts have happened twice before in modern times. In 1945, the first postwar Labour government in the UK legitimized the welfare state and full employment capitalism. It also paved the way for the rise of labor movements in other countries, from France to New Zealand. Keynesianism was the alternative paradigm to laissez-faire capitalism of the interwar period, with its belief in self-correcting markets.[10] New ideas about modern state practice brought about a revolution in public policy and birthed the modern administrative state as we know it. But by the 1980s, monetarism and market fundamentalism had emerged as the ideological alternative to the collapse of the Keynesian consensus.

Privatization and deregulation launched a second measurable global electoral shift in 1979, when Margaret Thatcher won a whopping majority. Thatcher, along with President Ronald Reagan in the United States, ushered in the neoliberal era of deregulated financial markets and the privatization of state-controlled enterprises. This market-first revolution was copied by dozens of governments regardless of their political orientation over the next forty years.[11]

Even five years ago, mainstream political scientists didn't think it was possible to force a seismic electoral realignment, but the populists were ready to try. And they've tried before, too, because populist movements are cyclical.[12] We saw their rise in the 1930s in Western Europe and North America, in the 1960s again in Europe, and in another small surge around the world in the early 1990s. Is there a correlation between cycles of anti-systemic activism and electoral realignments?

According to the academic research, there is a complex relationship between popular anger and the emergence of new electoral constellations. History never repeats itself, but our evolving societies are always borrowing recurring themes from the past to spiral into the future. We saw the rise of right-wing populism in Europe in the twentieth century. Today, we again see a similar set of traditionalist, nativist, and racist ideas rearing their ugly heads.

Think of it this way. The political stage is set for yet another great realignment, this time stemming from popular rage at the crisis-prone financial system that offers ordinary people less and the wealthiest more. To admit the failings of the postwar liberal order is not to justify authoritarian populism, but rather to point out that populists are popular for a reason: their message resonates with a large plurality of national voters who are already primed to fear future change. Great realignments always follow a catastrophic set of events, after which well-organized interests demand an expanded role for the state and a cultural revolution for the true people. This populist upsurge followed a well-trod path. It began as a critique of economic openness in the early 2000s, but it really took off after the disastrous meltdown of global markets in 2008.

In the United State for example, right-wing anti-China interests shared the same ideological space as reactionary culture warriors who were busy denouncing multiculturalism and equal rights. Both saw an opportunity for the state to protect its own economic interests while shoring up the cultural ramparts of "Western civilization." But the story is similar in other countries too, whether we're discussing Russian orthodoxy, the Hindutva movement in India, or Evangelical Christianity in Brazil. Authoritarian populism comes from a potent blend of cultural bigotry and the fear of narrowing economic opportunity.

What has been different this time around is that mass political parties have proved to be vulnerable to takeover by extreme ideologues on the inside. As American political scientist Frances Lee has argued, "parties may be more vulnerable to populist internal challenge than they were at earlier points, given (1) developments in communications technology, (2) the unpopularity of mainstream parties and party leaders, and (3) representation gaps created by an increasingly racialized party system."[13] As in a spy novel, double agents inside mainstream political parties worked to turn mass parties like the Republicans in the United States and the Bharatiya Janata Party (BJP) in India into fully radicalized arms of an authoritarian populist cult-like movement. This radicalization process occurred in most of the party systems in the states we have already discussed so far, including the UK, United States, India, Brazil, the Philippines, Poland, and Turkey.[14]

How did we get into such a mess? Ask psychologists and they will tell you about online radicalization, the loneliness of modern life, and the cult-like movements that promise people a return to simpler times. Ask historians and they might give you an answer about the rise and decline of great powers, the end of the American Century, and the ascendancy of China. Ask economists and they might tell you about the offshoring of jobs, the stagnation of middle-class wages, and the increasing inequality that has come to define Western capitalism since 2000. Ask political scientists and they will tell you that post–Cold War American hegemony has been replaced by a multipolar system of competing states pulling in different directions. The tectonic shift of geopolitics is creating earthquakes domestically and internationally. They will tell you the "big one" is coming. A philosopher would tell you that demagoguery has been the bane of democratic societies since the Greeks. Open societies are always targets for the bigoted nativist and the authoritarian despot. Each of these explanations is right to a degree, and each plays a role in our narrative.

If right-wing populism were just a problem in one or two troubled countries, it might only have been a curiosity for experts working in universities or bond-rating agencies. The populist tsunami has appealed to people from all sections of society across the world because it has captured the commanding heights of the twenty-first-century social media landscape. Donald Trump's Twitter account had more than eighty-five million followers before he was banned for inciting a violent coup attempt. Narendra Modi, the populist prime minister of India, boasts 133 million followers across Twitter, Instagram, and Facebook.[15] A recent empirical analysis of eighty-six million tweets has revealed extreme politics drives user engagement, which is a good thing for social media companies whose business is placing advertisements in front of captive eyeballs.[16] It is always in the interests of Mark Zuckerberg of Facebook and Jack Dorsey of Twitter that people fight about politics on the internet, because it increases engagement with their platforms. More eyeballs for more hours in the day translates directly into more advertising dollars for tech billionaires and their social media sites.

The Inequality Squeeze

The dynamics of structural change disproportionately impact the working poor. The wealthy are insulated from the worst of market volatility. The net worth of the wealthy is increasing much faster than middle-class incomes. This is the dynamic captured so eloquently by French economist Thomas Piketty's simple equation $r > g$ (if return on capital is greater than income growth, inequality rises).[17] This means that the investment income of the 1 percent is growing faster than the national economy and the salaries of the middle class. Liberal internationalists and their conservative counterparts used to broadly agree that free trade, investment, immigration, and human rights are in everyone's best interest, but this axiomatic truth is now being contested from the right.[18]

Sky-high inequality fuels the resentment of middle-class members of the dominant ethnic group who feel that they are "losing out" to the rich, who keep getting richer, as well as to immigrants and women who are ascending the income ladder behind them.[19] In response to this perception of being left behind, they attack other marginalized and racialized groups as the enemy. This dynamic of "comparing up and punching down" helps explain why most of the people who attacked the US Capitol on January 6, 2021, were gainfully employed, white middle-class men.

For the true believers of global populism, hyper-globalization hasn't made the world more equal or safer. Liberal internationalism has become a "globalization of the worst."[20] It's true that it has turned the income gulf between the rich and the rest into a Grand Canyon. And it did so very quickly. The wealth gap between America's richest and poorest families more than doubled in a single generation. In 1989, the richest 5 percent of families had 114 times as much wealth as the lower–middle class (defined as the quintile second from the bottom of income earners). By 2016, that number had jumped to 248 times.[21]

This pattern of rising wealth concentration is not only an American or Western European story. In its *World Social Report 2020*, the United Nations found that 66 percent of the world's population lives in countries where inequality has grown.[22] In China, inequality has grown enormously even as poverty has fallen. In the United States, the developed country with the most wealth polarization, the fifty richest people have as much wealth as the 165 million poorest people.[23] *That number tells you a lot of what you need to know about the politics of resentment and the structural dynamics driving these changes.*

If we do not want to live with ugly ethno-nationalism for decades to come, the nutrients of society's soil must be replenished. This can't happen as long as inequality runs rampant across our societies and, indeed, the global economy. The populist insurgency has a lot of fuel, as the authoritarian leader, social media activist, and true believer are dominating electoral politics with the big lie and hate speech.

The Rise of Extreme Speech

In the places that populism has won big at election time, the leaders don't often command a majority of the electorate. Still, they find a way to win. They are like magicians who through the alchemy of digital media turn "not quite good enough" into a skintight victory. How do they do it? Often, it is accomplished through electoral fraud, but more often, it happens through the activation of otherwise disengaged voters using angry, violent, and polarizing political speech.

Social scientists have been tracking the rise of populist speech for two decades. A group of American academics has developed an extensive database of more than a thousand public speeches by politicians in sixty-five countries given between 1989 and 2015.[24] The database gathers a sample of public speeches from party leaders, which the researchers defined as "populist" if their words evoked the moralistic language of "the people" versus "elites."

Out of more than a thousand speeches, 264 were coded as centrist, 342 as left populism, and 472 as conservative populism. The data shows the increasing frequency of conservative populist language. (See fig. 3.) In 1990, only four populist speeches were logged and coded. By 2003, that number had risen to forty, and by 2008, it had climbed to eighty. Not only is there a big rise in the volume of populist discourse, but there is also an intensification of extreme views.[25] Conservative populist words and images are now the dominant political frame.

Furthermore, the number of countries with populist party leaders has doubled to forty since the early 2000s. Notably, the database doesn't contain many of Donald Trump's speeches, so the upward trend does not even account for the biggest populist of all. If it did, his tweets alone would drive numbers through the roof. A 2019 article in *Presidential Studies Quarterly* showed that even compared to other populists, Trump's speech is way off the charts: "He stands out as an outlier among the outliers."[26]

Figure 3: The Dangerous Upsurge in Extreme Speech around the World, 1990–2016

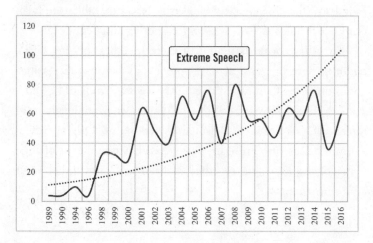

Source: "Global Populism Database," Harvard Dataverse, doi.org/10.7910/DVN/LFTQEZ

This steep upward trend in extreme speech needs to be emphasized because at the same time as it has become more prevalent, coarse political discourse has also become commonplace. We used to punish politicians for openly attacking immigrants and deploying racist dog whistles in the global public sphere, but not anymore. Viktor Orbán, speaking in Budapest in March 2018, told an audience of a hundred thousand people that European countries are losing their national characters, and this destruction is caused by an alliance between African migrants and a secret cabal of anti-Christian provocateurs.[27] This is a narrative lifted directly from the annals of twentieth-century anti-Semitism.

In Orbán's speeches, the enemies of the Hungarian people are portrayed as Jewish villains inspired by the *Protocols of the Learned Elders of Zion*, a notorious anti-Semitic tract widely circulated in the 1920s. Orbán said, "We are fighting an enemy that is different from us. Not open, but hiding; not straightforward, but crafty; not honest, but base; not national, but international; does not believe in working, but speculates with money."[28] He frequently refers to the founder of the Open Society University Network, billionaire financier George Soros, as "Uncle George," another anti-Semitic taunt.

There have been thousands of these speeches spewing vitriol, and this sort of political hate speech has become increasingly commonplace in almost every country we have studied. Le Pen in France, Nigel Farage in the UK, the players we have already introduced such as Duterte, Bolsonaro, Netanyahu, Orbán, Salvini, Trump, Berlusconi, Erdoğan, Putin, Assad, Modi: the list of angry demagogues who glue together coalitions of disgruntled voters continues to grow.[29]

The Anxiety of the Underclass

The late Zygmunt Bauman, the influential sociologist, compared the perilous present and its excess of frenzied individualism to a molten world of perpetual change in which base instincts and short-term self-interest destabilize the postwar compromise that has regulated capitalism.[30] We move backward, he argued, at an increasing velocity as society fails to meet the challenges posed by ever more complex technologies. Between 2004 and 2009, Americans endured forty thousand mass layoffs in which seven million workers lost their jobs due to automation.[31] In a digital world, everything is moving faster, and people without college degrees are the new underclass.[32] This structural change has also birthed a new political calculus catering to the fears and resentments of déclassé middle-class and blue-collar workers.

The conspiracy theories all around us are a primary indicator of this heightened politics of mass anxiety and electoral rage. Those who traffic in unfounded accusation make assumptions that connect people and events through secret links that only they can see. The conspiracy du jour is pushed by a vast online network that calls itself QAnon. It accuses the US government of being controlled by a secret cabal of Satan-worshipping pedophiles.[33] Every conspiracy theory follows a familiar pattern in which evil people with vast wealth and influence conspire to increase their wealth and power at the expense of everyone else.[34] Conspiracy theorizing is therefore integral to the populist narrative in which evil elites conspire to rob the people. Every widespread conspiracy theory of the past hundred years, from the *Protocols of the Elders of Zion* to today's "new world order" revolves around this narrative, rooted in provocation and anger.

Conventional wisdom holds that conspiracy theories centered on the nation are a way to express growing distrust for the political class in a world spinning out of control.[35] Before the populist surge, most scholars of conspiracy would have told you that anxious people living in uncertain times produce conspiracy theories to make sense of forces they can't control and don't fully understand. American political scientists Joseph Uscinski and Joseph Parent have argued that conspiracy theories are coping mechanisms: "They tend to resonate when groups are suffering from loss, weakness, or disunity."[36] But even as populist governments have promised to meet the needs of precarious people, conspiracy theorizing has exploded. How can we explain the rise of conspiracies even when the "right people" are in office?

Populist leaders have no intention of working in the real interests of their electoral base. Their goal is to make noise on headline issues, and when they fail to deliver the goods, they fall back on rage, conspiracy, and the blame game. What's more, chaos and distrust are pretty good ways to undermine liberal values and institutions. Voters who choose populists view them as shouting reformers who will bring the people's vengeance to government, either by bringing the corrupt to justice or by smashing the corrupt system.

Rodrigo Duterte in the Philippines has also been a master practitioner of this jagged-edged populism. His calls for the extra-judicial murder of anyone involved in the drug trade became headline news around the world. In the summer of 2021, he turned the spotlight of his anger on people who were reluctant to voluntarily vaccinate. "You choose vaccination or I will have you jailed," Duterte declared.[37] He went on to threaten to inject unvaccinated citizens with an antiparasitic drug used to treat animals, as an unproven precaution against transmission of the virus. "I will order all the village captains to have a tally of the people who refuse to be vaccinated," he stated. "Because if not, I will have Ivermectin meant for pigs injected into you."[38] It is unclear whether forcibly injecting people with a veterinary drug was meant to be a punishment or a possible prophylactic against viral transmission. Only days before, Duterte had signaled his desire for more testing of Ivermectin's unproven efficacy.

Social scientists have argued that populist rhetoric is deployed for its emotional power rather than precision in communication. But what if the affective language of populist leaders is not so imprecise at all? Some populists indeed cloak their more extreme ideas in nuance and metaphor meant for the faithful. But others say exactly what they mean, and Duterte is a good example of that. His extreme language used in the war on drugs is being investigated by the International Criminal Court, which believes his public exhortation of violence led to the deaths of thousands of suspects at the hands of Philippine police forces. Would he really forcibly inject Philippine citizens with Ivermectin? Should we take him seriously but not literally? History suggests that use of language as a prelude to outright violence is the iron link between authoritarian populism and fascism.

Electoral Alchemy

The point of populist speech is to increase the perceived power of the leader, with the goal of increasing his dominance and visibility at election time. In this regard, extreme speech is an effective tactic. In Poland in 2015, the Law and Justice Party (PiS) topped the polls with 5.1 million ballots, a significant plurality in a deeply divided multiparty legislature. They won again in 2020 despite falling levels of popular support, partly because the party dominates television and social media.[39] The wall of populist support seems unbreachable, but they were more vulnerable on election day than they cared to admit, because urban voters began to turn away from the identity politics of populism.

Donald Trump discovered this vulnerability when he lost states in 2020 that he might have won: Arizona, Georgia, and Pennsylvania. Trump's failure to win makes him something of an outlier among the populists who have learned how to subvert democracy. He tried everything, including a citizen-led invasion of the US Capitol complex on January 6, 2021, but ultimately failed to overturn the 2020 election outcome.

In 2016, Philippine president Rodrigo Duterte scored an impressive victory in a crowded multiparty system. He received 14.8 million votes because he stood out for his proudly extremist and violent rhetoric. It empowered a highly organized and vocal minority of movement activists and party insiders. Some of these populist bosses can get away with saying terrible things, and even advocate illegality, because they are older and well-established political figures. Their extreme speech can be written off as just a way to stand apart in a crowded field.

In the final presidential runoff in France in 2017, Emmanuel Macron received twenty million votes, or 66 percent of those voting. Marine Le Pen, his xenophobic rival, received one-third of the popular vote. This was a major improvement from her previous results, due to her impressive army of internet activists, enthusiastic trolls, and extreme speech.[40]

In Germany in the same year, the anti-immigrant Alternative für Deutschland (AfD) attracted 5.8 million voters, a record-breaking performance that is connected to lurid stories of Syrian immigrants swamping the German system of social support. Again, it legitimatized a highly vocal minority. In comparison, Angela Merkel's Christian Democrats (CDU) won the support of fifteen million Germans. Support for the social democratic Sozialdemokratische Partei Deutschlands (SPD) continued to slide.[41] The pattern of rising nationalist support and losses on the further left repeats itself in eastern Europe. In the Hungarian national election of 2018, Viktor Orbán was elected by 2.8 million voters, winning 49 percent of total votes cast, a very narrow victory and a divided opposition.

Italy also rode the tidal wave of populism. The right-wing populist led by anti-immigrant politician Matteo Salvini made a temporary alliance with the Five Star Movement, another centrist populist party, and took about 70 percent of the popular vote in 2018. Following the election, in true Italian fashion, the coalition fell apart in 2019. Salvini lost his government portfolio and responded by forming the Northern League, a hard-nationalist movement for "Italians First."[42] Less than two years later, in February 2021,

President Sergio Mattarella called upon Mario Draghi, former president of the European Central Bank, to form a government. The Five Star Movement became a key supporter, and the far right was marginalized, although they maintain a formidable, dangerous political presence in Italy.

Salvini's League has made inroads in Calabria, a significant step in one of the poorest regions of Italy. But they failed to fully dominate in poor regions as they'd hoped to. The socialist opposition has held so far in Emilia-Romagna, which is the traditional industrial heartland.[43] The League's social media presence, however, is far stronger than that of its socialist opposition. A strident minority retains its presence in Italian politics as its legislative power plummets to record lows. But due to the cyclicality of extreme movements, we can expect to see more organized anti-immigrant sentiment in the future.

Even in Canada, often portrayed as a haven of moderation, the Conservative Party recently ran a populist campaign and received more votes, but fewer seats, than the ruling Liberals in the 2019 federal election. The Conservatives managed to harness the popular anger of the western provinces to capture 34 percent of the popular vote. The ruling Liberals managed only 33 percent but nevertheless returned Prime Minister Justin Trudeau to power.

In 2021, the Liberal Party called another election. The Conservatives, chastened by their recent loss, ran a notably anti-populist campaign. But it didn't pay off on election day. The Liberals won another minority government, and the populist People's Party of Canada (PPC), despite not winning a single seat, doubled its popular vote, to about 5 percent of the electorate. This was a lower tally than the PPC expected. They had hoped to win up to three seats.

Regionally, populism is much stronger. The province of Alberta has its own secessionist movement, led by the Maverick Party.

Furthermore, United Conservative premier Jason Kenney has responded to dissatisfaction with his leadership by ramping up his fight with the federal government. He has recently demanded that Canada change the constitution to better suit his province's oil and gas interests. He channels a popular belief that the federal government failed to protect Western Canada's oil and gas industry when Biden cancelled the Keystone XL pipeline. He also plays to his base's belief that they are being cheated out of a prominent place in confederation and promises that he will fight for them. Unsurprisingly, his strongman persona plays well on the extremist edges of Facebook and Twitter.

In India, Narendra Modi won unprecedented support from 270 million electors who cast votes for the nationalist BJP and its coalition partners in 2019. With 45 percent of the vote, the BJP won the largest parliamentary majority in recent Indian history. Modi's victory decimated the Congress party, once the mighty political juggernaut of Indian independence, led by the fading Nehru dynasty. We will show later how "Modi the Ringmaster" dominates through a combination of constant campaigning, social media presence, attacking the rights of Muslims, and the bullying of journalists and news editors. But the turbulence upon which he thrives have periodically shaken his own government. A year-long mass farmer protest and occupation on the outskirts of New Delhi opposed BJP-sponsored market reforms and forced the Modi government to withdraw the legislation at least temporarily.[44]

Mass Electoral Anger and Anti-Politics

Some people may be tempted to believe that the populists are a spent force in world affairs. It may look like global populism lost its parade marshal, Donald Trump, in 2020. But he has tightened his grasp on the Republican Party, silenced dissent, and cemented the myth of a stolen election among his millions of followers. Since losing the White House, Republicans have closed ranks, pushed out any members who do not repeat the big lie, and pursued an aggressive campaign to reframe the January 6 insurrection as "legitimate political discourse."[45]

In places where the populist tsunami accomplished its goals, such as in the UK with Brexit, their policies have been a disaster. Britain had its worst year of growth in three hundred years in 2020, due to the compounding effects of leaving the EU and the pandemic.[46] Export businesses are failing because of mountains of red tape, border inspections, and endless paperwork.[47] Inequality is up, and growth is disappointing. In other places, populist leadership is facing a rising opposition and anger over failure to contain the pandemic.

It's not just the right-wing populists who are angry. Popular anger has been effectively mobilized by opposition parties and progressive movements too. Vladimir Putin and Narendra Modi fear the opposition today more than they did five years ago and have jailed thousands of them.[48] Even in the most authoritarian countries, civil society activists have not let up their opposition, despite mass arrests and indefinite detention. Highly motivated, focused, and with new reservoirs of money, the populists are regrouping and strengthening their global movement. Dismissing the anti-system now would be a grave error.

The defeat of Donald Trump was an inflection point in right-wing populism, but the movement's influence on world politics is likely to continue over the next decade. The deep structural and psychological conditions that gave rise to conservative populism have not been addressed, and until they are, the populist mentality has few limits. What's worse, "social bads," like societal instability, rising inequality, racism, and large-scale unemployment, have been made much more prominent by the pandemic. This can only help the cause of angry populism controlled by the charismatic leader.[49]

Populist leaders like to portray themselves on the global stage as "system smashers." Each is a battering ram, smashing a system that supposedly holds their country back from greatness. They undermine electoral freedom, degrade constitutional checks and balances, and attack the legitimacy of government at all levels. Russia's Putin wants to poison American liberalism. Britain's Boris Johnson wants to break free of European bureaucracy. India's Narendra Modi wants to transform his country into a great power alongside America, Europe, and China. At first glance, populists have only their raging animal spirits in common. What does British prime minister Boris Johnson share with Narendra Modi? What does Brazilian president Jair Bolsonaro share with the president of the Philippines, Rodrigo Duterte?

To most people, the answer is—nothing. Their policy goals make sense only in their own countries. The Conservative Party promised to take Britain out of the EU and return the nation to a pre-EU level of autonomy. The Republicans in the United States supported building a wall on the border with Mexico to keep out unwanted immigrants who were wrongly blamed for taking jobs away from homegrown Americans. In India, BJP has supported many moves to disenfranchise Muslims throughout the country. The Law and Justice Party has rolled back the rights of women in Poland with the support of the conservative wing of the Catholic Church. With so many disparate and extreme goals, the intellectual and policy establishments did not take them seriously at first.[50] These ideas were dismissed as outlandish—ridiculous, even. Who would vote for such a cartoon villain? Would the United States really build a castle wall against Latin American migrants? Would there be a moat with crocodiles?

Authoritarianism in a Post-Truth Age

Conservative nationalism, nativism, and populism are barometers of the health of a nation. The more extreme and angrier the tone of politics, the more worried we should be that something is going badly wrong with liberal democracy. Are we facing a new period of troubled peace as prelude to violent conflict? We cannot rule it out. Each populist leader crafts narratives that are designed to stoke division and push the buttons of their army of true believers. They slander their opponents and paint themselves as the only available alternative. Their strategies always rely on negative campaigning.

The most extreme leaders, such as Bolsonaro, Duterte, Orbán, begin with cultural dog whistles and progress into character assassination, fear mongering, and conspiracy. The stories the leader tells on the campaign trail are designed to rankle opponents and, in so doing, assure the tribe that their leader is battling for them. It is essential that the tribe sees the leader fighting their fight, because most of the time populist leaders are not the sort of people you would expect to see leading a working-class revolt.

Think of it this way. The Bermuda Triangle is a region in the North Atlantic Ocean near Cuba where tropical storms have resulted in hundreds of ships and planes being lost without a trace. It is the perfect metaphor to describe the way that the absence of intellectual authority, toxic identity, and mercantilist logic combine to sink unwary ships of state. This dark triad forms a giant sucking hole in global politics today. It absorbs most of our attention, and its gravity well plays havoc with traditional political compasses.[51] American author Barbara Ehrenreich has likened the effect to a "fear of falling" when faced with economic or cultural shock.[52] We teeter on the edge of something dark and dangerous.

Populism is most often associated with authoritarianism and dictatorship for one very good reason: right-wing populism utilizes the political style of fascism. Jason Stanley, an American political philosopher, has shown that modern fascism is a style—a way of doing politics that develops a particular method of propaganda that relies on a nostalgic narrative that followers internalize.[53]

For populists, the facts are relative. With alternative facts we can create new narratives and recreate the stories we tell about ourselves. In the new political narrative, the good guys are the "forgotten men and women," and the bad guys are global elites. But their main article of faith is that the people will prevail. All that matters is the belief in the movement and the strength of will of the true believer. The narrative is premised on going "back to the future." It telegraphs the message that together we can seize power and restore our country to greatness, purity, and strength.[54] All that matters is the will to power and the energizing fanaticism of the tribe. These zealous authoritarians rooted in the blind certainty in blood (people like us) and soil (the fatherland, our patrimony) must be defeated. There are no half-measure compromises to be made with fascists.

Populism and Fascism

We don't conflate populism today with historical fascism to demonize opponents. But rather it enables us to draw the historical links that are necessary to identify extreme populism as it is currently practiced in many countries. In his essential book *From Fascism to Populism in History*, Argentinian historian Federico Finchelstein demonstrated that the defeat of Hitler and Mussolini created a rupture in right-wing politics that has persisted to this day.[55] Modern right-wing populism is its own creature. It bears a resemblance to reactionary movements of the interwar period, especially in the use of narratives of grievance and the encouragement of violence. Right-wing populism today trades in pernicious theories of white supremacy, glorifies a false utopia of national self-sufficiency, and lionizes "Western civilization" as the natural order in world politics.[56]

Just like the ideologues of previous eras, the swaggering chiefs of our day believe they can control the beast they've created, and that despite the chaos and cruelty, they will usher in a new world order. Every authoritarian movement today has a unique historical path, a challenging political context, and a distinctive potential for success, as they measure such things. Some are more radical than others and more willing to use violence to meet their goals. Social scientists agree that the use of violence to attain exclusionary goals is what separates conservative populism from fascism.[57] Most of these movements have at one point demanded violence, sometimes rhetorical and sometimes real, from true believers such as the Proud Boys, an American paramilitary group.

We have painted a bleak picture because in the United States, Turkey, Hungary, Russia, India, and other countries, the populists are fundamentally undermining what is left and what is right, and with them the electoral calculus that has sustained liberal democracy. Populists represent an antidemocratic solution to the problems facing liberal democracy, of rising inequality, decaying institutions, and political cultures that emerged in the twentieth century and no longer capture the many pressing concerns of twenty-first-century citizens.[58]

Italian philosopher Norberto Bobbio identified "the composed middle" of moderate voters as those people who look both left and right in modern societies.[59] American pundits often call these people "the undecided voters" around election time, but to do so downplays their importance for deliberative democracy. In a healthy democracy, we need people who see both sides of a policy issue, and who look beyond the headlines and ideological theatrics. Nevertheless, this idea of the moderate middle has lost much of its appeal because identity politics has made such large inroads into the hearts and minds of voters across the spectrum. To be undecided is characterized as weak or unintelligent. But to seriously weigh and measure the promises and accomplishments of political leaders is an indispensable job, and one that democracy cannot survive without.

In highly polarized settings, authoritarians are learning the advantages to be gained by attacking courts and creating an unbridgeable "us versus them" divide between the leader's tribe and the legal system. Their distrust of the legal order unites the populists and gives a form to a movement that is defined in the negative. In Mexico, López Obrador threatens judicial independence by adjusting term appointments for the chief justice of the supreme court in contravention of the Mexican constitution.[60] Never one to avoid controversy, López Obrador has been criticized for openly questioning the judgment of those on the bench.

Throughout 2021, the president of Mexico resisted calls to vaccinate children. When a judge ordered the government to vaccinate all youth from ages twelve to seventeen, López Obrador dismissed the judge's order as "not definitive." He hinted that his government might challenge the ruling in court, declaring, "We are going to the relevant authority to clarify."[61] Most experts assume he meant that he was exploring his legal options, but he was also taking the case into the court of public opinion, testing constituency support for the idea that the president, not judges, should decide who gets vaccinated.

López Obrador draws much of his support from among the poor in rural Mexico, where vaccines are mistrusted. By mid-July 2021, about 30 percent of eligible adults had received a vaccine in Mexico, but in Chiapas, the take-up rate was less than half of the national average. In some of the poorest villages, the BBC reported vaccination rates of around 2 percent.[62] A combination of fear of adverse reactions, belief in the protection afforded by rural location, and misinformation spread on WhatsApp created a perfect storm of resistance.[63] López Obrador knows that for the rural poor, vaccines are often seen as a tool of the elite. Likewise, courts are viewed with mistrust. He must not be too pro-vaccine if he wants to maintain the support of the rural poor. If that means foot-dragging on a court order or other forms of passive obstruction, so much the better, because this sort of theater builds his mystique as the defender of the people.

In late 2021, the Israeli government announced that it was banning six civil society organizations that advocate for the human and civil rights of Palestinians. This policy closely follows Netanyahu's decade-long strategy of using government resources against human rights groups that advocate for Palestinians. His coalition government began a program of orchestrated legal attacks on human rights defenders, using the little-known Ministry of Strategic Affairs first created by Ariel Sharon as a sort of consolation prize for a coalition partner. Under Netanyahu, the ministry was granted an annual budget in the tens of millions of dollars with a mandate to fight the Boycott, Divestment, and Sanctions (BDS) movement with every tool it could muster.[64]

Even though the Ministry of Foreign Affairs maintained a branch dedicated to fighting the boycott, Netanyahu's government preferred to pour money into the secretive Ministry of Strategic Affairs because it operated as a public affairs "commando unit" with very little oversight.[65] By 2016, the ministry's rising costs and lack of accountability were flagged in a comptroller's report. The media dug into the scandal of secret agents working against democracy, and in 2021 the ministry was disbanded. But the Netanyahu government had proved that a concerted application of state money could effectively protect government policy at the expense of human rights.

Yet it would be a mistake to underestimate the strength of the populist insurgency by charting its ups and downs only in individual countries. We are deep into a once-in-a-generation process of rethinking the basics: representative democracy, capitalism, and the liberal international order. In this chaos, many things are possible. We need markers to navigate the future. As we grapple with populism and a global public health crisis, authoritarian leaders are being denied a victory lap for the time being. They are nationally important at home, but they are still little men abroad—controversial and craving recognition.

CHAPTER 3

Charismatic Big Men and the Volk

The Archetypes of Populist Leadership

Archetypes are a powerful tool for thinking about the strategies used by the modern populist "big men." If we look at the ideas that populists use to motivate voters, we can see four types, with their own strategies and overarching goals. The *First Citizen of the Empire*, the *National Defender*, the *Holy Crusader*, and the *Conspirator-in-Chief* are the most prominent identities embraced by the modern would-be populist rulers. (See fig. 4.) Some populists want to consolidate power and build an empire. Others want to defend the true people from invaders or transform the international system to make more room for their tribe. Conspirators try to destabilize their nation's constitutional order to maintain themselves and their loyalists at the center of power. Of course, the populist leaders want to do all of these things and more, but they prioritize depending on the context.

You probably recognize most of these masks because each of the leaders wears their favorite identity like a uniform. But a mask conceals as much as it reveals. The purpose of the mask is to hide their own insatiable lust for wealth and power. The most readily identifiable is that of First Citizen, as embodied by Roman emperors. Carl Sandburg's poem "I Am the People, the Mob" captures the potential for reform that is invested in the political agency of "the people" who trust the "first citizen" to protect their interests. It is a paean to transformation and must be read as a powerful invocation to a more expansive and inclusive politics. "I am the people . . . The Napoleons come from me and the Lincolns."[1] For Sandburg, populism was not a dirty word. His poem perfectly captures our present moment with its conflicted representation of populist promise and betrayal.[2]

Figure 4: The Archetypes of Populist Leadership

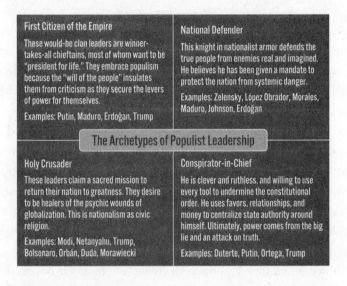

First Citizen of the Empire

These would-be clan leaders are winner-takes-all chieftains, most of whom want to be "president for life." They embrace populism because the "will of the people" insulates them from criticism as they secure the levers of power for themselves.

Examples: Putin, Maduro, Erdoğan, Trump

National Defender

This knight in nationalist armor defends the true people from enemies real and imagined. He believes he has been given a mandate to protect the nation from systemic danger.

Examples: Zelensky, López Obrador, Morales, Maduro, Johnson, Erdoğan

The Archetypes of Populist Leadership

Holy Crusader

These leaders claim a sacred mission to return their nation to greatness. They desire to be healers of the psychic wounds of globalization. This is nationalism as civic religion.

Examples: Modi, Netanyahu, Trump, Bolsonaro, Orbán, Duda, Morawiecki

Conspirator-in-Chief

He is clever and ruthless, and willing to use every tool to undermine the constitutional order. He uses favors, relationships, and money to centralize state authority around himself. Ultimately, power comes from the big lie and an attack on truth.

Examples: Duterte, Putin, Ortega, Trump

Source: Authors' Data, 2021.

The *First Citizen* embodies the tribe's restless energy and the people's will to power.[3] Sandburg hoped for a time when American democracy would mature, when people would "learn to remember," and "use the lessons of yesterday and no longer forget who robbed [them] last year." Certainly, there is a glint of optimism in Sandburg's vision of populism. He trusts the people to make wise decisions. But the First Citizen knows that given a choice between inclusion or retribution, truth or the big lie, the latter is a more certain pathway to the consolidation of personal power. The people may desire justice, freedom, equality. But these desires can be bent toward the darkest impulses of the popular will: for bullying, ostracism, adulation, and revenge.

The *First Citizen* is an emperor in everything but name. He is the people's savior and their *grande maladie*. He despises democratic limits even as he claims to love the implication of justice embodied in the "triumph of the will." Think Putin, Maduro, and Erdoğan, all twenty-first century dictators. In the name of the people and law and order, they rely on police and the military to silence civil society activists and imprison their political rivals. When this isn't enough, they reach out to paramilitary hard men, like the American far-right, neofascist Proud Boys and other vigilantes from the police and military for muscle and extra-judicial "dirty" enforcement. These leaders are the big men who come to power democratically and then turn the state against itself to create a cult of personality and a system of personalized institutional control.

Not every imperial autocrat wants to be president for life, but enough do that the removal of term limits is usually high on their to-do list. Some of these men don't appear to have the personality to enjoy the kinetic obligations of populism, such as a self-motivated social media presence, numerous rallies, a big charismatic public persona, and other means of courting grassroots support. That is because the "will of the people" is the best cover for consolidating power. In short, they are autocratic by temperament, and populism is a functional tool to further their ambition.

The second mask is that of the *Holy Crusader*. This is the identity worn by populists on a mission to defeat the enemies of the people, all the so-called outsiders who don't look like us. The *Holy Crusader* wants to change the world to protect the tribe. The best defense is a good offense, and the crusader takes the fight to banish the heretic and silence the apostate. He is aggressive and a risk-taker, a provocateur ready to go to the limit to give the true people their place in the sun. For Narendra Modi, Muslims are the enemy of the sacred land of Bharat. For Netanyahu, it was the Palestinians, Muslims, and any liberal who stood in the way of reuniting the historic territory of the Kingdom of Israel.

Jair Bolsonaro of Brazil and Mateusz Morawiecki of Poland likewise take on a crusading identity in which they struggle against the evils of secularism, women's rights, and cosmopolitan liberalism. Like Roland in the eponymous medieval epic poem, the *Holy Crusader* always faces daunting odds, but the cause of the people is righteous and sacrifice is patriotic—but only if other people pay the price. The *Holy Crusader* is a hypocrite who wraps himself in the flag and genuflects at the Stations of the Cross as long as they and their tribe benefit from the convergence of church and state in the populist heartland.

The third archetype is the *National Defender* of the sovereignty project. Boris Johnson is a significant example here. Certainly, much of his rhetoric sounds like that of the *Holy Crusader*. For example, he claims the EU is filled with French heretics who don't believe in the sacred sovereignty of Britannia. But Johnson shares a deeper affinity with the *Defender*, for whom protecting the country by pulling up the drawbridge is more important than changing the entire international order. He wants to secure his castle against the advances of globalization. Clearly, the *National Defender* shares some commonalities with the *Holy Crusader* but sees more value in building defenses at home than in adventuring far beyond the castle walls. Perhaps the biggest difference between *Defenders* and *Holy Crusaders* is that *Defenders* don't believe they have the hard-power capabilities to reshape the entire system. They may also operate in a political culture that doesn't value ostentatious forms of civic and religious piety. These two points are the essential differences between the narratives and strategies of a bellicose authoritarian Putin and the defensive anti-EU rhetoric employed by Johnson, for example.

The final populist leader archetype is the *Conspirator-in-Chief.* He is not a fired-up crusader or a stalwart knight of the people, at least not right now. Nor is he an autocrat with kingly pretensions using populism as a disguise for empire-building. Rather, he is a populist because it works for him, and he is open to using extralegal means, big lies, unfounded accusations, fear and innuendo, and the religious community of zealots that gathers wherever conspiracies are spread. Think Duterte, Bolsonaro, and Trump. Conspiracy-minded populists know that secret cabals, evil plans come to light, and dirty deeds are the stuff that energize bored and anxious people. And so they spin webs of lies.

The *Conspirator-in-Chief* is the day-to-day manager of a populist regime. He is a master of the manipulation required to keep its enemies guessing. For example, Duterte is tough on crime, loves to hear himself speak, sleeps late, and works far into the early morning hours. According to the *Washington Post*, his style "serves to further his interests as a performative, populist leader."[4] Certainly, he shows no signs of slowing down, despite his advanced age. He publicly flirts with the idea of subverting the constitutional terms limits for the Philippine presidency. He muses about creating a dynasty, running with his daughter or maybe a close associate who will be a figurehead to Duterte, the power behind the big chair. There have been many protests against the thousands of extrajudicial killings, but Duterte is a master of the dark arts of populism. He constructs enemies for voters to hate, bolsters his government's strength by attacking them, and trivializes the concerns of his critics. It seems to work, at least for now. At the height of the pandemic in October 2020, when Bolsonaro was struggling to maintain his position and Trump was losing the American election, Duterte had a 91 percent approval rating, according to a Pulse Asia poll.[5]

What matters most is that the true believer internalizes the lies as a set of cardinal beliefs that define the movement. Conservative populist movements are always rooted in a perceived existential threat: the threat of cultural swamping, of evil global governments, of elites stealing the wealth of the tribe. That none of these threats can be certified by independent analysis is important. Belief hinges on a shared language, a way of expressing certainty, and a shared credulity about what is "really going on." They use many terms and expressions that make sense only to insiders: "Uncle George," "microchips in the vaccines," "WWG1WGA (where we go one, we go all)," "stop the steal," "the white left."[6]

This form of "speaking in tongues" on a mass scale is culturally rooted in religious and political context. It resonates with subsets of national populations, with some concepts making the leap from one society to another. The language of QAnon has jumped from its American context into far-right groups in Europe too. It appears that American conspiracy theories are exportable, like soft power and boy bands. Anglo-German historian Katja Hoyer has estimated that Germany has the largest group of QAnon adherents outside the Anglosphere.[7] They enthusiastically engage with the growing universe of conspiracies and add their own as well. Germans have as long a history with conspiracy theories as the Americans. But the fact that American conspiracy theories have proved to grow so readily in foreign soil is a troubling feature of the populist moment.

The *Conspirator-in-Chief* understands that his political career demands that he combine canny messaging with strategic relationships with power brokers. The conspirator is a gossip and a wag. "A lot of people are saying" becomes a way to lie without triggering a lawsuit.[8] He exploits faith and credulity like a revivalist preacher, but with deadly results. He is a spider, spinning webs of narrative, entrapping the unwary and credulous. As always, there is power to being at the center of a lie. In this cult, loyalty to the leader is everything. We have come full circle. We can now see clearly that populism is always a tactic and never a principle.

A Wide-angled Portrait of Populist Leaders

Of course, not every leader fits easily into every box. While holding high office, a leader's relationship to certain aspects of his archetypal mask predictably evolves. A Holy Crusader may develop into an imperial autocrat. The manipulative populism of a Conspirator-in-Chief often progresses into a Holy Crusader when he discovers the narratives that will secure him another term in office. The invocation of "we the people" as both a call to liberation and a reason for desecration binds all these masks together. As an archetype of archetypes, "we the people" is the meta-mask and brings together all the nostalgia, hatred, and resentment of modern fascism. So, skeptical reader, don't get too caught up in individual masks. They mean a lot to the true believer, but for the rest of us, it is the big lie that matters most.

We have raised the issue of the multi-masked populist so that you can think of the masks as being interchangeable. A smart populist wears the right mask needed for each occasion. So if you were reading about these masks and thinking, "Trump was a First Citizen, but he was also a Crusader, a Defender, and a Conspirator-in-Chief," you'd be right to think of the masks as being interchangeable. He wore many masks, as do all of the most successful populists. He was duplicitous and quick to cycle through his political identities on Twitter and at his rallies.

So what about the rest of these charismatic authoritarians? Where do they fit in? Imagine a class photo of the thirty leaders of populist parties and governments, a global potpourri of grandiosity and eye-watering mediocrity. On this list of the top guns are the leaders of the UK, the United States, India, Turkey, Russia, Israel, Brazil, Venezuela, the Philippines, Mexico, Hungary, Poland, Austria, the Czech Republic, and Nicaragua. Most of the populist leaders have extensive connections to television, newspaper, and social media empires, either as talent or as owners. Zelensky and Trump were television performers and even Johnson got his start in British public life as a tabloid journalist. Their careers veered in different directions, but most of the populist leaders live among the upper echelons of their societies. They were rich before they entered office or became rich through corruption once they were in power. They are entirely at home among the 1 percent (or even 0.1 percent) of their societies. But to their followers on social media, they are scrappy underdogs who never back down from a fight.

They are overwhelmingly traditionalist, male, in late middle age, with deep ties to religious fundamentalism and radical nativist groups. Most are white, but it's more important that they come from the dominant cultural group in their society. They wield their beliefs like a weapon and advance behind a shield of religious moralizing on issues of women's reproductive health, gender equity, and civil rights for the LGBTQIA2+ community.

Even in the UK, a more secular country than Brazil, Russia, or the United States, religion has been seeping into electoral politics once more. As Vince Cable, the former leader of the UK Liberal Democrats said, "Identity is sometimes about religion, sometimes about color, sometimes about nationality. And I think what is happening is that traditional left-right class alignments are becoming less and less relevant, and it's identity, in those different forms, that becomes salient."[9] Me against my cousin, me and my cousin against our friends, me and my community against outsiders, me and my nation against foreigners.[10] The oppositional binary is the oldest method of identity formation.

The Unholy Trinity of Populism, Tribalism, and Religion

In this breakdown of left-right identities, religion is central to tribalism and predates the nation-state, capitalism, and political parties. But the fact that tribalism is primitive and combustible is a dangerous feature, rather than a tiny complication in our liquid world of shifting identity. It is dangerous because you, the populist, feel your tribe in your bones. Identity is affective and alive inside your head, giving you something supposedly authentic and "woke." It has the immediacy of emotion, and negative feelings make it even stronger. Even the enormous loss of life in the pandemic of 2020 failed to overcome partisan identity.

White evangelicals voted overwhelmingly for Trump in the autumn of 2020 when they were hard hit by the pandemic and clearly hurt by his reckless failure of leadership.[11] In the UK, where they "don't do God," religion has become a somewhat surprising factor in modern elections. Both Labour and the Conservatives have charged each other with religious bigotry, against Jews and Muslims, respectively. Vince Cable went on to say, "This isn't America, it's not Poland, we're a fairly secular country so it's not the vast majority of people wanting to express a religious view. But I think it's one manifestation of the politics of identity that is becoming increasingly common."[12]

In Central Europe, populist leaders frame the conflict as one in which the identity of the people must be protected against globalization and "a plague of Islamization." For recalcitrant nativists, African and Muslim refugees are the shock troops of a secret Jewish cabal trying to overthrow the Christian cultural base of the old Austro-Hungarian Empire. These ancient bigotries of religious traditionalism have once again become the cultural glue that binds the lowest common denominator of the populist electorate. This is the stuff that rallies low-education, low-information voters—tattoos, football songs, and the nationalist pride of the populist tribe.

In Russia, like the czars, Putin has built his power alongside the new oligarchic aristocracy, the Orthodox Church, and the millions of impoverished Russians east of Moscow. Putin is not a czar but acts like a modern version, ruthless toward his opposition, assassinating them with poison. Thousands are in jail or living in exile. He likes to be identified with the big men of Russian history— Michael Romanov, Peter the Great, and Joseph Stalin. He is a twenty-first-century strongman who fancies himself a patriot and patriarch of Mother Russia. His iron-fisted leadership protects the country from hostile forces, whether it be the "West" writ large or Pussy Riot.[13] Putin caricatures toxic masculinity, but he is a ruthless operator who rules through the security establishment, the state-controlled media, and the military.

As Alexander Nikolayevich Yakovlev, a former member of the Politburo, has explained, Russia has been long ruled by autocrats, and obedience to the terror of arbitrary authority is baked into the national culture.

It's the "leader principle." It's a disease. It's a Russian tradition. We had our czars, our princes, our secretaries-general, our collective-farm chairmen, and so on. We live in fear of the boss. Think about it: we are not afraid of earthquakes, floods, fires, wars, or terrorist attacks. We are afraid of freedom. We don't know what to do with it . . . That's where the fascist groups come from too—the shock troops of tomorrow.[14]

To rule "the people," Putin looks back to authoritarian models that are older than communism. He cloaks his raw power in religious authority by associating state leadership with the pageantry and traditionalism of Orthodox Christianity. A communist no more, Putin now thinks that it has been Christianity, not the contradictions of capitalism, that has driven Russian history. In the Russian Federal Assembly in 2014, he stated, "It was thanks to this spiritual unity that our forefathers for the first time and forever-more saw themselves as a united nation." Strong language from a former Soviet NKVD agent obsessed with restoring Russia to its imperial greatness.[15]

Finland is a small country, but it is an important one in our class portrait because it's a driving force in modern European populism. Timo Soini is a larger-than-life figure and a veteran tribalist. As a traditional Catholic and sometime theorist of conservative populism, he has been working since the mid-1990s to bring conservative populist democracy into mainstream Finnish politics. In the early years, he built a career in municipal and then later national politics, which helped him spread the gospel. He connected with rural and urban blue-collar voters who felt left behind by European progress.

Soini's party is another example of a true-believer movement. The True Finns (now known as the Finns Party) gained enough votes to form the opposition in the Finnish national legislature, and Soini was deputy prime minister between 2015 and 2017. As an outspoken traditionalist, he has described the ascendancy of populism in religious and mystical terms: "Populism is a *secular gospel* [emphasis added]. It brings good news for the poor and those in difficulty. Its message cuts to the heart of the matter. In today's world, such a secular gospel must be understood in terms of spiritual as well as material well-being."[16]

Like Soini, former Brazilian president Luiz Inácio Lula da Silva (Lula) was an iconic populist too. As an icon of the left, he was loved by the poor and disenfranchised but disgraced by corruption and ultimately ousted and jailed by a bloc of even more powerful, corrupt right-wing populists. The court overturned his conviction and Lula is running once again for reelection. So is his successor, anti-corruption crusader Jair Bolsonaro. An electoral showdown between Lula and Bolsonaro is peak populism.

Jair Bolsonaro and Mike Pence have a lot in common in terms of a self-consciously faith-based rhetoric and style. But Bolsonaro also parrots the "urbane tough guy" act of Donald Trump—bold, brash, macho, and loud. Bolsonaro's base comprises conservative evangelical voters who used to be poor but have risen to prosperity through the long resource boom. These voters have seen their prospects decline in recent years along with commodity prices. The pandemic has worsened their economic outlook, and the truest believers have clung to Bolsonaro even tighter.

Bolsonaro has broadened his support among Catholics by calling for fasting and prayer in the midst of the pandemic. He met with conservatives associated with Renovação Carismática Católica (Catholic Charismatic Renewal) in early April 2020, a meeting at which they declared him to be part of God's "salvation project [to] liberate us from Communism."[17] Francisco Borba Ribeiro Neto, a sociologist at the Catholic University of São Paulo, has argued that Bolsonaro practices a form of "outsider fundamentalism."[18] He views himself as a savior of the country and often plays up his middle name, Messias—or Messiah, in English. His followers nicknamed him "Mita," which means "myth." Isabela Kalil, a Brazilian anthropologist, has likewise suggested that "the staunch Bolsonaro supporters blend a combination of anti-system politics with a refusal to process information that is not created within the Bolsonarista universe."[19]

In Mexico, President Angel Manuel López Obrador stands out in our group portrait for his ecumenism and disinterest in the authority of religion. Mexico's political traditions have a strong vein of anti-clericalism fed by refugees from the Spanish Civil War and right-wing dictatorships in Chile and Argentina. Even so, this is a deeply Catholic country that embraces traditional values, the foremost being patriotism and national integrity. López Obrador is a secular outlier, but he fits the populist profile because he combines charismatic patriarchal leadership with a pugnacious nationalism. He is determined to turn back to an older developmental strategy of nationalization that reverses a generation of privatization since the signing of the North American Free Trade Agreement in 1994.

Finally, there is a lesser-known leader, President Daniel Ortega of Nicaragua, a political survivor who marries centrist populism with religious traditionalism.[20] Ortega is a former leftist revolutionary who has thrived in the gray zone politics of family connection and foreign money at the top of Nicaragua's social hierarchy. He rose to power as a firebrand opponent of crony capitalism but is now a stolid patriarch of neoliberalism. Like the rest of the populists here, he brings together traditional narratives of the foreign elite oppressing plucky Nicaraguans. He plays different Indigenous groups off of each other and maintains his position through a combination of savvy messaging and media control. Ortega knows how to combine left nationalism and nativism, but we must not forget that it is easier to hone a winning political message when your family owns a third of the television market in Nicaragua.

A Portrait of the Populist Voter

Populist leaders are chosen by angry voters who demand belligerent leaders. Conservative populist voters form a hybrid of white-collar business owners, blue-collar industrial worker castoffs, and middle-class service workers with no place to rise. Populist voters are activist political animals goaded by anger who cast their votes across party, race, class, and gender cleavages. Large swaths of economically precarious voters have thrown in their lot with snarling, impetuous demagogues who continuously attack the basic principles of liberalism. The movement also attracts older conservative voters who reject the global rules-based economic system. These new blocs of voters are impulsive, responding to the forces of change without concern for a just society or a code of rational law and ethics.

Political scientists Pippa Norris and Ronald Inglehart studied the comparative data on right-wing populist voting and were among the first to identify the rising nationalist gale.[21] They characterized the populist multitudes as more male than female, and often white with only a high school education. They are more often young than old. Most are in their prime working years, between twenty-five and forty-five. Contrary to the cliché of the white male loser deployed on both the right and left, they are often gainfully employed. Many are single parents and women with little support.

But are these voters "true believers" in the most extreme arguments offered by nativism? Perhaps; perhaps not. In political science terms, these are contingent voters whose support is up for grabs in a system of retail politics. In other words, nativists can be found among the much-courted swing voters of established democracies. Today there are more of them in liberal democracies. Some experts put the number of swing voters among suburbanites, minority ethnic groups, first-time voters, and women as high as 25 percent in highly polarized electoral races.[22] The upsurge in populist voting is in no small way explained by this volatile, fluid change in voting habits. It is important to reiterate that many of these voters are willing to vote for politicians on the left *or* right who craft a platform that clearly identifies what's going wrong in their society.

These are "low information voters," and sometimes pundits use this term dismissively, but there is truth in it. These exurbs are information deserts where people with little education get their news from Facebook and other social media platforms. The local newspaper is just for flyers, and there is endemically low civic engagement. People are awash in words on screens, but little of it is of much use to help them move forward in life or to assuage their fears of a bleak future. They build communities online and in churches. They want to be part of something that matters. They want to be part of the solution to the anomie and inequality of modern life. They are bored. They want something more for themselves but don't know where to look for it, beyond the traditional circles. What they find online is no different, but it's available 24-7, and that is important too.[23]

In the past, these voters used to form communities in kinship networks, make friends at work, and attend church, temple, mosque, or synagogue. In plain terms, their lives revolved around sporting events, family, and steady work. They were the blue-collar salt of the earth, only a generation removed from family farming. Now they spend their time on Facebook, Twitter, WeChat, Weibo, or Zhihu. More and more often, they live apart from their extended families, socialize online, and find their voice at raucous political rallies.[24]

Who are they? In France, the *gilets jaunes* (yellow vests), working-class protesters who live in the suburbs and towns beyond Paris, brought the country to a standstill through massive demonstrations and strikes against the rising cost of living. Their raucous demonstrations week after week beginning in 2018 and lasting for more than a year pressured the Macron government to promise far-reaching reforms.[25] In Britain, these disrupters are disproportionately Brexiters from the Midlands and Northeast England. In a shocking turnaround, they abandoned their long-time Labour Party loyalty to vote Conservative in 2019.[26]

The Pivotal Role of the Low Information Voter

In North America, white American men without a college degree supported Donald Trump in massive numbers in 2016 and 2020. Their wives, girlfriends, and sisters did too, to a slightly lesser extent. Many of these voters are former Democrats who have lost manufacturing jobs. For example, auto workers who have lost their incomes due to globalization shift their political loyalties when their hourly wages are cut in half. At the local level, these shifts are barely perceived at first. But in Michigan, when income per person dropped from 110 percent of the national average to 87 percent in the past decade, Republicans' share of the presidential vote rose by six points, from 48 to 54 percent—an enormous shift in a crucial swing state in 2016.[27] There is a strong correlation between income loss and rising support for political figures whose bellicose language and scapegoating strategies best reflect popular fears.

In 2020, an article in the *New York Times* reported that "by 2016 the Republican Party won almost twice the share of votes in the nation's most destitute counties . . . than it won in the richest."[28] Today, populist and nativist parties position themselves as the champions of those left behind by austerity and market fundamentalism. They win big among globalization's losers. Donald Trump won the presidency despite losing the popular vote because of significant support in inland swing states, which have been hardest hit by the hollowing out of manufacturing. These are members of the American working class with a singular agenda on election day. They don't want a nice guy. They want a big man with a big personality who promises "you're going to win so much, you're going to be so sick and tired of winning."[29]

Voters stuck with Trump as long as he could take credit for low unemployment and record equity prices. But once jobs were decimated by the pandemic, they turned on him. The swing states of Michigan, Wisconsin, Pennsylvania, Arizona, and Georgia turned blue and dumped Trump. The Electoral College giveth, and the Electoral College taketh away.

True believers used to have good jobs and stable incomes. Some of them still do, if they have held on to work in shrinking segments of the economy devoted to manufacturing, corporate sales, mining, or energy. Many used to own their own homes but lost them in the 2008 financial crisis. Some who held on to underwater mortgages lost them anyway, while others rode the housing bounce and are far better off. Either way, their perspective shifted and the Anglo-American middle class has become increasingly convinced that markets are casinos manipulated by the rich.

White, working-class Christians aren't most Americans anymore, but they are still a potent Republican voting bloc numbering in the tens of millions. As job markets for semiskilled workers decline and university tuition rises, these largely white blue-collar workers feel that they and their children are on a slippery slope of declining incomes and debt-driven downward mobility. Many weaponize their declining cultural position by embracing the populist cause. They are the lost middle-class generation in many countries that have embraced populist traditionalism and supported the rise of authoritarians.[30]

The Populist Disruptors' Deep Loyalties

Many of these people—in India, Brazil, Turkey, and even the United States—are not poor, at least not yet. They fear that if things continue as they are, they will become a new underclass, pulled down as much by cultural factors as economic precarity. This is why populists are such a puzzle for political scientists; more than ever, voting is emotive and subjective across all jurisdictions we looked at. Voters choose leaders who mirror their identity, even if they don't necessarily reflect their rational interests.[31]

Does this make voters who break toward conservative populism racist and xenophobic? They themselves don't think so, but many scholars and policymakers would disagree.[32] They are believers in French cultural superiority, American ingenuity, the British stiff upper lip, and the "git 'er done" work ethic of rural everywhere. They are proud of their peasant roots in Finland, Hungary, and the Czech Republic, but they don't extend that solidarity to Black farmers from sub-Saharan Africa. They venerate their rural heritage in western Canada and rural Australia, but they openly distrust migrant workers and political refugees from Pakistan and Afghanistan. In Brazil, they used to be called the "new middle class," because they had climbed out of poverty in the 1990s. When the 2008 global financial crisis decimated commodity markets, their incomes plunged as well.

Unique in the relationship between voters and populist leaders is the deep rapport the leader cultivates and the rapt devotion with which the voter reciprocates the leader's attention. But what's the attraction between these voters and populist leaders? We must assume it is more than mere charisma. Tribes are communities of choice, and as such they represent both ancient touchstones of identity and modern forms of political community. While social media has made joining the community easier, the movements themselves are not recent digital creations. Hindutva zealots, Hungarian true believers, or Islamist Turks have millennial-old roots. But today they are not the old tribes of kin; rather, they are digitally linked, amorphous clans of fealty held together by constantly shifting narratives maintained by adept activists. They are organized around the twin poles of the charismatic leader and his deeply loyal base that resonates with the archetypal masks of populist leadership.[33] But that base's loyalty does not come cheap.

The leader must publicly embrace their cause and stay in sync with activist narratives. These voters want their leaders to stop saying that there is no alternative to globalization, and to start putting their interests first. As the agent of change, the populist disruptor therefore offers a concerted attempt to reorder political relations at home and, just as importantly, rearticulate state interests abroad. It is a prickly bundle of conflicting political projects to manage, with the leader having an outsized role in disentangling domestic authority from its international obligations.

Big Money at Work

The populists talk a big game about representing the *volk*, but their marketing strategy is also carefully calibrated for big business. The alliance between system-wrecking populists and business leaders who value continuity seems contradictory at first glance. But a big part of capitalist success is knowing how to scent the winds of change and back a fresh face.[34] In India, Brazil, the United States, and the UK, populist movements have been backed by powerful economic interests both inside and outside the state. Some of that money has come from wealthy and connected individuals. Other funds have come from donors outside the country intent on using their wealth to reshape liberal democracies beyond their own borders. Even when business owners are liberals, they still sometimes support populist campaigns, because backing the winner is the best way to assure access to governmental decision-makers later.

As political economists Eric Lonergan and Mark Blyth remind us, "when we see tribal energy being fueled for electoral gain, or to generate fear, we are alert to manipulation by media and politicians motivated by vested interests."[35] Facebook and Twitter have given American conservatives a global megaphone under the false pretense that all speech ought to be equal in the public sphere. In the UK, the right-wing tabloid culture does the same for Nigel Farage, Boris Johnson, and their fellow travelers. Modi has whipped the fractious Indian media firmament, and they also do his will against Pakistan or in the simmering confrontation with China over the wilderness Ladakh border region between China and India. The same can be said for Russian, Turkish, and Hungarian media as well.

Every nation with a populist leader has a sovereigntist messaging strategy for bringing together the coalition of nationalism and big money. In Russia, Putin is not beholden to democratic mechanisms. Therefore, he doesn't have financial backers in the Anglo-American sense because he has centralized the levers of clientelist control of the oligarchs in his own hands. Doing business requires a form of tithing, in which one pays the leader for the privilege of profiting in Russia. In this way, Putin has amassed a huge personal fortune in the range of US$70 billion to $200 billion. His takings dwarf the wealth of other Russian kleptocrats.[36] The relationship between money and nationalism in the United States and Russia are only the best-known examples. Let's look at the economic staying power of populism in other national contexts.

One of the reasons Modi is so successful is his ability to shape his message and with it exert broad-spectrum control over the mass media. He is financed by India's leading capitalists, including heavily indebted industrial conglomerates. The BJP, Modi's party, spent lavishly on the 2014 election, burning through at least $670 million.[37] Modi is broadly supported by private-sector India, many members of which are high-caste Hindus. Most importantly, Modi's BJP has a significant hold on the collar of the Indian media.[38] Modi, like Trump and Johnson, believes strongly in the importance of charismatic leadership to hold together the coalition of true believers and big money backers. He uses an authoritarian grip on the fractious Indian media to cement his place at the top of the pyramid.

India is a vast media universe unto itself, with seventeen thousand newspapers, a hundred thousand magazines, and 178 television channels. The BJP uses an army of unpaid party trolls to police social media, labeling those critical of government policy as #antinational.[39] Salaried workers send directives to news editors to stipulate how to cover the prime minister's activities. Modi's party uses other pressure tactics too, such as raiding news channels, tax investigations of journalists and editors, and stopping government advertising in major newspapers, which is a significant source of advertising revenue.[40] The party also controls the selective handing out of lucrative television licenses.

So far, the media is knuckling under. An investigation by the *New York Times* corroborated what many independent Indian news outlets have whispered about for years. Modi's government "has tried to control the country's news media, especially the airwaves, like no other prime minister in decades."[41] And he has been largely successful. "Even skeptical journalists censor themselves," an article reports, "afraid to be branded anti-national by a government that equates patriotism with support for Mr. Modi."[42]

Rodrigo Duterte in the Philippines, like Modi, Netanyahu, and the rest, intimidates and silences opposition critics in the media and uses the power of the megaphone to rally his nativist supporters. He is quick to sue for libel and defamation, and sometimes he wins. He also follows the populist playbook of appealing to the financial elite for money while simultaneously portraying himself as a swamp-draining nationalist. He is supported by old money in Davao City and Manila, although he pretends to be funded by "Emilio Aguinaldo," by which he means ordinary Filipinos—Joe the Plumber, in American terms.[43]

Duterte has a complicated relationship with his moneyed backers. His populist campaign for president mocked the elite as "illustrious idiots" and a "cancer on society." He openly declared that his intention was to "destroy the oligarchs embedded in the government," and then he named and shamed his political rivals.[44] But Duterte did not want to destroy the financial elite. Rather, he wanted to bend them to his will and create a new network of money with his movement at the center. In early 2019, he threatened to sue and arrest members of the families who control two major Philippine corporations over water contracts that he thought disadvantaged the state. When he made peace, the entire Philippine stock market enjoyed a large bounce. The story is not about the corrosive influence of money in politics anymore, but rather about how Duterte made himself the chieftain of the elite.[45]

Finally, Viktor Orbán of Hungary rounds out our examples of authoritarian populists who beat down journalists, court dark money, and forge a coalition of nationalists and domestic financial interests. Hungary used to be a beacon for post-Soviet democracy, but it has spiraled into corruption and crony capitalism. Hungary is still an agrarian country and Orbán's funding is quite different from that of the other populists. Orbán's family wealth, and that of their peers, comes from land rents, European subsidies on agricultural production, and the structural funds doled out by Brussels. Hungary is a major beneficiary of EU funding, and received more than €6 billion (US$6.5 billion) in 2018. The EU payments are equivalent to 5 percent of the country's GDP. At the same time, Hungary contributed only a billion euros back to the EU.[46]

Orbán openly intimidates all critics of his government. For example, he has forced the Central European University, funded by George Soros's Open Society Foundations, to pick up stakes and move to Vienna from Budapest. He is obsessed with the prospect of foreign influence and outside money strengthening the opposition.[47] The fact that Orbán is so obviously dependent on EU transfer payments makes his quest for sovereignty look both hypocritical and self-serving. A truly independent Hungary would be poorer. As it stands, the EU contributes agricultural funding that directly benefits Orbán's inner circle, most of whom own large farms.[48] So Orbán rattles his sabre and intimidates his opposition without actually meeting his stated goal of more sovereignty, because to actually leave the EU like Britain did would be to cook the goose that lays the golden egg.

A Welcome Mat for Conspiracy Theory

Rumor, innuendo, and salaciously cruel gossip have always been a method for influencing political outcomes.[49] And it's not just here that conspiracies thrive. We showed above that QAnon is alive and well in countries with the highest standard of living, including Germany and Austria. The belief in conspiracy theories has spread much farther than Western Europe.[50] Conspiracy theories live on because, like the bogeyman, they rely on heightened emotion, not reason, to maintain their place in our imagination. According to British psychologist Jovan Byford, "conspiracy theories seduce not so much through the power of argument, but through the intensity of the passions that they stir. Underpinning conspiracy theories are feelings of resentment, indignation and disenchantment about the world. They are stories about good and evil, as much as about what is true."[51]

In Russia, conspiracy theories are spread by Russia Today television network.[52] In Latin America, conspiracy theories have also been central to the politics of cronyism and corruption. They have spread under Jair Bolsonaro, for example, who takes an active role in the long-standing Brazilian tradition of anti-communist conspiracy peddling. Flávia Biroli, a political scientist at the University of Brazília, notes that "it's important to remember that the idea of moral decay was behind anti-communism too—the threat to the family was mentioned then and is back now. Bolsonaro brings these elements together and he does it very well."[53]

Conspiracy theories may appear unbelievable to the unconvinced, but the feelings of helplessness in the face of monumental change are very real.[54] Anytime discredited elites must contend with the forces of change and uncertain futures, populists peddling conspiracies and fear enter the picture. According to the 2020 Edelman Trust Barometer's international survey, people increasingly distrust government, business, non-governmental organizations, and the media. None of society's main institutions are considered to be trustworthy. Among those surveyed in South Asia, Europe, Hong Kong, and the Americas, there is a growing sense of inequity, a rising pessimism about economic prospects, and a fear of being left behind.[55]

Conservative populism has similar poisonous effects wherever it takes root. It is not a mysterious hothouse bloom. The noted American political theorist Benjamin Barber first warned thirty years ago that reactionary populism could become the dominant force opposing globalization: "The mood is that of jihad," he said, "not as an instrument of policy, but as an emblem of identity, an expression of community, an end in itself."[56] Nationalism was once a force of integration. Now it is used to pummel enemies real and imagined.

We know the archetypal masks worn by populist leaders. We know their methods. We know how they use chaos and fear to undermine civil society. We know they want to consolidate their grip on power. To that end, they seek to undo the constitutional limits on what a leader may do in the name of the state. Once they have that power, there will be a revolution at the top. The unraveling will move down the pyramid of power, recruiting loyalists along the way, firming up its connections to money and finance. Spin doctors, rich donors, communities of experts, and a mass media propaganda machine will help the movement reach its exclusionary goal: the end of liberal democracy as we know it.

PART II
THE INSURGENCY

CHAPTER 4

The Sovereignty Project

An Old Idea Gets a Makeover

All of the populists are united in their goal of regaining the sovereignty their state supposedly lost in the past four decades of globalization. Rhetorically, we need to ask: Who doesn't want their country to have more control over its own destiny? Of course, the question of whether we must regain our sovereignty begs a more basic one: have we really lost any sovereignty? Many conservative commentators would answer with a resounding yes! In an era of globalization, have we not delegated sovereignty to a range of international actors? Does that not make our states weaker because our governments don't control aspects of governance that they used to?

Liberals would say, no, we have not lost sovereignty absolutely. Rather, we have become more interconnected, and the challenges that states face require specialized actors to deal with them, including international organizations. Every nation is linked through global supply chains and also socially interconnected with its neighbors. Even North Korea, the isolated Hermit Kingdom, has an interdependent relationship with China. So when populists beat the drum of sovereignty, liberals assume that it is little more than performance art. After all, a lot of the political swag worn at nationalist rallies everywhere is made in China.[1]

But the sovereignty project is much more than red meat for the base. The foreign policy lens empowers populists to frame the problems facing their societies as a foreign threat. The leader's stature grows when people rally around the flag. It is all well and good to recognize foreign policy as a tool of populism, but we haven't explained what makes sovereignty such a powerful tool in the populist bag. One way to explain the power of sovereignty narratives is to look at how mainstream the idea of sovereignty is, and how conventional. Who would oppose autonomy for their government and more power for their elected representatives? No reasonable person opposes popular control of their own country's policies.

Of course, the problem isn't sovereignty itself. Liberal internationalists are correct that powerful states don't gain and lose sovereignty. Sovereignty is not a commodity that can be traded away, even though we often use the metaphors of delegation to explain how states deputize other organizations to carry out governance activities. But the story is a lot more complicated because conservatives are correct too, in their assertion that sovereignty ought to be safeguarded because, despite four decades of intense globalization, it is still the lifeblood of national community.

What ought we to think about populism and its obsession with sovereignty? Can it be dismissed as rhetorical nationalism or explained away as pandering to a nativist base? We argue that the way powerful states are reorienting their foreign and domestic policies suggests that we are entering a new era of sovereignty-first state relations with less investment in multilateral cooperation, and the populists are at least partly responsible. For example, Xi Jinping has pivoted China away from a narrow focus on export markets toward domestic priorities, which use economic tools to address issues like poverty, common prosperity, and the environmental crisis.[2] For the Communist Party of China, a return to the basics of sovereignty is necessary to consolidate the gains of globalization. The sovereignty focus and a transition toward domestic autonomy are the narrative frames for Xi's third term in office.[3]

Likewise in the United States, Joe Biden's foreign policy incorporates a sovereigntist frame. Biden is continuing Donald Trump's America First policy, just under a different guise. Whereas Trump emphasized that America is getting ripped off, Biden emphasizes the importance of social protection of families and communities for "building back better." But the substantive thrust of both presidents when it comes to foreign policy is that America needs to take back control globally as the foremost power setting the international agenda. In fact, US support for Ukraine has the obvious consequence of both emphasizing the importance of the NATO alliance while framing American power as essential to the protection of liberalism once more. In Washington, there is a bipartisan consensus on rejuvenating American leadership, through infrastructure, technology, and competitiveness.[4] In fact, the single issue the Democrats and Republicans agree on is that America must win the bare-knuckle boxing match against China and Russia, and that means weighting the American heavyweight gloves with more sovereignty.

European nations can see which way the wind is blowing, and they are battening down the hatches in the EU, pivoting toward a policy of "strategic autonomy" on trade and finance, in which they understand that their interests are diverging from those in the United States. Gérard Araud, former French ambassador to the US, recognizes that the new sovereigntism carries fewer certainties: "After Biden, it may be Trump again . . . so we Europeans, we have to learn to be grown up, we have to learn to defend or to handle our interests by ourselves."[5] The war in Ukraine has only heightened Europe's perception that security relies on building pro-active policies to both safeguard sovereignty and protect the economic interests of the bloc.

Weaponizing Sovereignty

The main problem with the new sovereignty project is that populists are weaponizing sovereignty for chauvinistic purposes to mobilize their base, which benefits only a segment of the electorate, and this is enormously destructive. Authoritarian populist movements have taken their criticism of modern liberal democracy in a dangerous direction. The populists are trying to revitalize a form of sovereignty that reflects an older world of ethno-cultural supremacy.[6] This sovereignty project is perilous because it seeks to return to a violent imperial hierarchy in which wealth and status were typically won through coercion, armed violence, and conquest.[7]

Today, the concept of sovereignty has newfound urgency to bludgeon liberal internationalism, the high standard of international relations. The populists want a new, narrow, inward-looking approach to sovereignty because they know that reducing a state's obligations to international institutions also reduces the fixed costs of operating in the world, at least temporarily. In the long run, it increases the costs of maintaining global order, but they don't concern themselves with the future. Their myopia only increase future transaction costs, the best example being the case of the global pandemic and the massive state involvement required to protect public health.

The populists want to revamp the international order according to their own values, to dismantle the invasive internationalist dimensions that they believe are not part of its pure essence. This originalist vision of order imagines that there was a time long ago before the industrial age when states were completely independent, and governments made decisions that were only about maximizing their own power. It wrongly claimed that values don't clash in international relations because no state is trying to make the world better. Rather, in this flawed view of history, states operated according to national interests with no need to worry about human rights, international law, or massive systemic change caused by a warming climate.

Of course, like other big lies, the lie about international history is self-serving and false.[8] The conservatives don't want to be bound by treaty obligations for human rights, or even for trade and investment, if those deals limit their authority here and now. The sovereignty project is about retrenchment around the immediate interests of the leader and his tribe. Modi, Orbán, Maduro, and López Obrador have tightened control over borders.[9] Johnson, Trump, and Duterte tore up economic agreements that conceptualized sovereignty as a shared arrangement. For all of these figures, the new concern with national integrity has the toxic populist side effect of increasing cultural polarization, and for ultra-rightists that is beneficial to the movement.[10] The populists judge that a narrative in which the true people are beset on all sides by the tyranny of evil foreigners is the best way to maintain their grip on their base.

But it hasn't been a cakewalk. Until recently, there has been no pressing reason to place territorial control front and center on the public agenda. Talk of sovereignty, the national interest, and raison d'état was mostly on the margins of international public policy.[11] It wasn't a central part of the grand strategy articulated by policy chieftains in the United States. In such an interdependent age, the state itself, with its bricks and mortar bureaucracy, was increasingly seen as analog—old, inefficient, and an obstacle to progress.

Predictably, governments were caught flatfooted as public opinion shifted. After decades in cold storage under neoliberal regimes, the idea of state power as a tool to defend the national interest has returned with a vengeance. "Sovereignty now!" is the rallying cry of the conservative anti-system of charismatic leaders, social media followers, nativists, white supremacists, militia members, "sovereign citizens," and other conspiracists.

What matters most is that they tap into the psyche of the nation in a deep way with their powerful icons of flag and country, race and privilege, rule of law, and constitutional history, all of which are powerful totems of identity. These symbols evoke powerful emotions of the land, inviolability of borders, and the necessity of national sacrifice. Rhetorically, they are about holding one's head up high, national respect, and hope for better days ahead.

But in reality, slam-bam nationalists have taken control of the national narrative for their own interests. For example, Duterte declared all-out war against crime, even advocating vigilantism. His embrace of lawlessness for the purposes of law and order made the Philippines more unstable, and more dangerous.[12] Johnson declared war on the idea of the common market and lost some of the UK's biggest export markets in the process.[13] Trump declared war on the swamp, which he defined as the professional consultancy class who work as lobbyists and advisors. They populate the upper ranks of public administration, the military, and think tanks in Washington, DC. Putin declared war on all domestic opposition and arrested thousands of his main opponent Alexei Navalny's supporters, as well as the leader himself in January 2021 on Navalny's return from Germany after being poisoned by Russian operatives.[14] Supercharged populism throws out the old rules and takes on an "every state for itself" approach to nation-building that benefits the leader first and foremost.

Sovereignty captures the political imagination of conservatives because it is intellectual and emotional shorthand for patriotism and freedom. Conservative populists use terms like "sovereignty" and "freedom" to act unilaterally and to cast political rights as finite resources.[15] Once you give some away, you have less for yourself. Most significantly, however, when it comes to acting unilaterally, the anti-liberal disrupters identify sovereignty as the freedom of autonomous action only when it is action that they initiate and control. They don't like the idea of unilateral action when it is their rivals acting unilaterally. The message to the base is wrap yourself in the flag and stomp on your enemies.

One final point that needs emphasis is that sovereignty has struck a deep note with people who don't want to be left behind. They don't want to fear the impersonal forces unleashed by the market anymore. They need to make sense of a world of monumental shift. From a psychoanalytic perspective, Sherry Turkle gives us a way to understand the potency of the sovereignty narrative: "Theories most easily pass into popular culture when they offer a way for people to think through a collective issue of political and social identity."[16] So what is the psychological appeal of sovereignty for the true believer? A cynic might say that populists are telling a simplistic story that is easily believed by people who don't think much about globalization. But that isn't all of it. The populists are asking a very important question about the indispensable presence of the state in everyday life and twisting it into something else. To dig into the nuance of sovereignty in an age of globalization, we need to know something about its origins.

Sovereignty in Principle and Practice

For historians the concept of sovereignty is inevitably traced back to the Peace of Westphalia that ended the Thirty Years War in Europe in 1648.[17] The development of the concept in which states did not interfere in the internal actions of their neighbors put a punctuation mark on the religious wars between Catholics and Protestants in the sixteenth and seventeenth centuries.[18]

By definition sovereignty is both a legal category and a standard for governmental legitimacy. It is the power of a country to control its own territory and make its own decisions inside its borders. Secondarily it is about symbols such as the flag, borders checkpoints, and national myths. National narratives of exceptionalism are as much a part of the sovereignty story as are territory and control of borders.[19] Sovereignty is the value of *maître chez nous*—being independent. It is the power to protect citizens from criminality at home and from foreign invaders. It is equally about dominance over geography and effective economic regulation.[20] Sovereignty is articulated through governmental action in every policy domain. It is the power to tax, to spend, to regulate, and to incentivize. To be clear sovereignty is not a state of being. It is a constant, dynamic process of becoming.

Of course, the basic definition is still operative. Today, sovereignty is a foundational principle of international law and a central pillar of every one of the 193 nations that comprise the United Nations. Article 2 of the UN Charter states that "the Organization is based on the principle of the sovereign equality of all its members."[21]

Sovereignty is accepted today as a right of self-determination and a responsibility to maintain law and order. A state may be recognized as sovereign if it exercises control over its territory and its citizens. States maintain their sovereignty through agenda setting, decision making, and policy implementation and the military capacity to defend its territory and people. It is widely accepted that the converse is also true. According to the fragile state index, territories where a government cannot assert active control, such as Yemen, Syria, and Afghanistan, are called failed states depending on the degree of state vulnerability. There are more than twenty-five countries whose central government is weak and ineffective or dangerously debt stressed, heading for potential default.[22] A territory without effective control is a sitting target for civil war, a military coup, transnational crime gangs, and terrorist groups.[23]

The Story of Louis Napoleon

The links between populism, authoritarianism, and traditionalism are as old as politics itself. But we don't have to go back to Greek philosophers to show how this works. It is enough to tell the story of the last king of France. The nineteenth-century populism of Louis Napoleon has uncomfortable parallels with conservative movements today that use nationalism to gain and hold power. Louis Bonaparte (1808–1873) was the nephew of Napoleon Bonaparte, the military officer from Corsica who rose to power after the French Revolution. Napoleon's defeat at Waterloo ushered in the Concert of Europe, a new era of conservative stability, in 1815. For decades after, his family continued to look for a way back to power. With the popular revolutions of 1848 and the abdication of King Louis Philippe, the Bonaparte nephew saw an opportunity. He ran for the presidency and won.

But right from the beginning, his administration was beset on all sides by critics and hampered in its reform efforts by term limits. Louis decided to silence his critics and gain the power necessary to make France great again. He launched a coup d'état, arresting his enemies and launching a wave of propaganda. The Paris proletariat failed to revolt against the coup plotters, despite Marx's great hope that the working class would be a bulwark against tyranny. In the end, despite a republican distrust of autocrats, the machinery of the French state was too weak to resist Louis Napoleon. President Louis Napoleon became Napoleon III, the last emperor of the French.

Those of us in the English-speaking world remember this story because it was immortalized in *The Eighteenth Brumaire of Louis Bonaparte*, a classic account of class relations by Karl Marx. Are we living through another Bonapartist moment? Will these authoritarians become kings? What makes the populist upsurge such a train wreck is that when you mix ambitious egomaniacs with popular anger and big money, if luck is against you, you get dictators and kings. Marx teaches the cautionary tale of how an ambitious populist with a messiah complex can take over a dysfunctional political system.[24]

The current crop of charismatic leaders is not interested in representing social need, but only wish to weaponize grievance for their own ends.[25] For populist leaders, the people are an abstraction, reducible to affect and taste. And this is where they meet with our friend Louis Bonaparte. The flimsy rhetoric of populism failed to galvanize the radicals into a resistance movement. The same is true today when the conservative populists sneer at reform and desire to channel popular rage for their own ends. Is the machinery of the liberal democratic state at the present time too disorganized to resist the well-orchestrated attack of the populist big men?

National Identity Is Sticky Like Crazy Glue

Polls have shown that people don't want to be defined by their consumption patterns. They would rather be known for their national, ethnic, or family identities.[26] They identify as Japanese, Pakistani, Argentinian, and Italian. They have not moved heart and soul into a post-national era in which communities are created by choice rather than dictated by fate. National identity is sticky. You can buy a book by an award-winning French author on Amazon, read it in your book club in Austin, Texas, and share it with your sister-in-law in Toronto, but none of those affiliations—Francophile, book lover, Texan, bi-national family—surpass national identity. I can criticize your taste in literature, but I'd better not rag on your nationality.

In a world in which "all that is solid melts into air," the nation has a mysterious and quasi-spiritual solidity—or so we'd like to believe.[27] If it can be rediscovered and reconstituted by the populists, is it any more solid than the rest of modernity? And so the populist movement proceeds supposedly secure in its nationalist foundations and yet convinced that it needs to reverse the undertow of liberalism or face imminent demise. "Sovereignty now!" is the perfect rallying cry to fire up a movement of alienated voters, because as a big lie, it is tremendously compelling. All that's necessary is to identify a scapegoat, a countermovement, a traitor, a wolf among the sheep.

That is why the populist leader needs to fight symbolic battles that are hugely important to their tribe's self-worth. Populists inevitably choose large, amorphous forces to wage war on: the global order, institutions, immigration, ideologies, or the media. The liberal international order is public enemy number one. The American tribe attempted to dismantle liberal internationalism by attacking the legitimacy of international organizations such as the WTO and WHO. They swung their wrecking ball wherever they found a moving target.

The Indian tribe is transgressing the Indian constitution, occupying Kashmir, and in so doing attempting to take the entire subcontinent for Hindus.[28] The British tribe is fixated on reconstituting an ancient trading empire in which they dictate terms to the rest of the world from their tiny island. China is very much a part of this geopolitical jockeying and is carving out an expansive sphere of control in Asia for its growing tribe.[29] This is a new period of dangerous, unstable, great power rivalry. These are political wars, but

also wars of ideas in which sovereignty is the weapon to be bran-
dished at every turn. It is not surprising that states have returned to
the ideal of national autonomy. After all, the bloodline of modern
conservatism is long and deep and anchored in empire. What's
more, the arbitrary exercise of authority has been the norm and
liberalism the exception for most of political history.

For populists, all the ills of the modern era spring from their
nation's losses, real and imagined. Is this not the common lament
of Modi, Netanyahu, Bolsonaro, and the rest? Their nations have
lost something that is almost indefinable—*un éclat, élan, esprit.*
Sovereignty becomes the treasure at the end of the hero's quest
that populist movements use to define their progress toward state
restoration and the end of a long-imagined period of national
humiliation. But at a time when entire societies must face daunting
challenges from systemic climate change, the hero's quest to
single-handedly make his nation great again looks less like a heroic
pursuit for achievement and more like a lonely form of narcissism.

Sometimes they have an antagonistic relationship to the pursuit
of sovereignty, sometimes they want a revolution, and sometimes
they are petty reformers whose rhetoric doesn't match their lower
expectations. They want a return to sovereignty in the most mech-
anistic sense of a national will to power. But if one scratches the
surface of the rhetoric to reveal the economic interest beneath,
the end goal is not really more sovereignty. The real prize is more
power and latitude of action for the executive office, which is held
by the populist *el jefe* leader. Populists like the idea of enhancing
state sovereignty because they want to use the sovereign authority
vested in the leader to clip the wings of global governance and
enhance the hard power of the state. And then they want to use
that power to gain advantages in the global economy.

Theoretically, all of the tribe will benefit from the return to
the simple ideal of absolute sovereignty. The insurgents have been

primed by thirty years of neoliberalism to instinctively believe that a rising tide for the tribe will lift everyone's dinghy. But in reality, one can see benefit flowing in only one direction. These advantages accrue directly and indirectly to the populist chieftain and his inner circle as practitioners of paternalism and clientelism. So how does the sovereignty narrative play out in different countries?

The Sovereignty Narrative in Russia

Vladimir Putin is the prime example of the populist leader who has repurposed his own security state apparatus, which is indispensable to the sovereignty project. He has fully shaped it in his own image since coming to power twenty years ago. He has surrounded himself with highly competent loyalists such as Russian foreign minister Sergey Lavrov and the oligarchs who control much of the Russian economy, including strategic commodity and financial sectors.[30] This economic and political elite group is entirely reliant upon Putin's favor, but in return for loyalty, he offers a deep network of economic and political connections. Putin became a politician only after a career in the Russian intelligence service. He doesn't fear the deep state because he is the deep state.

More than anything else, Putin is a master tactician who uses the element of surprise to keep his rivals off balance. He believes above all in security-driven counterbalancing, in which Moscow has the right to organize the affairs of its subordinate states which must look to the imperial metropole for guidance in political affairs, foreign and domestic. Like the rest of our class portrait, he sees no reason to consider ethical niceties in the realm of global governance. He is a realist and a ruthless strategist in the classical sense.[31] He brutally persecutes the political opposition through extrajudicial killings and imprisonment. Temperamentally and stylistically, he simultaneously resembles the grandiose ambitions of Peter the Great and the lethal cunning of Joseph Stalin.

Like the many Russian autocrats before him, Putin is not a populist like Trump, for whom populism is a part of his personality. Rather, Putin wears his populism like a mask of global command. He can put it on and take it off as his realpolitik requires but he fools only the naïve and the uninformed. For populists like Putin, stability in a multipolar system is the result of calculating leaders seizing the momentum when they can, and taking the high road only when there is no other alternative. Fairness, justice, and human security are only rhetorical cover for harder interests. He understands the implications of American war fatigue in the Middle East, and he has calculated that the politicians of the Anglo-American states would rather appease him than mobilize their enormous resources to defend the principles of the liberal order.[32] Putin was partly correct in this assessment. But he did not expect that in response to the invasion of Ukraine, Europe and the United States would cooperate to seize central bank assets, launch a punitive boycott of a huge portion of Russian business and society, and supply billions of dollars worth of the latest generation of weapons to the Ukrainian government.

The Sovereignty Narrative in Mexico

Mexico's Andrés Manuel López Obrador (AMLO) is a unique personality in the populist class portrait. López Obrador represents a break with older norms of anti-American nationalism common in Latin America. But he is not a neophyte in Mexican politics. He is a big booster of Mexican sovereignty, which he does not see as a single issue but as a framework for addressing corruption, privatization, inequality, deregulation, and the management of the border.

If AMLO shares a worldview with the other populists, it is in his contempt for the North American economic elite and in his belief that they are working to undermine him. And he would not be entirely wrong, although he likes to play up the extent to which he, as an everyman, faces overwhelming domestic elite opposition. It is true, however, that banks and multinational firms have been his enemy, although they reluctantly admit that he has been a stabilizing force. In the words of one banker, "We may not like López Obrador's economic policies—in fact, we hate them. But we have to recognize that he has delivered a few years of political stability, which has spared us from the mess engulfing countries f[a]rther south."[33] He is by far the most popular national leader in Latin America and this grudging acknowledgment, even if only from a select few in the financial community, is rare for a leftist in Mexican politics.

His likeness to other populists is also seen in his willingness to take idiosyncratic positions that are based in his own experience, rather than in a more traditional ideological frame. For example, López Obrador hates debt-fueled public spending, a fact not easily reconciled with the business community's attempt to paint him as an out-of-touch leftist. According to one former minister, "AMLO turns into a panther when you suggest that he should take on more debt. It's simply not something you can discuss. He will not spend."[34] His debt aversion comes from a belief that Mexican governments he admired in the 1960s and '70s were crippled by too much debt, and that Mexican sovereignty therefore requires a higher degree of financial autonomy.

As a populist, AMLO wears the masks of archetypal populist leadership. In particular, he relishes the role of National Defender. After he won the presidency in 2017, he continued to position himself as an outsider in the Mexican establishment. In 2020, when the pandemic struck, he resisted all calls to take firm and swift measures. He preferred to counter with rallies, warnings from public health officials, and in the final instance when it was clear that he had miscalculated, a fatalistic bravado. Even so, Mexicans have stuck by him, despite the criticism. In midterm elections, his party fell just short of a supermajority, and this level of support is almost unprecedented in modern Mexican politics.

Donald Trump and his followers painted Mexico as the source of all illegal immigrants and criminal gangs, but surprisingly, López Obrador did not seem to hold all this negativity against Trump.[35] By temperament, AMLO is cautious about maintaining entangling alliances but quick to take advantage of geopolitical circumstances that will enhance Mexico's prestige.[36] Like the rest of the populists, AMLO is skilled at creating symbolic public policy that is rich in rhetoric and short on big results. For example, he changed the Pemex company logo to include the words "for the recovery of sovereignty" to highlight his goal of using the state champion to rebuild Mexico's energy sector.[37] Like those of the other populists, his sovereignty project is both an economic symbol and a strategy for national renewal. Even so, AMLO is convinced that Mexico can profit from changing configurations of global power. His retrenchment behind fossil fuels is startlingly traditionalist. And his willingness to bet his political future on national champions and the politicization of Mexican industrial policy is contemporary populism through and through.

Dumbing Down the Sovereignty Narrative

After having listened to the populist chiefs and their confident pronouncements about the stunning success of the sovereignty project, you might be tempted to think that sovereignty is cut and dried—we've worked out all the bugs in the concept and we know how it is used and abused. While nationalists obsess about lost sovereignty, liberals went to the other extreme. In a digital world of global information flows, sovereignty was analog tech. For postwar liberal internationalists, defending sovereignty seemed unnecessary because the welfare state reinforced the basic concept of state authority. For the neoliberals of the 1980s, the regulatory state was still a fact of life. But experts such as Kenichi Ohmae were looking forward to an imminent future in which wealthy and secure citizens participated in international markets on their own terms and states would wither away.[38] In one form or another this Hayekian vision for a post-state future stayed with us for the next four decades.

The global financial crisis of 2008 refuted the idea that globalized society had no further need for the regulatory state, but we still weren't worried much about national sovereignty. Conventional wisdom sold us the platitude that our future was secure because big tech was producing the social media platforms that would bind us all together in a tighter form of interdependence. It is amazing to recall that a Google employee became the symbol of the Arab Spring in North Africa. We watched livestreams of the protests in the Maidan Uprising that toppled a corrupt, Moscow-aligned regime in Ukraine in 2014. This was the global village we were promised by media guru Marshall McLuhan. Timeless concerns about sovereignty and national community were looming, but according to the commentariat, the problems of interdependence would be resolved through more technological interconnection, more economic flows, and greater mutual benefits from online life for everyone.[39]

As neoliberal policy undermined the welfare state, it became apparent that it also corroded people's sense of national community, leaving a big opening for the populists. The sovereignty project is the perfect fight to fire up a movement of alienated voters. The populists know a lot about selling this quasi-religious attachment to hearth and home. The sovereignty narrative promises advancement for the masses through tribal renewal and national transformation.

But as we will discuss next, sovereignty is a bigger and more complicated issue than ever. Repatriating sovereignty is a daunting task in which the ideals of interdependence and shared community collide with the hard power of the armored state. For the populists, the needs of the state are always more important than the desires of people, regardless of their invocation of belonging and meaning. Welcome to the post-liberal world.

CHAPTER 5

The Post-Liberal Order

The Latest Diplomatic Dance

The populists are putting the liberal international order on trial. They accuse it of creating too many rules, of ineffective institutions, and of continuing to pour resources into a creaky alliance system that is no longer fit for purpose. They don't like the legal thicket of rights and obligations, the secrecy, the bureaucracy, the legalism, and the diplomatic dance in the face of Chinese power politics.[1] Their biggest complaint is that unelected officials—at the EU, the WTO, and the UN—are undermining the state's ability to pursue its national interests. The bean counters and rule-book thumpers and all the rest of the bureaucrats want to tie the hands of the alpha male leaders, and that can't be allowed to happen.

Populist movements want to put as much space between themselves and Anglo-American liberalism as possible. For them, liberal internationalism is synonymous with elite interests, brokerage of power, and management of affairs of state in the interests of a professional class. Or at least, that's the official story.

Recall how we showed in Chapter 3 that the populists are themselves privileged and wealthy members of the top strata of their societies. The fact that the populist leaders only play at being the humble everyman, and are in fact members of the same elite they pretend to hate makes their disdain for liberalism all the more untenable. They became rich in global markets. If they really believe that throwing over human rights, open markets, and collective security will make the world a safer place, they are fools. But if their position is a smokescreen and their true goal is to gather more power to themselves, then their willingness to throw away *our security* makes them an existential danger to everyone. But let's take them at their word for the moment so that we may better understand their case against the liberal international order.

The Sovereignty Orthodoxy

Trump wanted to drain the swamp in Washington, but how do you drain the swamp in Geneva? The answer is by dismantling the WTO's legal system and paralyzing its dispute resolution mechanism by refusing to appoint new judges.[2] In Trump's America, not only does the president have authority over international trade at home, but he must be allowed to step around WTO rules too.

Of course, for British nationalists like Boris Johnson, the WTO is not a great Satan. British nationalists hope it will be useful in shaping a different relationship with the EU. Significantly, the institutions of global governance are differently perceived by different populists. There is no single orthodoxy to be found. Even so, the Anglo-Americans represented by Johnson and Trump were united in their desire for a grand realignment that returns sovereignty to the state via Brexit and the Make America Great Again (MAGA) campaign.

For the populists outside the Anglo-American bubble, like Indian prime minister Narendra Modi and Hungary's Viktor Orbán, the goal is to profit from the dismantling process and to benefit from a checkerboard of transactional alliances and security agreements. In both respects, right-wing populists in both rich countries and emerging economies are betting big on the return of the nation-centered system to replace liberal international order where there are fewer international rights and obligations that reach behind borders.[3] This would lead to fewer incentives to collaborate on climate change, less international oversight of human rights violations, and fewer codified rules governing trade between countries. At least in theory, every big boss wins something.

For the MAGA men, there is always a way to bend the trading system to use it against a rising China. For Little Englanders, there are advantages to be seized in European commerce by opting out of the EU. Before their invasion of Ukraine, the Russians had assumed correctly that they could benefit from European commodity markets and American financial services without giving in to liberal ideas of fair play. As the cracks spread across postwar liberalism, an increasingly selective application of international law is still the norm.

Robert Zoellick, former head of the World Bank, has succinctly captured the dysfunctionality of this position in which law is simultaneously an important piece of governance and a hindrance that must be pushed out of the way:

> Today, the US, the innovator and guarantor of the late 20th-century order, is recklessly deconstructing its own framework. China, which rose successfully within this supportive international system, threatens it from within while exploring an alternative design based on tributary states.

Ageing Japan, fearful of China and uncertain [about] America's reliability, treads cautiously. India drifts back to the diplomacy of "strategic autonomy." Russia manipulates for external advantage while withering internally. The EU struggles to preserve internal coherence while waking painfully to dashed dreams of a postmodernist international legal order. Britain debates with itself. Middle-weight economies struggle to calculate where they will fit within the fractious new world. Billions of people in developing countries do the best they can.[4]

Most states used to accept, at least in theory, that institutions of global governance could legitimately wield delegated sovereignty that reduced a state's scope of action but increased the world's collective benefit. The Bretton Woods and UN institutions were premised upon the assumption that international rules are in the enlightened self-interest of all countries. In the 1950s, this was a radical idea whose time had come. Keynesian-embedded liberalism was the lynchpin, improving on the older idea of laissez-faire capitalism by regulating labor markets and creating a social safety net.[5]

We have argued that the populists don't have a positive vision in terms of ideals and values for the world because they are nationalists first. But they do have a vision *for their nation's place in the world*. The populists exaggerate the hypocrisy of liberalism and take their own hypocrisy to a new level, which only highlights the contradictions of the aging liberal order. They constantly look for inflection points where the liberal rules benefit themselves, while using every trick in the book to hurt their most threatening rivals with tariffs or punitive sanctions. But perhaps the most significant development is the fact that international order has become so central to domestic political considerations. Populist leaders view their victories in the international realm as burnishing their record of winning domestic wars for their political base.

The Return of the Nation-Centered System

Ian Bremmer, a risk consultant and author, argues correctly that this global reboot order is driven by an intense inward focus: "every nation for itself."[6] The practical consequence is that each nation defines its national interest with little regard for collective security and economic reciprocity in the global community of nations. For the global polity, this means fewer rules, more subsidies, more unilateralism, more tunnel vision, rampant short-termism, less cooperation, less stability, and a great deal of pushing and shoving on the high beam of international relations.

It also results in the proliferation of low-ambition international agreements that are long on rhetoric and short on substance. The best recent example is COP26, the UN system for enacting the Framework Convention on Climate Change. Even UK prime minister Boris Johnson confessed his disappointment in the final statement, which watered down the goal to end the use and subsidization of fossil fuels. Jennifer Morgan, head of Greenpeace International, said the final outcome was weak, adding, "Glasgow was meant to deliver on firmly closing the gap to 1.5°C and that didn't happen."[7]

What does "every nation for itself" look like? It is less global regulation and less regulatory oversight from international organizations. It is against value-driven foreign policy and for ad hoc deals that favor nationalist movements. The populists call themselves realists and sneer at the so-called idealism of liberalism. They are creatures steeped in the culture of transactional politics in the Anglo-American sphere, where cooperation is never free, and interdependence comes with hidden costs. But the fact that they recognize that every worm hides a hook doesn't make them wise. They are simplistic realists who never admit that nationalism is itself a value orientation with tangible opportunity costs. They are for an alliance system that delivers material benefits. But those benefits are frequently counterbalanced by enormous costs associated with short-term deal-making. National security takes priority over human security in every instance. For example, Morawiecki and Orban see little practical value in cooperation as an absolute principle and are strong believers in unilateral solutions to collective problems. This nationalistic form of order will bring with it unprecedented uncertainty, great power rivalry, and the proliferation of armed conflict. It rejects the older international consensus embodied in the United Nations that a rules-based order is in the enlightened self-interest of every state.

The populists know that their electoral base loves a good military parade. They invest heavily in weaponry because they believe in peace through strength. But they are not believers in the old balance-of-power system, per se. Rather, it is an international order of bluffs, trade-offs, and naked advantage playing to the home crowd they seek. "Every nation for itself" as an international order is therefore volatile and unpredictable with heightened risk of conflict between regional rivals and a rising global confrontation between Russia, China, the United States, and India. It is not a world for the meek and weak. For the authoritarian big men, primacy and national security are the name of the game.

Through national populist rhetoric, these leaders portray themselves as bold disrupters who are reorganizing the global order, just as Steve Jobs and Bill Gates did with the computer industry. The product they are selling is nativism at home and transactional mercantilism abroad. War, land-grabbing, specious national security policies, militarizing existing borders, defying international law, destroying treaties, and ignoring the rights of migrants and refugees are all strategies in the service of a return to the mythologized armored state.[8]

They have a very different understanding of the international hierarchy of rules, with top billing given to national security and state sovereignty rather than cooperation and trade.[9] For them, human rights and climate change are very low priorities. Their immediate goal is to hollow out the international system to create a bigger place for their own states. Theirs is a strange position that reflects the narrowest possible vision for international relations, and it is important to look at how they are doing this. Donald Trump is the prime example in this regard because so much of what happens in the United States filters through to the populist insurgency in the rest of the world, from Australia to Brazil.

The Charge of the Trump Brigade

American conservatism has had an outsized influence on populist discourse around the world. American cultural narratives celebrate hyper-individualism with an in-your-face disdain for government. There is an obvious close connection between the political culture of disdain for rule-breaking at home and the system-smashing that was at the center of the Trump administration's foreign policy.

The mechanics by which right-wing populism dismantles the administrative state follow the playbook of the bully. Always push aggressively one step further. Don't be afraid to step across the red line. Never accept responsibility for things you've broken. Furthermore, never offer a grand vision. Planning is secondary to the act of breaking a promise or commitment. In this way, Trump proceeded in a piecemeal fashion, chipping and cutting without ever developing a master plan. But there was a Trump doctrine: to bring jobs back to America and beat down friend and foe alike. We can more clearly see its objective: American supremacy requires the fear of enemies and the submission of friends.

The metaphor of system-smashing might give you the incorrect impression that Trump and his crew were attacking the order with a sledgehammer, attempting to break it with one mighty blow. But that was not the case. Rather, he attacked obliquely and incrementally, which was far more effective because he never crossed directly into criminality by imprisoning his rivals or formally deputizing paramilitary fascists like the Proud Boys. Ultimately, he didn't pull the United States out of the WTO or NATO, although he kept these options on the table right up until the last day of his presidency.

Similarly, pulling the United States out of the UN was not outside the realm of possibility. But everything must be driven by happenstance and motivated by the need to retaliate against those who are perceived to have wronged the leader. Those who wish to minimize the destructiveness of Trump point out that presidents who rule by executive order are easy to reverse by the same method. But this misses the main point that once a president has passed hundreds of executive orders reordering the regulatory machinery of the United States, dozens of countries alter their own regulations and practices. This domino effect can never be completely undone by Joe Biden's executive orders. Over time, Trump's policy footprint may fade, but for the next conservative nationalist president, his brand of disruption will remain a model to emulate.

Trump invoked the presidential prerogative to rule by decree more than any of his immediate predecessors. George W. Bush passed 291 executive orders in his two terms in office. Barack Obama used his executive privilege 276 times in eight years. Donald Trump used it 220 times in a single term.[10] But for scholars of the presidency, it was not Trump's use of a particular set of tools that set him apart from his peers. Rather, it was his narcissism, his unwillingness to work with his own divided party to craft legislation, and his disturbing pattern of attacking friends and foes alike with big lies. In 2019, Trump forced Britain's ambassador to the United States to resign after a brief he had written was critical of Trump's administration and was leaked to the media. This is one of those small stories that tells a lot about the motivations of the administration. Everything was personal, and there was no larger method to the madness. This is one more feature that sets the populists apart. The personalization of authority goes hand in hand with a governance style that brings everything down to individual sins. The personal is political in a terribly literal sense.

If there was one place where Trump pursued an improvised strategy that played to his strengths in bullying and name-calling, it was in his foreign policy toward China. The Trump administration believed two things: that China had stolen American jobs and that multilateral obligations hobbled America's ability to push back against unfair trade practices. If the United States was truly committed, then the gloves needed to come off.

Trump had originally argued that his tariffs on China were part of a negotiating strategy to drive the Chinese to the bargaining table. But once it became clear that the tariffs would not do that, the narrative was replaced with the explanation that a Cold War tariff and quota system would better promote American industry. To that end, the so-called Phase One of the trade deal with China committed the Chinese government to buying billions in US agricultural products while leaving in place more than 75 percent of US tariffs. In fact, even the limited trade deal did not do what it was supposed to. Chad Bown, a leading US trade authority, has shown that state enterprises did not buy nearly as many commodities from the United States as China had agreed. In fact, the US trade deficit with China continued to grow under Trump, despite his promise to rebalance trade flows.[11]

Trump was like every other populist leader who aimed his heavy fire at the global order wherever he found a moving target. Trump loved the symbolism of transactional tit for tat and used the trade deficit to bully friends and rivals alike, but none more than China. Toward the end of his term, Trump stopped talking about the deficit. His silence was not because he had seen the light on trade balances. Rather, it reflected the fact that he could no longer use them as a scorecard for "America First." In fact, America's trade deficit with the rest of the world reached a fourteen-year high of $67 billion by the summer of 2020.[12]

When Bullies Triumph

When bullies get away with their behavior, it's because others standing by lack the courage to push back. For example, the EU has been slow to push back against egregious abuses of its system by Poland. The EU reluctantly laid a complaint against the Polish Law and Justice Party's attack on judicial independence when it fired duly appointed judges and replaced them with their own partisan supporters. They levied fines when it became apparent that Poland was not complying. Marcin Matczak at the University of Warsaw called the partisan populist attack on judges in recent years an "extreme escalation by the Polish Government. It has run out of arguments, so it is resorting to brute force."[13] That it has taken a major constitutional crisis to push the EU to stand up to Warsaw's attack on the core principles of European law is upsetting but understandable because populists portray themselves as emissaries of grassroots popular will.

In their political logic, the right-wing populist government in Poland has always claimed that any regulation beyond the state is illegitimate because it does not flow directly from the will of the people, defined as the ones who voted for them. But when they can't claim that law is toothless, as in the case of Poland, they will try to wrestle the law into submission.

Even when hard-edged populists reluctantly compromise, as they must, they never admit to making concessions at the bargaining table. Contrast this cartoonish nationalism with the realist diplomacy and hard-edged deal-making of master negotiators like Henry Kissinger, the larger-than-life former US diplomat and advisor to presidents. Kissinger wrote his doctoral dissertation on Prince Metternich, the nineteenth-century Austrian architect of the Concert of Europe.[14] Kissinger is widely considered to be deeply conservative for his insistence on the balance of power, counterbalancing treaties, and his overarching belief that statesmanship is the art of the possible rather than being reflective of values and belief. For America's premier diplomat, war was the continuation of policy by other means. But in his toolkit, diplomacy was always an option when American interests were faced with military defeat. Kissinger always looked for a face-saving compromise that allowed the Americans and their battle-hardened adversaries to accept grim trade-offs in Vietnam and Afghanistan.[15]

Now compare the old master with Peter Navarro, the former special assistant to President Trump. Navarro has written books with titles like *Death by China* and *The Coming China Wars*.[16] He believes that there is no common ground to be found between the United States and China, and that China has to be hammered into submission. Nobody thinks Navarro is a giant statesman or a grand strategist. Trump surrounded himself with capos and enforcers, not thinkers and diplomats. As Kishore Mahbubani, former Singaporean ambassador and current public foreign policy intellectual, noted, "One of the most disastrous decisions America made after the end of the Cold War was to walk away from diplomacy."[17] Certainly Trump and his Lilliputian policy advisors are proof of that.

Many decisions large and small contributed to the shrinking of American diplomatic muscle under Trump, from the selling of ambassadorial posts to the rise of "hashtag diplomacy."[18] Certainly, diplomacy seemed less important while America was the undisputed superpower after the fall of the Berlin Wall. But the rise of China and the emergence of a multipolar world has highlighted the dangers of its degraded diplomatic capacity. With both China and the United States engaging in the rhetoric of nationalism, traditionalism, and thin-skinned grievance, we are in greater danger than ever. Diplomatic failure could easily, by error or intent, lead to war.

President Xi has referenced the Thucydides Trap on at least three occasions, and he is alert to the possibility that the United States and China could fall into deadly conflict due to the lack of mutual understanding that comes from great power arrogance, and overreach. *The Thucydides Trap* is the title of an influential book on US foreign policy that described the competition with China in terms of the historical rivalry between Athens and Sparta that led to the ruinous Peloponnesian War.[19] Will the rise of a multipolar system in which growing Chinese power threatens the American status quo lead to war in our time?

As Wang Jisi, president of Peking University's School of International Studies, has said, "China and the US are shifting from an all-round competition to a full-scale confrontation, with little room for compromise and maneuvering. We cannot rule out the possibility that the two powers will fall into the Thucydides trap."[20] Clearly, we have entered a dangerous new phase of power transition, and the nationalists are ratcheting up uncertainty.

After the Liberal Order, a Nation-Centered System

With fewer embedded ties that bind the different international organizations, the emerging nation-centered system "accords higher value to national sovereignty than the liberal international order," says Amitai Etzioni, a major theorist and founder of the nonpartisan Communitarian Network. "[It] is based more on agreements among nations and less on the promotion of individual rights, democratization, free movement of people and goods, and the quest for democratic global governance."[21] This return of the state has been facilitated by the pandemic, for each state to act in its own self-interest to procure masks, ventilators, and vaccines. Populists in the worst-hit countries, including Brazil, Mexico, and India, successfully exploited fears about the uncertainties of interdependence and used COVID-19 as a case in point.

In a time of global shifts, interstate rivalry pushes state actors to think more carefully about their entire toolkit and the resources at their disposal. It must also take more responsibility to row and steer the economy through economic crises and recessions. Voters want a state that can protect the public interest from the predatory behavior of ruthless actors, from foreign competitors to hostile dictators. The populists came to power promising to be ambitious, if false-faced reformers, in many areas of social life. They were going to sweep out corrupt bureaucrats, clean up cities, stop the flow of drugs, bring back jobs from China, and most importantly be a bulwark against the impersonal forces of the international. As if that wasn't a tall enough order, they also promised to revitalize faded national prestige with long-term investments in infrastructure, but that hasn't happened.

Nevertheless, a combination of smart technologies, security analytics, and new border practices enables countries to move beyond liberal internationalism, manage more of their national political space, and privilege the return to a nation-centered system. American right-wing provocateur Steve Bannon saw this nation-first shift coming a long way off. He argued the controversial proposition that in a post-truth world, populism is the only viable rallying point. The only issue for him was whether progressives or conservatives would weaponize populism first: "The question is whether it is left or right—the deconstruction of the administrative state, or democratic socialism."[22] Bannon saw that in the absence of a common project to build political community, people are left with few inspiring choices.

He believes polarization is like a zero-sum game that the nationalists are winning, and he has a point in that conservative populism is successfully reframing national politics as a winner-takes-all game of brinksmanship that benefits risk-taking autocrats who are willing to fight mean and dirty. The ideology of populism is a hell of a drug for the multitudes, and it is increasingly clear that many, perhaps even most, right-wing voters will not readily return to the liberal democratic fold.

A New Era of Anti-Liberalism?

We now have a surging ideological position on the modern political spectrum that is strongly anti-liberal and opposed to universal rights. Liberal democracy is losing its once solid middle ground where consensus was carefully achieved. Since the global populist tidal wave, there are fewer swing voters in Western democracies than a generation ago. The fair-minded, middle-of-the road consumer of politics who is not committed to any party's worldview is rapidly becoming an endangered species.[23]

Already, it is evident that the big lie and extreme speech have altered the rules of the game across many continents. Western democratic traditions are more fragile and vulnerable than most of us would care to admit. What makes this moment so dangerous is that illiberal populists are so evenly matched electorally with their liberal democratic opponents. Their tribe is smaller, but more loyal and hyper-motivated. Even with so many outrageous mistakes and blunders on the part of their leaders, the people refuse to abandon them. In the end, the populists have an edge in this process of transformative change because they are bolder, hungrier, and more ruthless than their liberal opponents.

Historian Michael Kazin has astutely observed that the main challenge facing politics today is that this is "a time when there is no real dominant ideology which can unite people."[24] Every country has coming-together moments that are mythologized as collective efforts of sacrifice. The Allied victory over Germany shaped an entire generation in the postwar world. The fall of the Berlin Wall and reunification changed Germany forever. The last time the United States came together was in the aftermath of the 2001 attack on the World Trade Center and the Pentagon that resulted in the loss of three thousand American lives and transformed America's political culture in the "endless wars" in Iraq and Afghanistan in myriad ways.

Today on the global electoral map, the *stigma against compromise* is accepted as a normal, and indeed integral, part of competitive elections. The populists have succeeded in creating a post-truth, identity-first political environment that is transforming international relations, destabilizing the liberal order, and rewriting the modern political theory of democratic engagement. Populist politicians don't offer many workable solutions to the very real problems faced by liberal market economies.[25] But so far, their lack of practical solutions, from poverty eradication to climate warming, hasn't slowed down the populist express one iota.

With international liberalism at its lowest point ever, is the turn to populist authoritarianism inevitable? The nationalists cannot be dismissed as an aberration or a once-in-a-century storm that will blow away by the next electoral cycle. In an age of the emergent nation-centered system, the problems of twenty-first-century international anarchy are mounting: winner-takes-all mercantilism, degraded global governance capacity, and a new deadly strain of political rivalry in which democracy is no longer equated with growth and social stability. The trend toward violence in nations with populist movements is destabilizing for the entire world order.

Populist violence in the United States takes the form of reactionary militias that set themselves up as the protector of honest people against the straw man of Antifa. In Israel, it is the violence of settlers against Palestinians.[26] In Brazil, it is truck drivers blockading highways in support of Bolsonaro. In France, it is physical attacks on Muslim immigrants.[27] In Peru, it is violent protests on the part of left populists attempting to oust a corrupt president.[28] In Nicaragua, populist violence is also state violence and election-rigging.[29] In Chile, months of mass street protests by students and the unemployed against the political elite erupted in running battles between the police and protesters that paralyzed the country and ended, in 2020, in the defeat of the president by Gabriel Boric, a former student leader.[30] All of these violent clashes between communities and the state have given global populism the extra push to ride on for another decade.

The Paranoid Style of Global Politics

Nobody thought the international order would be so vulnerable to the paranoid style that has surfaced in American politics and so many other jurisdictions, to paraphrase Richard Hofstadter's classic study of domestic extremism.[31] Yet, the wave of twenty-first-century populism struck the international system like a battering ram.

In the space of a few short years, the hard right proved them-selves electable and capable of governing despite their scandals and lies. For the populists moving fast into retail politics, this trans-national trend toward extremist political discourse has paid off on election day. But it is undeniably bad for democracy, bad for our societies especially, and bad for the old compromises that have shored up the foundation of postwar capitalism. That should make all of us very worried.

At the beginning of our narrative, we described the anti-system surge. We have shown how this rising tide of nationalists has reprised the sovereignty project. It has harnessed identity politics to destroy the empire of liberalism by repatriating sovereignty and slashing the constraints of international law. They want to leave the Bretton Woods post–World War II vision far behind and advocate international cooperation only when it clearly bene-fits them. This motley crew of sovereigntists and chancers has become more than the sum of their parts, if only because once the Americans elected a hard nationalist whose populist rhetoric was off the charts in 2016, the entire insurgency doctrine movement was given an adrenalin shot.

On a trip to France to meet President Emmanuel Macron early in 2021, US Secretary of State Antony Blinken declared, "We will stand up" to any country that challenges the liberal order.[32] But we've already seen through Biden's continuation of Trump's trade policy that his administration is not fully committed to upholding the values of liberal free-trade internationalism. Even facing a land war in Europe, the nation-centered system is a large step down from the optimism of coopperative interdependence and multi-lateralism. The nation-centered order's overarching concern with competitive unilateralism and short-termism will only make the problems of global disharmony painfully worse.

CHAPTER 6

Pandemic Nationalism

The Populists versus the Pandemic

What the pandemic taught us is that the loudest of the populist shouters were the worst prepared and least effective at containing the outbreak. Think back to the spring and summer of 2020, when the pandemic first raged across the world. President Trump sought to fire Dr. Anthony Fauci, his top public health advisor. But he didn't dare. Fauci had quickly become a mass media icon of plain-spoken American resolve in the face of a tidal wave of new infections. If Fauci was trusted by both sides of the electorate, Trump's hands were tied. He feared a public relations disaster if he dumped his trusted director of the National Institute of Allergy and Infectious Diseases. But he had a card to play that had worked with other troublesome employees in the past. He needed first to smear Fauci in public and humiliate him. Then Trump would be able to fire him and avoid any blowback.[1]

Of course, the virus cannot be defeated with such a crude media strategy; it cannot be crushed by spinning the narrative. Massaging the message was always a losing strategy because so much of the planet's health is the result of complex interdependent systems for the financing, coordination, and implementation of public policy. Future historians are likely to conclude that populist governments were not simply poor leaders in challenging times, hapless bystanders to tragedy. In fact, they acted as an accelerant of viral transmission in at least five ways. Populist leaders

- minimized the risk of the pandemic in the first months even as they watched it explode in Wuhan, China;

- opposed an orderly limitation of cross-border flows as a preventative health measure, preferring to protect the economy at the expense of citizens' lives;

- did not develop robust national programs of contact tracing and quarantine, laboring under the mistaken belief that COVID-19 would fade away after a single wave of infection;

- attempted to pass the buck by blaming China for the initial outbreak in order to distract from their own lack of preparation; and

- politicized the wearing of personal protective equipment, talked up miracle cures, and opposed public health mandates for vaccination, even as they promised vaccines at "warp speed."

Finally, and even more importantly, the populists failed to provide a plan for subsequent waves. As a group, each successive wave was the last one, as far as they were concerned. How can we judge the populist response to the pandemic when all countries seemed to do quite badly at different points? The best-organized, such as Germany, and the least-prepared, such as Mexico and India, faced calamitous and horrifying scenes of death and chaos. Thousands of doctors and medical assistants died and the elderly and children alike perished in hospitals when supplies ran out.[2] The final toll of the pandemic on first-responders is not yet known.

Economist James Galbraith has shown that the worst-performing countries initially were large and decentralized.[3] The best performers, at first, were smaller and more homogenous countries, such as Greece, Scandinavia, Taiwan, Singapore, New Zealand, South Korea, and the Atlantic provinces of Canada. On average, these were middle-to-high-income regions that embraced immediate intervention. They had the capacity to scale up their response with great speed and accuracy. Even small countries led by populists responded quickly to the pandemic. Under Netanyahu, Israel moved very fast to vaccinate its population, and ranks among the first in the world for having delivered two doses of vaccine. Similarly, Hungary moved faster than the rest of Europe to provide vaccines because it was the only EU nation to buy the readily available Sinopharm doses from China.

In the first eight months of the crisis, there was no established public health model for pandemic response. Almost everywhere, despite differences in cultures, values, and political orientations, governments were flying blind, hoping that drug companies, universities, and overstretched public health agencies would work together and produce something to save millions of lives—and they did! But not before most countries lived through a mayhem of grief and self-inflicted loss. Somehow, they forgot the public health lessons of earlier pandemics such as SARS and complacently believed that the worst outcomes always happen elsewhere to other countries and their citizens.

Countries like the United States, the UK, India, and Brazil, which are large, decentralized, and politically polarized, and which have populations who have little faith in their public authorities, did poorly. Even the rest of Canada felt the crunch. Western provinces British Columbia, Alberta, and Saskatchewan looked a lot like Oregon, Montana, and North Dakota in their response during the first year of the pandemic.[4]

In a Pandemic, We're All Losers

The populist right moved from the internet into the streets in 2021, beginning with the storming of the US Capitol in January, and continuing into the autumn with mass demonstrations against pandemic restrictions in major European cities. In many countries, there is a seamless tie between authoritarian activism and people protesting the temporary restrictions of certain liberties in the form of lockdowns, mask requirements, and mandatory vaccines. In Vienna, Rotterdam, The Hague, Paris, Brussels, and Berlin tens of thousands of demonstrators took to the streets in November 2021 in some of the largest political protests in years.[5]

Despite relatively high rates of vaccine uptake in Europe, new variants promise more trouble ahead, and populists have pivoted toward an antiestablishment form of populism to channel popular frustration into political energy they can use. In the United States, right-wing populism has always had a strong libertarian flavor, with most true believers strongly supportive of more capitalism and smaller government. In Europe, where governments are trusted more, a US-led libertarian form of populism is on the rise. Political scientist Ivan Krastev at the Centre for Liberal Strategies in Sofia declared, "Suddenly populists all over Europe have had a libertarian baptism."[6] Their message resonates with European youth movements on the left and right, who believe that their lives have been significantly curtailed by pandemic restrictions.

Across the developed world, most people wanted to believe that the virus would burn itself out after the first wave as healthy people contracted asymptomatic forms of the disease and built up a natural herd immunity in national populations. But the coronavirus was never the sort of disease in which a single infection provides immunity for life, like chickenpox. It operates more like the flu, with constantly evolving variants that people can catch again and again, and subsequent infections can increase in seriousness.

This is perfect soil for populists, and many conservative media personalities are jumping onto the populist bandwagon, from television personality Éric Zemmour in France to celebrated American memoirist J. D. Vance, a Trump loyalist and rising political star of the Republican Party. The Cleveland-born son of Turkish immigrants, Dr. Oz, a man best known for wellness commentary on afternoon television talk shows, wrote in the *Washington Examiner* that the official response to COVID was part of a political cover-up by health authorities and the political elite. He said that the pandemic "has been mishandled by 'elites' who stifled dissenting opinions, 'mandated' policies and 'closed our parks, shuttered our schools, shut down our businesses and took away our freedom.'"[7]

If there is a grain of truth in what he said, it is that governments have not been using vaccines to their best effect by vaccinating the elderly, the vulnerable, and the frontline workers in every country first. The mad scramble for vaccines meant relatively high rates of vaccination in wealthy countries, leaving poor populations open to continuing viral mutation. The WHO's chief scientist, Soumya Swaminathan, said, "If we had used the vaccines produced so far in a rational and fair manner, we wouldn't be seeing the high death rates, two years into the pandemic. Even now it's not too late to act. We need vulnerable and high-risk populations everywhere to be protected urgently."[8] The populists are, of course, making a bad situation worse, but it is a predicament they created.

At first, they demanded vaccines for their own countries and took personal credit for scientific advance. Then when their base turned against the "elite" message of vaccination, they shifted stance and turned against vaccines, even though they themselves had been vaccinated. The anti-vaccine movement has attracted renegades from the top echelons of the ruling class. Robert F. Kennedy Jr., the son of the assassinated civil rights era US Attorney General Robert F. Kennedy, has drawn enormous crowds with his venomous message opposing vaccination. "The minute they hand you that vaccine passport, every right that you have is transformed into a privilege contingent upon your obedience to arbitrary government dictates . . . it will make you a slave."[9]

The Deflection Game of False Narratives

The anti-vaccine message is yet another surreal big lie: Don't fear the virus, don't listen to the chief medical officer for your region. Don't listen to the best epidemiologists in the world. Don't listen to national centers for disease control. In their ideologically charged worldview, masks are for timid liberals and vaccines will make you sick. Only "sheeple" follow public health orders. Medical freedom has become the number one wedge issue in their war with the public health authority.

The second year of the pandemic brought more waves of infection despite the widespread use of vaccines in wealthy countries. The issue of vaccine passports became more pressing for authorities. Such passports would make vaccination a requirement for all entry into indoor public spaces such as schools and shopping malls. A meme making its rounds on Facebook decried the heavy hand of the state: "If you have to carry a card in your pocket (or a pass on your phone) proving you injected a drug into your body to gain access to grocery stores, receive medical care, or freely move about society, then you no longer live in a free country and you are no longer sovereign over your own body—and that should concern everyone—regardless of political or medical choices." There aren't any legal issues because people weren't being denied access to grocery stores or medical care.[10] Anti-vaccine activists flooded social media with misinformation. Republican governors in the United States made requiring masks or vaccines in schools illegal. In the Canadian general election in the fall of 2021, anti-vaccine protesters pelted the prime minister with gravel.[11]

The message of medical freedom created a false narrative in which untrustworthy scientists and power-drunk politicians were forcing the skeptical public to inject unproven medicines into their arms. In North America, between 25 and 40 percent of state and provincial populations bought into some aspect of this narrative. Some people believed the conspiracies and encouraged others to "drink the Kool-Aid." Others feared the new vaccines because they distrusted the speed and urgency with which they were introduced. Still others hesitated because they feared side effects or couldn't take time off work if they felt sick.

For a die-hard few, the issue was about individual freedom versus state regulation. Simply because the government wanted them to, they wouldn't take the vaccine. It was the Darwin effect in action, because those who most forcibly rejected vaccines welcomed miracle cures, from hydroxychloroquine to vitamin C and even Ivermectin, a veterinary medicine for deworming live-stock, which causes sterility in human males.

On the popular social media platform, Reddit, users created a forum for posting the social media activity of vaccine skeptics who contracted COVID-19 and later died. Called the Herman Cain Award, it was named after the former Republican presidential primary contender who was one of the first high-profile politicans to die in the pandemic. The similarities among the many hundreds of posts are striking.

Most often the victim is a white, blue-collar man in his 50s or 60s, overweight, and with other health issues. He is deeply concerned that his rights are not infringed by state authority, and posts dozens of memes about how Covid is a hoax, health authorities are lying, and pharmaceutical firms are corrupt. The posts usually end abruptly with a Facebook status update announcing that he has Covid, but he's going to fight it. The final post comes from family members describing the victim's final moments. Critics of r/hermancainaward have argued that the forum is disrespectful to those who have died. Its proponents counter that it is important to document the impact of political disinformation on the lives Americans who are misled by authoritarian populism.

Yet the Republican Party in the United States continued to play to the worst fears of their constituents. Dr. Peter Hotez, a co-director of the Texas Children's Hospital Center for Vaccine Development, recently said, "The most dangerous thing that could happen is the Republican Party [adopting] anti-vaccine, anti-science to the major platform. This is the nightmare situation I'd hoped to avoid."[12] The medical freedom anti-vaccine falsehood amounted to little more than "no masks, partying, carrying on like crazy, people doing all the stuff they did before, not even any consideration," according to one man who lived through the tragedy in Florida.[13]

A Parade of Covid-Infected Leaders

Political leaders were often among the first to contract the virus because they encounter hundreds of people on a weekly basis. Among the very first was Prime Minister Justin Trudeau of Canada. The populists also were also quick to contract the illness, and they frequently used the experience to burnish their image as iron men with bullet-proof constitutions. Prime Minister Boris Johnson became seriously ill, but the experience did little to stiffen his resolve to fight the virus. He recovered and praised the efforts of the National Health Service, but his government did almost nothing to organize to meet the second wave. By the time the winter holidays were over and 2021 had begun, Britain's death toll surpassed one hundred thousand, more than twice as many as those killed in the Blitz.

Johnson took a tiny measure of symbolic responsibility, declaring, "I am deeply sorry for every life that has been lost." But he did not take responsibility for de-emphasizing the pandemic, keeping universities open, or moving slowly on the Christmas lockdown. At that point in time, the *Financial Times'* modeling of UK mortality placed the British death toll even higher, alongside Spain and Italy as the worst in Europe, and even higher than the United States.[14] The BBC's coronavirus tracker painted a worse picture. The UK death rate of 158 people per hundred thousand was higher even than Italy, at 146 people, and the United States at 134.[15]

In Brazil, populist machismo also undermined public health authority. As Brazil's death toll rose to become the second highest in the world, Bolsonaro embraced an extreme form of fatalism, arguing that Brazilians should stop being "a country of sissies," because "everyone is going to die" sooner or later.[16] Bolsonaro postured and swaggered, and his fellow citizens continued to die in alarming numbers. As the second wave gathered momentum in the fall of 2020, the virus began to mutate, making it more transmissible.

In Manaus, where doctors were preparing for a second wave that resembled the first, hospitals ran out of beds within twenty-four hours. They ran out of oxygen by January 14, 2021. The next day, dozens of people died gasping for air in their hospital beds. One epidemiologist described the overflowing COVID wards as "chambers of asphyxiation." Doctors were forced to ration their scarce resources: "You choose who lives and who dies, who gets oxygen and who doesn't. It's like we're living in a horror film."[17] Nothing in Bolsonaro's public demeanor recognized the terrible toll of the pandemic on the people of Brazil.

There is a line between courage under pressure and callous disregard for suffering. As Brazilians continued to suffer through months of chaos and death throughout the spring of 2021, João Doria, governor of Sao Paulo state, summed up the feelings of many Brazilians: "We are in one of those tragic moments in history when millions of people pay a high price for having an unprepared and psychopathic leader in charge of a nation."[18]

Bolsonaro's reckless approach to the pandemic is not a one-off. He showed the same attitudes toward his most fervent supporters. He slashed the social safety net in Brazil, with no regard for the needs of the poorest. Brazil's internationally recognized anti-poverty program called the Bolsa Família system of social support required that children receive regular health checkups and attend school in order for parents to receive financial payments. After Bolsonaro was elected, the number of families accepted into the program dropped from 275,000 a month to fewer than 2,500. *The Economist* reports that "the number receiving benefits has fallen by one million. The government says that 700,000 are on the waiting list. That may be an underestimate."[19]

Extreme nationalism requires an unfeeling leader who treats every challenge as if he is storming the beach at Normandy in 1944. Trump, too, played a tough guy on TV even as the second wave brought the death toll in America to new heights: 2,000, then 3,000, and then higher still, to 4,000 people per day. He played down the seriousness of the virus, and when that didn't work, he blamed China. He mocked the "kung-flu," he promoted pseudoscience, he touted ridiculous cures—malaria medication, bleach, ultraviolet light.[20]

Like Bolsonaro, Trump also contracted the virus.[21] He celebrated his iron constitution even as the virus almost killed him. But once he had recovered, he lost interest in aggressively containing it for regular Americans. He judged it to be no longer a threat, personally, and therefore it was no longer of any importance. Behind the scenes, he ranted about how he had been robbed of a second term. By the time he lost the election in November, he had abandoned the daily television briefings and showed no interest in American suffering.

Of the eleven countries with the highest number of coronavirus cases, seven of them had populist governments. By the end of the first wave, in the spring of 2020, countries led by populist leaders, such as India, already had the highest rates of infection and some of the lowest levels of public health coordination. The scenes of death were horrific as public health systems teetered on the edge of collapse. Not only did conservative nationalist governments have high infection rates, but they also scored poorly on recovery rates.

By contrast Israel was an outlier, with one of the highest rates of vaccination in the first year of the pandemic. Based on WHO statistics, their mortality rates ranged from 4 to 6 percent of those who tested positive for the virus.[22] Because populist leaders minimized the severity of the threat, countries led by them, such as Russia, India, and Mexico, showed significant community spread. Some, like the UK, had a mortality rate that briefly reached as high as 15 percent of those who contracted the virus.

We won't know the official death rate for this pandemic until social scientists analyze excess deaths around the world during the years before COVID-19 evolves into something less deadly. But even official death rates, which systematically undercount mortality, are startling. By May 2022, more than a million people had died of COVID-19 in the United States alone, and more than six million globally.

The Anti-Science Resisters

Overall, the United States, India, Brazil, the Philippines, Mexico, Turkey, Russia, and Italy are standouts for high case counts and high mortality rates. These eight countries accounted for 58 percent of coronavirus cases, and 55 percent of deaths by early July 2020. In fact, the top four countries by case count—the United States, Brazil, India, and Russia—accounted for 51 percent of all cases globally by the end of that first summer. As for the soaring death rate, the numbers tell a tragic story. The top five countries led by science-denying leaders— the United States, Brazil, the UK, Italy, and Mexico—accounted for 57 percent of all deaths globally in the first year of the pandemic.

The pandemic showed very clearly that when every country is pulling for itself in an emergency, wealth and power are the deciding factors that create huge disparities of outcome. The self-interested nationalism that was on full display in 2021 was not the creation of the populists per se, but it did serve their larger purposes to discredit and destroy the liberal order. Indeed, it is a small glimpse into the future of the "every nation for itself" system they want to enact.

As the pandemic entered a second year, efforts to create a vaccine to counter COVID-19 paid off. In North America and Europe, Pfizer, Merck, Johnson & Johnson, and relative newcomers to vaccine production AstraZeneca and Moderna announced the creation of highly effective vaccines. Governments partnered with Big Pharma, linking the spending power of the public sector to the scientific creativity of universities and the corporate sector to beat every record for vaccine development.[23] In China, the state was a partner in the development and production of the Sinovac shot. Likewise, the Russian Direct Investment Fund bankrolled Sputnik V, Russia's state-coordinated vaccine effort.

Countries clamored to purchase these miracles of modern science. Unsurprisingly, the wealthiest and most powerful countries, partners to their pharmaceutical firms, were at the top of the list for Western jabs. Wealthy countries bought up great quantities of the best brand-name vaccines, concerned first and foremost with protecting their own citizens.[24] They failed to divide available doses equitably, and observers quickly termed this unjust response "vaccine nationalism."

A power-based scramble for the scarce resource of the vaccine was the ideal environment for the populists to preach about their own genius in procuring medicines. The relative shortage of vaccines, at least in 2021, created perverse incentives for countries to jockey for position in the queue instead of prioritizing the most vulnerable around the world. Netanyahu made a secret deal with Pfizer to turn Israel into a model country with the majority of its population protected.[25] Israel also agreed to share information about its vaccine drive with Pfizer. Similarly, Orbán secured large quantities of the Chinese vaccine in the early months of 2021, demonstrating that in a public health crisis populist leaders bring home the bacon.[26] Later, some populist leaders would turn against the vaccine and support anti-vaccine movements.

If the primary goal of the global vaccination drive was saving lives, it would have made sense to vaccinate the elderly, the vulnerable, and health care workers around the world first, and then open purchasing programs to governments buying shots for general use. For epidemiologists, vaccines were part of a holistic treatment that included social distancing, masking, testing, contact tracing, and quarantining sick people. Vaccines were never supposed to be the only line of defense. They were never meant to prevent the spread of infection entirely, but were to be used along with testing, social distancing, and masking.[27]

Governments who put up public money for vaccine development, such as the Trump Administration's Operation Warp Speed, cared only about vaccinating their own citizens. The notion of the pandemic being something we were all in together disappeared as governments vied to be the first to stamp out the pandemic in their own jurisdictions. By 2021, the idea of public solidarity for collective protection, and with it the language of "bending the curve," quickly disappeared from public discourse. Instead, it was the embodiment of the nation-centered sovereignty project—every country for itself.

In China, vast quantities of vaccines were produced and shipped to developing countries to prove that China cared about poor people in the global south, even if the West didn't make it a priority.[28] The export of shots produced by Sinopharm and Sinovac Biotech as "peoples' vaccines" were a case study in China's strategic use of soft power to build bilateral relationships worldwide. In the race for herd immunity, the populists have a keen nose for public sentiment. We look back on this time in disbelief because Bolsonaro and Orbán, who at first were so strongly opposed to protecting their people when the pandemic was dismissed as "just a flu," were also the first to cut a massive deal with China's Sinovac for vaccines.[29]

India at the WTO

The pandemic has been a game-changer, and the populists are scoring big political points. In India, Modi was quick to portray himself as the champion of the people and a pharmacy to the world. India has the potential to become a health and wellness powerhouse, selling not only generic drugs but also traditional medicines, wellness products, and lifestyle accoutrements.[30] Partnering with South Africa, India proposed at the WTO that formulas for making vaccines should be shared freely with developing countries.[31] So far the progress has been painfully slow.

The formulas for vaccines are the exclusive intellectual property of big pharmaceutical companies, and they are protected by treaty at the WTO. Twenty years ago, activists and Global South governments went to war against drug firms over HIV medications and won significant concessions that lowered drug prices across the globe.[32] This time, Modi was confident that he could lead the charge once more against unjust Northern patents. If he were to win, the Indian pharmaceutical companies would get fast access to the newest mRNA vaccine technology, the industry would attract more foreign investment, and ancillary health and wellness industries would also benefit.

The Global South uses 25 percent of the world's vaccine demand but produces only 1 percent locally. Countries in the Global South do produce some vaccines, but they don't yet produce the newest mRNA vaccines developed by Pfizer and Moderna.[33] India's pharmaceutical industry produces the AstraZeneca vaccine, and Russia produces its own creation, and Global South countries will likely have to wait years as these countries take care of their own populations and then begin to export large shipments to Africa. Transferring the newest mRNA technology to Africa would drive down its cost and create new centers of vaccine production.[34]

This is a pretty good plan, all things considered. India would lead the way in domestic drug production in the Global South, exporting medicines and the materials needed to make them. India's goal is to champion open markets and health equity while maintaining its sectoral lead over other rapidly developing nations in Africa, which likewise plan to produce more medications and vaccines in the next decades.[35] Technology transfer is essential, and looser patent restrictions would be a much-needed public good. African nations are not waiting for a WTO waiver that will likely never happen. Instead they have begun to sign agreements for vaccine production partnerships in Morocco, Ghana, and South Africa.

The Indian–South African push for an intellectual property rights waiver is the right move. In an "every nation for itself" system, the populist leaders grab every opportunity to tilt the rules in their own favor. Furthermore, from oil in Mexico to medicine in India, the populist leaders are champions of national industry and a "made at home" industrial policy. So painting themselves as leaders in opening markets is useful even when they are openly nationalist in so many other areas of economic life.

After two years, this is the way the world looked. (See fig. 5.) We have included this chart because it drives home the point of the enormous global divide between the capacity of health systems in high-income countries and the health systems in low-income developing economies without adequate access to vaccines.

Figure 5: The Global Vaccine Divide: The Advanced Economies versus "the Rest"

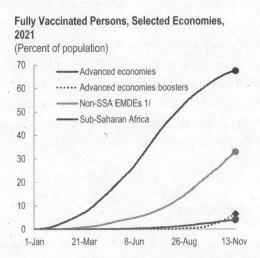

Fully Vaccinated Persons, Selected Economies, 2021
(Percent of population)

Source: Our World in Data, and IMF staff calculations. 1/ Excludes China.

The rich countries, with 20 percent of the world's population, controlled 80 percent of the vaccine doses in the first wave of vaccination in 2021. By the time 5 percent of the world had been fully vaccinated in the spring of 2021, only 0.2 percent of people in the Global South had been.[36] By the middle of November that same year, only 4 percent of sub-Saharan Africa had received a vaccine.

In the Global North, more than 70 percent of the population had received two shots, and governments were gearing up to offer a third. Even children between the ages of five and eleven years were being offered vaccines in the United States, while most health care workers in Africa toiled without any vaccine protection.[37]

The populists did not invent self-interest, but the problems of inequity, of which vaccine nationalism is the foremost example, are made worse in an international system of "every nation for itself." A power-based system may have a seductive allure when populist big men are promising that they will use national power to avenge grievances, but the dark side is increasingly evident. It is more illness, more naked self-interest, more death, more poverty and less security for everyone. The WHO's goal to immunize 70 percent of the world's population by the end of 2022 is failing. High levels of Covid vaccination may never be attained by most low income countries as badly needed funding from the US and the EU begins to dry up. Only four of 82 poor countries have reached the 70 percent vaccination threshold. Most are under 20 percent. By contrast, two thirds of the richest countries have exceeded the target.[38]

Pandemic Nationalism

Vaccine nationalism distorts who gets access to vaccines and how quickly they are vaccinated.[39] A young healthy person in the United States had a one in three chance of being fully vaccinated by April 2021, four months after the vaccines were released. In Africa, those odds stretched to one in a million.[40] Vaccine nationalism has cost millions of African lives. Whether it was the issue of hoarding, gatekeeping, or just the fact that money and legal jurisdiction give northern countries a leg up in the buying frenzy, state power guided the flow of vaccines. The post-liberal international system that the populists are so eager to implement will make these problems of cooperation worse. The pandemic is increasing the social instability and polarization that feeds the populist insurgency.[41]

Populists in different countries have responded to vaccine nationalism differently. Russia, India, China, and the United States boasted of their abilities to produce vaccines. But as the pandemic has worn on, they have also capitalized on vaccine skepticism and anger over the fact that wealthy people have seen their wealth increase over the past two years, while the working poor, who have borne the brunt of the risk of exposure, have also been hardest hit by lockdowns. This is where inequality and pandemic instability collide.

IMF researchers studied the long-lasting social impacts of SARS in 2003, H1N1 in 2009, MERS in 2012, Ebola in 2014, and Zika in 2016. They found that following each pandemic, inequality rose, growth fell, and social unrest increased significantly in the countries affected.[42] None of these pandemics were as big as COVID-19 and none impacted as many countries. The economic crisis that inevitably follows a pandemic is fallow ground for their narrative of resentment. We don't have a crystal ball, and neither do the populists. They can only try their best to keep their noses above water and take their opportunities as they come. As chancers, this is their world, and they can't ask for more.

As global response to the COVID-19 pandemic moves in fits and starts, very few populist big men have been punished by their electorates for their terrible decisions, cynicism, and indifference. It didn't happen in the regional Spanish elections in 2021. Nor in the regional and council elections in the UK in the same year. In India, despite horrific scenes of death and the collapse of the public health system, Modi remains popular with his base. Even Trump enjoys unparalleled support from 80 percent of Republicans, or more than fifty million Americans, despite losing the general election in 2020.[43]

Some people thought that the pandemic would sink the populists because they don't lead well-organized governments. In fact, voters associate their brand with system-smashing and punishment rather than the competent management that is required to produce and distribute vaccines. People who thought the pandemic would sink the populists pointed to Joe Biden's defeat of Donald Trump, a victory for sanity over grievance politics. But that would have been true only if we had experienced a single-wave pandemic.

As the pandemic ground on throughout 2021, the populists, buoyed by their support from the anti-vaxxers, were "building back better" among younger voters and activists who became increasingly dissatisfied with established populist parties. In Germany, the Alternative für Deutschland won fewer votes in the federal elections in 2021 than they did previously. But they have not lost any of their organizational muscle on the streets or at protest rallies against masking and lockdowns.

Protesters like the "Swiss Free Left," the "Freedom for Democracy Party" in the Netherlands, and "People Freedom Rights" in Austria have taken their antiestablishment message into the populist heartland and galvanized far-right parties that are already in parliament.[44] They work to heighten people's fear that governments will introduce stronger curbs on personal freedom and future shutdowns that are so painful to small-business owners and workers. This hard line against lockdowns, and masks and vaccines, has given populist parties a renewed relevance in public life.

Hyper-Individualism and Vaccine Freedom

The system smashers' future is now inseparable from ending the global pandemic. The ranks of the insurgency are being swelled by the anti-vaxxers who live outside the Metropolitan capitals, largely without university education, predominantly male and 25 to 40 years old. They have embraced vaccine freedom and a belief in hyper-individualism, "I alone decide what's good for my health not big brother government." It will likely take until 2024 to fully control new infections. As new waves of infection in the global south cause new infections in wealthy countries, public fear continues to play into the populists' anti-immigrant message as well.

The anti-vaccine movement started out as a collection of eccentrics, contrarians, cranks, and libertarians at the margins. Now it has millions in its ranks in Germany, Austria, the UK, France, Italy, and Spain, not to mention the United States, where most of the anti-vaccine conspiracy theories began. By a conservative estimate, in the advanced economies there are more than one hundred million EU vaccine sceptics who don't plan to vaccinate under any circumstances.[45] The anti-vaxxers have swelled the ranks of the global populists and their ascendance from marginal to mainstream opposition has given them a grand public far beyond their own tribe. The introduction of mask mandates and obligatory vaccination protocols have lent the anti-vaxxers newfound credibility as frontline defenders of freedom against "intrusive" public health regulation.

Unwitting mainstream politicians could even open the door to a hostile takeover of government by attempting to accommodate their demands or bring them into power-sharing arrangements, as happened in Europe in the 1930s. The introduction of mask mandates and obligatory vaccination protocols enraged the populist right-wing movement in North America and Europe and the anti-vaccine activists have anointed themselves frontline defenders of freedom. In a recent interview, Steve Bannon approvingly noted that "anti-vaccine outrage is beyond totemic for Trump's base . . . It's almost defining."[46]

We worry that we are on the brink of another disastrous wave of populist rage because the left appears to be largely disoriented by the populist advance. There is good reason for this confusion.

As noted social critic and author Paul Mason has argued, working people "have accepted the post-2008 logic of neoliberalism—that because the wealth of the super-rich is untouchable and always growing, redistribution can only happen between sections of the working class."[47] The left has not been able to use identity politics as an effective electoral strategy like the right has done. Even in the US, Joe Biden's election was a victory for centrism and competence rather than rage against the machine. So far, in practical terms, no governing political party has a solution to out-of-control inequality and the breakdown of liberal consensus.

Certainly the insurgency shouldn't be regarded as a uniquely American problem any longer; today it is global at its core and demands a coordinated international response from citizens networking and governments working together to renew liberal democracy. Something must be done, because if we can't make our societies more equal, and safer, we are going to have even bigger problems in the future than we have now.

The pandemic struck when liberal democracy was already fragmenting along the cultural lines of religion, race, class, gender, and education. Is it a wakeup call for democratic renewal or a harbinger of our ur-fascist future? The populists are mobilizing their global movement with their network of informal linkages and transnational coalitions. They are more globally connected than ever on many levels, from civil society to business and government. The deep structural and psychological conditions that gave rise to rightwing populism aren't going away. Ending the pandemic is crucial to tamping down the flames of populism. Without an end in sight, populists will have a lot of dry kindling to set on fire.[48] To protect ourselves and crush the pandemic we must vaccinate the world. But the logic of the new nation-centered system works against collective action, and that is exactly what the populists want—more chaos, more division, and more lies to feed their insatiable movement.

CHAPTER 7

Darkness at Noon

The Antidemocratic Answer

In his chilling novel *Darkness at Noon*, Arthur Koestler describes the way that a political revolution devours its own children.[1] The protagonist is an old Bolshevik revolutionary who is the last of his generation of scrappy fighters who brought down the czar. His friends have slowly disappeared into the bowels of the state, chewed up by the same revolutionary machinery they invented. When he is finally imprisoned on trumped-up charges of disloyalty to the regime, he faces an impossible choice: confess to crimes he didn't commit or plead his innocence and be subjected to a show trial with staged execution as a foregone conclusion.

Koestler's book is about the betrayal of revolutionary Marxism in the Stalinist era, and at first glance it has little to do with our present crisis. But the overarching themes of revolutionary fervor and the overreach of extreme ideology resonate with us once more. How many of the populist leaders will be caught in nets of their own misdeeds? Some perhaps, but certainly too few. For those of us watching all of this take place, our "darkness at noon" moment may be read as the hollowing out of the political center and the slow implosion of liberalism. The worst of us are creating the political environment that will shape the lives and livelihoods of the rest of us.

The tragic irony of "darkness at noon" is that our current difficulties are always self-inflicted. We listen to the lies; we are seduced by conspiracy theories. We don't want to do the heavy lifting required of an informed public. Hannah Arendt describes the sensation of our dawning awareness as an "iron band of terror" that we cannot escape.[2] For some, it needs to be said that the pandemic has turned public attention away from nostalgia and the big lie.

So how can we break the fever that has taken hold of our minds? Almost a century after defeating fascism, we have arrived at another "darkness at noon" moment, when the political contradictions of the present threaten to overwhelm us.[3]

Populism's siren song that calls to the darkest part of our nature has always been underestimated as a driver of modern societies for organizing politics. It was not until the birth of social media and the polarization of political silos of information that populism became a tool to whip resentment into new heights of rage.

Inevitably a big man with all the answers is always ready to push his way onto center stage and take control. There will always be activist true believers and angry contingent voters for whom the interests of the tribe outweigh everything else.[4] They see themselves as "the true vanguard," said retired Green Beret Joe Kent, now running for Congress as a Trump loyalist. "We need warriors in Congress who are going to use their intellect, their ability to stand up strongly . . . to take on this totalitarian regime. A lot of us will be shaming Republicans. I need to be going after the people in the Republican Party who want to go back to go-along-to-get-along. It's put up or shut up."[5] That is why populism is so toxic to liberal democracy: because many aspiring candidates have cast themselves in the image of the big lie and rely on hate speech to win office. At their most controversial, they give unparalleled license to their worst impulses—the id run amok.

But the "darkness at noon" moment has another significance. This moment is threatening for the authoritarian movement as well. Some will be held responsible for their pandemic complacency, short-sightedness, and policy disasters. Other extremists will be made redundant by fickle voters who want to use the machinery of the state to improve the lives of ordinary people. Some will fall to party infighting and the long knives of rivals. "Darkness at noon" is a tragic time when their fevered revolution devours the true believer and the cyclone of anger tears apart the guardrails of democracy.

Four Hard Lessons the Global Insurgency Teaches

The goal of democratic politics is to demonstrate to citizens the effectiveness of working together. Citizens must share enough to build consensus and when we lose the instinct to share, societies in trouble are fertile ground for authoritarian recruitment.[6] Fascistic movements have already blown away our expectations, and they will continue to churn with dark energy. What have they achieved? The populists have taught us four painful lessons.

Lesson One

The ur-fascist strongmen have demonstrated that in-your-face hate speech wins elections. They have built winning coalitions by driving hard to the right, and thereby marginalizing the center and the traditional left. This winning strategy of going big on hate defied the predictions of pollsters.[7] Even if people were ashamed to admit publicly to supporting extremism, in the privacy of the polling booth, they chose authoritarianism.[8] In doing so, they upended the comfortable expectations of the post–Cold War liberal accord, where electoral politics rewarded centrist parties and punished the extremes. Multilateralism will continue to unravel as domestic politics invests less in interstate cooperation, and new configurations of power move to the forefront of international relations.

In the last thirty years, conventional wisdom has argued that authoritarianism is something that happens in other countries, to poor people who are too deferential to corruption or whose cultural expectations allow fundamentalists or patriarchs to hold too much power. It was an article of faith that authoritarianism is a form of government led by kings, kleptocrats, despots, and dictators in the Global South. Northern citizens, supposedly democratic by default, are armored against authoritarianism. Were they not skeptical of anyone who promises the sun, moon, and stars? Were they not rugged individualists who don't want the state to tell them what to do? But the populists have showed how faulty this baseline assumption has always been.[9]

After decades of wage stagnation, angry voters are ready to sacrifice some of their vaunted individualism if a strongman will fight in their corner. The big lie has ripped through fortress democracy.[10] The past decade will be remembered by historians for the fact that the populist insurgency held a knife to the throat of liberal democracy and got away with it. In doing so, they forever changed the way the multitudes on election day think about political identity—as a contest between the law and order, the sheriff protecting the good folks against the foreigner, the sexual minority, or groups with special needs. Modern populism relies on this Manichaean wedge to polarize an already fractured polity to change the political terrain by stoking nationalist passions.

Today, being unthinkingly authoritarian is no longer a black mark against politicians and activists; rather, it signals a deeper commitment to country, tradition, family, the Leader.[11] The ur-fascist always assumes that premodern forms of social organization are necessary for returning to national greatness. He draws a link between personal identity, the mystique of the nation, and premodern social forms. This is blood and soil in a nutshell. It is also why the foreigner, the Muslim, the sexual minority can never be a loyal citizen in the eyes of the traditionalist.

In this premodern view, people are not agents of their own destinies. Rather, they are pigeonholed as interchangeable worker bees serving unquestioningly: soldiers, officers, mechanics, bureaucrats, ready to die for their country if called upon. This perverted form of group identity has at its core a society that is hierarchical, controlled, secure, and limited. This Hobbesian idea of a beleaguered collective is older than both capitalism and the early modern idea of national sovereignty. In *Game of Thrones*, the elite may win or die. But for the little people, it is always better to be inside the castle walls of the state for security.

The populists in North America, Europe, and South Asia are not anti-state. But they are against a world of radical freedom. They are against the liberal ideals of the free flows of people, information, and even lifesaving drugs. Remember what they champion. They are very much in favor of the free flow of capital. They believe that a scaled-back state with more money for militarized security and less for the public sphere to correct the overreach of hyper-globalization. You may lose free speech and free elections, but in their place, they are offering security for the chosen people. It is ironic that the populists promise to oppose the power of the global elite and then turn around and champion the rule of modern-day financial robber barons. The tribal chieftains like Brazil's Bolsonaro promise illiberalism because they believe the little people are a herd to be driven in whatever direction their betters desire.[12]

Before his death, historian Alexander Nikolaevich Yakovlev, the *éminence grise* of the then Russian prime minister and a leading architect of Mikhail Gorbachev's opening up, or glasnost, described this basic conception of the new authoritarian state riding roughshod over individual rights and civil liberties. In his last televised interview, he depicted a disturbing trend in attitudes in Putin's Russia toward a passive acceptance of authoritarianism, but he may as well have been talking about any of the strongmen in our story: "We still live with a simple trinity. The state is on top, and we keep making it stronger. Society is suspended somewhere beneath the state. If the state so wishes, society will be civil, or semi-civil, or nothing but a herd. Look at Orwell for a good description of this. And the little, tiny individual is running around somewhere down at the bottom."[13]

When authoritarianism reaches its logical end point, the militarized state takes command. As the populists tear up the rulebook of international law, impunity feeds the cycle of violence.

Lesson Two

One electoral victory is a fluke. Two is a problem. Three is a pattern. Our populists don't just win once. They win repeatedly. *And this is the second big way they have changed the entire global landscape of power. We now have to deal with populists as machine politicians of mass political parties.*

Most of the populists in our sample have gone on to second and third electoral victories. We often hear about how populism is a fluke of the electoral system, engineered by people who want to rig the game. It is true that voting rules matter, as we will touch on below. But we simply can't discount popular anger as a wellspring of tyrannical energy at election time. The re-electability of populist authoritarians is surprisingly high and explained by the fact that in the populist playbook winning is more important than ideological purity. So they are promiscuous courters of public opinion.

In the United States today, Republican nativism is as strong as it was in 2016 when Trump won.[14] There is one persuasive explanation for this: soaring inequality and the policies that trap the middle deciles of income earners in dead-end employment are not going away any time soon. Even though the Biden stimulus packages are worth more than a trillion dollars, they are nowhere near large enough to erase forty years of income stagnation. Average income growth in the United States stood at 2.1 percent annually.[15] The ranks of the downwardly mobile create an ever-expanding reserve army of voters for authoritarian populists.

The Republican Party expects to ride its angry nationalist narrative to victory in many state elections, with vast reserves of money, control of State legislatures, governorships in twenty-seven states, and an enormous force of motivated on-the-ground volunteers. Biden's big win was actually a razor-thin victory. In swing states, the Democrats' advantage is evaporating as Republicans enact changes to state-level rules that govern elections. A drop of 1 or 2 percent of voter turnout among suburbanites will sink Democratic chances to win in 2024.[16]

Forget about Trump as a one-term president. If you consider the number of times a populist politician has won by a whisker, you will stop asking yourself if these guys are lucky, and you will begin to wonder whether their luck comes down to controlling the rules. The likely American scenario is that the Republicans will recapture House and Senate and are on track to win in the electoral college again in 2024. There is a good chance that the Democrats will win the popular vote, but with the shenanigans of the US

Supreme Court in the disputed election, Trump could well be back in the White House. It certainly looks that way.

The modern voter is still an enigma despite the sustained attention of political scientists. The right is hacking a weak spot in modern electoral politics—the incentive to vote. Do citizens vote for a message that resonates with their values? Do they vote for a candidate they like and admire? Do they vote for a movement that makes the best promises? These are all good reasons to get out and vote, but are they good enough in the final instance? Will they guarantee a turnout on election day? Probably not. The right understands something that the left has failed to grasp: voters aren't always motivated to elect a candidate they believe in. Many times, they vote to defeat a candidate they despise.[17]

If they have a reason to hate, they will find a "good enough" reason to love the other option. They want to feel like they're getting ahead, but they are not. Their ship is sliding sideways, and they have lost their trust in the institutions of the postwar compromise. Once we have stripped away all the lies and hate speech, we see that brokerage politics isn't what it used to be. It is a dangerous and unpredictable enterprise. Without new institutional safeguards, it cannot protect the most vulnerable and precarious. Governments need to protect their citizens from the volatile swings in the international economy. Until they do, the driving force of electoral agency will remain antipathy. Everything else comes second.

In the past ten years, the right's message of anti-elite resentment has been perfectly tuned to voters because the right has had plenty of material with which to build a hate campaign. Hillary Clinton, Jeremy Corbyn, and Lula da Silva were eclipsed by political newcomers because enough voters knew who to hate and how to punish.[18] Grassroots donors, big financial backers, and political branding are of secondary importance. Now the populists' winning strategy is to relentlessly dominate the news cycle with social media negativity, controversy, partisan spin, and the constant artillery barrage of the big lie.

Most political scientists will tell you that the playbook of populism is a tried and tested method for winning elections by transforming a narrative of resentment and rage into a political machine to win office. And until recently, they would also have said that it is not an effective way to govern, for one obvious reason: Governments can't make good on their populist promises once they take power because they are no longer outsiders. They have to have obtainable goals and often need to make compromises to satisfy competing interests and regions. Real-world governance is about choosing imperfect solutions to intractable problems. In short, governing is harder than campaigning. And when the real world of compromise meets the simplistic narratives of populism, voters drift away, disillusioned.

But this new breed of populists has defied the experts. They've stayed populist, they've got a low C in governance, and they've still been reelected. As long as they are true to their narrative, it doesn't matter that they can't back it up with constructive policy. As long as the populists can maintain the momentum of hatred, a poor track record is no longer an obstacle to future electoral success. Poland is another good case in point.

Polish voters recently returned a second Law and Justice government to power. Outside a few metropolitan areas, Poland's exurb population is declining. People are leaving for better jobs elsewhere in the EU. A depleted, Catholic, conservative countryside faces off against Poland's more cosmopolitan, urban jurisdictions such as Kraków, Warsaw, and Łódź. This hinterland exodus and cultural insecurity was exploited by the Law and Justice Party, led by Prime Minister Mateusz Morawiecki and President Andrzej Duda.

Even so, Law and Justice's position has slowly eroded over the past five years as the party has doubled down on its cultural populist roots.[19] Their position was tuned to resonate with the most conservative members of the religious base when they effectively banned all abortion, including in cases where the fetus is not viable. The main problem with speaking only to the base is that it alienates everyone else. Hundreds of thousands of women took the streets in the autumn of 2020 to oppose abortion laws that place ideology ahead of reproductive health. The populists may not keep winning into the future, but they have showed that they aren't one-hit wonders. They balance on the knife edge of uncertainty and thrive on intolerance to a much greater degree than anybody thought possible in countries with free elections.

Lesson Three

The populists' third lasting impact is that they have scrambled the left/right binary. Ideology is so basic to politics that throwing it out seems an impossible feat. But the populists did it by substituting emotion and tribal loyalty for reasoned discourse. There is nothing new to this tactic. Hannah Arendt described it best when she argued that totalitarian movements organize "masses—not classes."[20] Masses are rallied using emotion, and strong feelings often appear to eclipse the logic of ideology and interests.

The populist leader always market themselves as something unique to modern politics: the maverick, the free thinker, the self-made person. They have jettisoned the traditions of the past and utterly personify the urgency of the present. The world is spinning out of control and only they can bring order out of chaos. Zygmunt Bauman, the noted public intellectual, called this the world of liquid modernity in which fears proliferate and anxiety dominates the affective field of politics. So who are they? And have they destroyed the left/right spectrum forever? Are they liberals mugged by reality, to paraphrase conservative American commentator Irving Kristol? Are the authoritarian big men the post-ideology messiahs they would have us believe? They promise to free us from our mental shackles, but their vision for the future of politics is not new. They are just conservatives who have learned how to scramble their opponents' radar with irony, dog whistles, a wink and a nod in the place of traditional ideological messaging.

The Brexit campaign is the clearest example of this intentional, ideology-denying tactic. Dominic Cummings, the architect of the Vote Leave campaign in 2016, argued that leaving the EU was not a conservative or liberal decision. He claimed that the EU was ripping off British citizens, draining away national resources, and not living up to its promise of an open market for British industry. Leaving was the only reasonable response. He portrayed the campaign as fresh, new, and unconstrained by the ideological baggage of Europhiles.[21] He was even happy to make common cause with "socialism-in-one-country" Labour supporters and the old order of aristocratic Conservatives. Cummings knew that as long as he could maintain a narrative about taking back control, he could transcend the left/right binary with a sovereigntist message that resonated across the political spectrum. And he was right.

Lesson Four

The final part of the populists' legacy is that by mainstreaming hate speech, winning elections, and disrupting the left/right divide, they have destroyed the case for a neutral, benign, globalized form of neoliberalism. We still maintain global production chains, and we still value a globalized approach to sourcing goods and services. But nobody is singing the praises of capital-G Globalization as an end in and of itself anymore. Let us recall that in 1999 *The Lexus and the Olive Tree* became a runaway bestseller. Thomas Friedman, leading globalist at the *New York Times*, painted a two-dimensional picture of the post–Cold War world in which market opening benefited even the poorest people.[22] Reasonable, center-of-the-road voters cheered for this neoliberal vision of global prosperity because they were promised a better living standard and higher salaries. Even the public policy cognoscenti began to get behind the idea that states and markets are a fluid set of interconnected practices and policies. The boundaries of the state blurred with the arrival of the latest chapter in this global order.[23]

Prior to this, we often believed that globalization had costs and benefits. The benefits of trade are broad and shallow while the costs are narrow and deep. But soon we were convinced that the benefits of wealth creation far outweighed the costs to factory workers in flyover regions of many countries. Friedman attacked skeptics and their outdated ideas about national community, the particularity of culture, and the importance of state sovereignty. He argued that anti-globalizers cared more about tribal vendettas—their metaphorical olive trees—than they did about the robotic factories producing the newest Lexus. It makes no difference to urban professionals if their cars are made by robots or armies of proletarians. But the distinction is a matter of life or death to the workers.

The world is more globalized than ever, but we have come to a bitter understanding of the downsides of interconnectedness.[24] Hyper-globalization is a dangerous system we can't easily control. We can no longer pretend that the market will always balance its accounts. Sometimes, taking jobs away from one place just makes that place poorer and people angrier, no matter that the entire world is struggling to be better off.

This Changes Everything

Every populist on our list believes the future is theirs if only their country can leverage its interests by dumping its commitments— to justice, to the rule of law, and to multilateral cooperation. Populism's Mad Max futurism resonates with people who see the alternative as one of more foreign control, Chinese techno-authoritarianism, and declining industrial competitiveness.

For the tribe and true believers, the rhetoric of disruption captures the zeitgeist of fear and offers an outlet for voters' anxieties. In 1951, Eric Hoffer published *The True Believer*, which became an American bestseller.[25] Hoffer was a character out of a Kerouac novel—a drifter, philosopher, laborer, and a theorist of working-class politics. His work grew to influence the American right thrown into disarray by the Civil Rights Movement and Barry Goldwater's crushing defeat by Lyndon Johnson in 1964. His work is especially prescient today because he demonstrated that populist movements succeed when they are led by charismatic authoritarian leaders commanding a wildly loyal tribe of devotees in thrall to the mystique of their movement.

Hoffer's insights about true believers were written about the left and the potential for socialist revolution in the postwar period. But his work drew inspiration from earlier research on fascist politics by storied contrarian and psychoanalyst Wilhelm Reich. Reich was part of Sigmund Freud's inner circle in Vienna and a leading figure in early theories of sexual development. In the interwar period, he conducted research that attempted to show how mass movement politics were rooted in human psychology and sometimes even sexual pathology. As Reich put it, "the fascist mentality is the mentality of the subjugated 'little man' who craves authority and rebels against it at the same time."[26]

Where do these little men first learn their hatred of women, of the foreigner, of everything they don't understand? Reich identifies the family as the first and most important incubator of authoritarian values: "From the standpoint of social development, the family cannot be considered the basis of the authoritarian state, only as one of the most important institutions which support it. It is, however, its central *reactionary germ cell*, the most important place of reproduction of the reactionary and conservative individual. Being itself caused by the authoritarian system, the family becomes the most important institution for its conservation."[27]

What was so revolutionary about Reich was that he recognized that the responsibility for defeating fascism rested with the masses of ordinary people who had supported it at home in the first place. When people embrace the cruder appeals of nationalism, it is not for an abstract love of country, but rather as a way to express their desires for freedom, autonomy, a voice in world affairs, and personal empowerment to shape the way they and their family live. That is why they make the connection between reducing the obligations of their state internationally and reducing the obligations of individuals in their societies. The freedom and autonomy they desire is the freedom to discriminate and the autonomy to ignore LGBTQIA2+ rights.

What Reich believed about the authoritarianism of interwar conservatism in Europe, Hoffer similarly believed about the left in America a generation later. And it is surreal that many of our modern authoritarian movements can be similarly understood through this lens of frustrated striving and precariousness.[28]

As Hoffer observed, "They who clamor loudest for freedom are often the ones least likely to be happy in a free society. The frustrated, oppressed by their shortcomings, blame their failure on existing restraints. Actually, their innermost desire is for an end to the 'free for all.' They want to eliminate free competition and the ruthless testing to which the individual is continually subjected in a free society."[29]

Nowhere is this truer than among the white working-class supporters of Donald Trump and Boris Johnson, who demand the removal of groups with whom they compete for state support and employment. For them, freedom is a mirage, and the only reality that matters is the way of life they cling to, the space they occupy, and the leader who will defend the flock and hold back the terror of liberal competition in an era of globalization.

What has made populism such a powerful force in the United States is that it has become an internalized language of the economically pressured true believer to galvanize anger against the political class. In Lacanian terms, the acquisition of this language is a ticking time bomb for these individuals.[30] In its most extreme, it evokes the demonic lynch mob, the absolutism of a cult movement, or the exorcism of blood sacrifice. Language that expresses a person's longing for systemic revenge against real and imagined enemies goes far beyond a political act of calculated defiance. For millions of people, populism has become a potent language of political revolt, a self-contained grammar of nativist anger that is almost impossible to neutralize through conventional electoral competition.

The Revolt of the Masses

With so much conflict baked into the system, the potential for fascist violence should never be underestimated. In the eyes of the true believer violence is always romantic because every militiaman is a Cincinnatus, guardian of the Republic, poor and proud, a paragon of the patriotic virtues of integrity, responsibility, and sacrifice. It is about posing with big guns, imagining that one's politics are imbued with a sanctity of spilled blood, courageous last stands, and the greater glory of the cause.

Sectarian violence in Israel, the electoral violence in Peru, the violence of rank-and-file American police officers who imagine themselves to be the thin blue line between order and racialized chaos are all part of the same turn to extremism and state violence. State-sanctioned extrajudicial violence of the police upholds authoritarianism in Turkey, the Philippines, Brazil, Nicaragua, Poland, South Africa, and Russia.[31] Conservative violence has become more visible, more regular, more accepted. There are red flags everywhere.

In 1929, before the rise of the fascist Spanish general Francisco Franco, José Ortega y Gasset published *The Revolt of the Masses*, a classic statement of modernist liberal political thought. His liberalism was far removed from the revolutionary fervor of the socialists, but he nevertheless shared Orwell's dream of a democratic Spain. It is surreal to think that almost a hundred years later, we are at a similar juncture today, witnessing the rage of the working classes, pressurized, and pushed to the edge.

Ortega y Gasset offered a pungent commentary on the rise of charismatic leaders; he had an uncanny ability to identify how people in the wealthiest societies might turn toward populist authoritarianism. He thought that urbanization, labor-saving technology, and the wealth afforded by open markets had made the masses soft and entitled. He explained: "The sovereignty of the unqualified individual . . . has now passed from being a juridical idea or ideal to be a psychological state inherent in the average man. And note this, that when what was before an ideal becomes a component part of reality, *it inevitably ceases to be an ideal* [emphasis added]."[32] He may as well have been talking about people in the Global North today, who take for granted that they live in liberal democracies.

The trampling of the democratic ideal was on full display as rioters ran through the halls of the US Congress waving confederate battle flags and shouting about conspiracy theories on

January 6, 2021. Popular historian Simon Schama observed, "When truth perishes, so does freedom."[33] Once democracy is taken for granted, it is easy to sacrifice it for short-term gain. "The prestige and magic that are attributes of the ideal are volatized," Ortega y Gasset said. "The leveling demands of a generous democratic inspiration have been changed from aspirations . . . into appetites and unconscious assumptions."[34] According to his old-fashioned patrician reasoning, it is easy for the people to forget the hard work that went into building the democratic institutions of their freedom.

To this old Spanish philosopher who distrusted majoritarian politics, the sovereign people were like spoiled children. Today, the populist insurgency is another putative revolt of the masses. Even in his ossified attitudes, Ortega y Gasset was forced to acknowledge the potency of popular agency: "Was it not this that was hoped . . . the average man should feel himself master, lord, and ruler of himself and of his life?"[35] Like many other philosophers in the classical age of liberalism, Ortega y Gasset was afraid that uneducated people with the right to vote would hand massive power to populist demagogues who promised them a seat at the table but instead gave them only bread and circuses.

Historian Anne Applebaum has argued that, given the right conditions, "any society can turn against democracy."[36] Of course, authoritarianism is not a foregone conclusion, but certain circumstances virtually guarantee its success. For a long time, it has been believed that our liberal institutions would insulate us from the worst elements of authoritarian populism. In liberal societies, interest groups compete for influence and peaceful competition is the highest form of cooperation. The difference today is that tribalism that relies on fear and anger to divide and conquer destroys the checks and balances of liberal democracy by arguing that it is okay to win by any means necessary.

Where Are We Now?

We need to think more critically about what comes next. Professor Rob Walker termed this a key problem of modernity in which we have learned to think globally, but not inclusively, something he termed, "after the globe, before the world."[37] The populists have taught us that despite decades of globalization, the allure of sovereignty is indestructible even in a borderless world. Trump taught us that ethno-nationalism can win the presidency and drive a stake through the heart liberal internationalism. Johnson showed that you could deploy the raw power of xenophobic sovereignty to reverse forty years of European integration and cooperation. Netanyahu demonstrated once again the universal toxic appeal of extreme sovereignty to win repeatedly at the ballot box. The contested claims of Israeli sovereignty over Palestinian territory carried him to victory defying the stillborn guarantees of international law.

Only a few of the populist governments have faced sanction by voters but, their inevitable demise is still a long way off. Even so, we can begin to see rumblings of discontent in their ranks. In the UK close to 100 members of Boris Johnson's Tory party voted against or to abstain on his motion to introduce new controls to reduce the spread of COVID-19 and it only passed when Labour voted to support the government's bill. Johnson's scandals and his erratic leadership have given the Labour Party a dramatic rise in the public opinion polls.

The disenchantment with others of the Big Men is already apparent. By the end of 2021 in Brazil, Bolsonaro's support plummeted. Voters were angered by his recklessness and indifference in responding to the pandemic and "Lula" the former leftist president pulled ahead with elections scheduled for 2022. In Turkey, Erdoğan is also facing a major economic crisis with runaway inflation and

Turkey's currency in freefall. Ankara's foreign currency reserves have fallen by billions of dollars and will probably continue to fall.

In the Czech Republic, Andrej Babiš was caught up in another corruption scandal when it was learned through the Pandora Papers leak that he transferred $22 million to a tax haven in the British Virgin Islands to purchase a luxury villa in Cannes, France. Already caught in a spending scandal involving EU agriculture subsidies, Babiš was severely weakened going into Czech parliamentary elections a week later in October 2021. Babiš's minority government fell and was replaced by a coalition of opposition parties forming a center-right alliance.

Do the political ups-and-downs of the Big Men mean that they are on the ropes? Certainly not in Hungary, India, Brazil, the US, and France, just for starters. This is what we know. First, the insurgency movement continues to win new converts across the world by recruiting hundreds of thousands of supporters from the ranks of the anti-vaxxers and other parts of civil society angered by elite politics. In France, the authoritarian right continues to draw major support. In April 2022 Marine Le Pen won 42 percent of the vote in the second round of the presidential election. The Le Pen family have been shooting for the presidency for twenty years, with her father winning less than 18 percent of second round votes back in 2002. Since that time their party has cleaned up its image, focusing on bread and butter issues and downplaying anti-immigrant policies. But as the Natonial Rally has tacked to the populist centre right, other right-wing firebrands, like Eric Zemmour have risen to fill the gap. Authoritarian populism is now a fixture in French politics at every level, and each new election, municipal, regional, parliamentary, and presidential brings a new opportunity for the far right to try again.

Some leaders will go down in defeat, but the conditions which elected them to high office in the first place and created the populist insurgency haven't gone away. The structural crises of a quickly changing liberal international order have given authoritarian movements a new lease on life. They continue to surge and spread their toxic message in ways that few could predict.[38] (See Appendix Two: The Reelection Prospects of a Cross-Section of Populist Governments and Far-Right Opposition Parties.)

Secondly, right-wing parties are looking at new ways to cooperate and form governments in Sweden and the Netherlands, two Northern European countries where populism has been historically absent. In Sweden, the Sweden Democrats, a far-right party with a neo-Nazi past and once a pariah, has now been invited into a grand conservative coalition.[39] In the UK, US, India, and Russia, populism in the streets continues to attract new followers, and authoritarian leaders have strengthened their grip on their supporters.

In the last five years society has become more divided, polarized, intolerant, and angry. In a study of public opinion conducted in 2021, Ipsos found that anti-elite sentiment is continuing to rise around the world and most citizens in twenty-five surveyed countries express feelings of alienation and anti-elite sentiment.[40] Of the nineteen thousand people surveyed in 2021, 81 percent agree that "politicians always end up finding ways to protect their privileges." Another strong majority, 72 percent, say "the political and economic elite don't care about hard-working people." A whopping 70 percent think "the main divide in our society is between ordinary citizens and the political and economic elite." More than half, 60 percent, say "the most important political issues should be decided directly by the people through referendums, not by the elected officials."[41]

It is not only Trump and the Republican Party that are in the vanguard of the global insurgent movement. Across the industrial world, the systemic fracturing of the social consensus is visible. Ur-fascism is not an infantile disorder but a social pathology running deep in the heartland of liberal democracies. In recent years white supremacist and nativist reactionaries have proven to be Teflon, bouncing back from scandal, and growing their base even when they are charged with crimes or lose civil suits. "While some of the messengers have been eviscerated, the more mainstream versions of their hatemongering continue to have real currency, with broad exposure guaranteeing that the violence of the far-right fringes will unfortunately continue,"[42] said Brian Levin, the director of the Center for the Study of Hate and Extremism at California State University, San Bernardino.

Has Populism Won?

It all comes down to this. Putin has been a wellspring of the authoritarian insurgency and Trump was the bottle rocket, soaring high, lighting up the horizon for a new generation of would-be autocrats and religious nationalists. Even in defeat, he has reordered American life, with dozens of subnational imitators and a Supreme Court poised to roll back the right to abortion for American women. At the end of our narrative, we must return to our warning: The populist insurgency is being radicalized in many countries and the radicalization poses a new threat to democracy. The populist insurgency received a jolt of energy from Evangelical Christians in January 2022 when a convoy of truckers and activists opposed to vaccine mandates converged on Ottawa, the capital of Canada.

The freedom convoy blockaded and occupied the streets in front of the Parliament buildings. The convoys of hundreds of pickup trucks, eighteen-wheel rigs, and farm tractors captured the imagination of the far right around the world. It became the top story on Fox News, and anti-vaccine supporters from Europe and the United States contributed millions of dollars in support. The convoy dumped Canadians straight into the pipeline of hatred that has been roiling the United States, and the overt anger and other forms of bigotry stunned Canada's political class.[43]

The occupation spread, with copycat civil disobedience in other Canadian provinces, as well as in New Zealand, Australia, Belgium, and France.[44] No one saw this coming, certainly not the Canadian authorities, not the media, not the specialists. All the same the most important lesson it teaches is that far-right populists have found a cause and are learning tactics and strategy from each other. The support for radical far-right militant activism underlines again that in a post-truth internet age these kinds of insurgency movements are born online and take flight.[45]

In the larger picture, the pandemic has made contingent voters around the world angrier, more impatient, more uncertain, and radically open to authoritarian leadership cults. Hyper-individualism and the big lie have raised many existential questions: Who is a citizen? What are our responsibilities to each other? What are our core national values? Despite the best efforts of young anti-fascist activists, the historic left has not been able to neutralize the big lie, vanquish tribal-based politics, and restore liberal democracy to a semblance of health. The populist insurgency will continue its ascendance as long as there is no end in sight to the pandemic. The "right to infect others" is not a core national belief, yet reckless calls for absolute freedom at all costs attract millions of true believers. It will require a much larger army of citizens to push the populists out to sea.

Until such a mobilization occurs, we must live in a world without a robust middle class in control of the electoral system. The middle class's dream is an inaccessible reality for many in the millennial age bracket. According to the Economic Policy Institute, CEO compensation has grown by 940 percent in the past four decades, and in that same period, the compensation of the typical worker has increased by 12 percent.[46] And that enormous gulf of economic inequality continues to widen.

Workers' wages rose an average of 1.8 percent in 2020, and CEOs' compensation rose by 16 percent, an average of $21.4 million in top American firms.[47] Is it any wonder that the populist reserve army of voters has grown? Mainstream parties have mostly lost the support of the social democratic left's traditional voters in the old industrial centers in England, France, India, and the EU. It is an open question whether these voters will ever return to their traditional political homes in significant enough numbers to rebuild the old "red walls." Every mainstream politician believes that they can win back the working class with a turbo-charged stimulus. Still, the populist insurgency maintains its credibility with the precariat in the service sector, white men without university education, as well as the large swaths of the old proletariat, furious at the political elite and hyper-globalization. Neofascism has given these strange bedfellows a common destiny and a language they can own.

The populists are right about one thing: the self-seeking political elite are unreliable allies who materially benefit from citizen apathy and indifference in every national political system. Millions of workers and families who lost better-paying jobs are poorer than they were before 2020. The World Bank has forecast a rise in global poverty today that is about four times worse than the global financial crisis in 2008.[48] Furthermore, the IMF has found that "COVID-19 has exposed and exacerbated inequalities between countries just as it has within countries."[49]

In this sovereignty-first order there will be more conflict, less consensus about trade and security, more violent border clashes, more regional wars, and more human rights violations behind borders. We are living through an exceptional period of instability and realignment with two parallels in modern history.

The full-employment Keynesianism of the post-war era was supported by a broad base of voters. The second realignment occured after 1980 when voters turned towards neoliberal capitalism and its promise of prosperity for all. Now we are living through a third realignment as voters look for security in sovereignty-first populism. What makes this time more dangerous is that these movements are exclusive, not inclusive of the majority, and they promise benefits to the chosen few rather than everyone. Even worse, leaders are willing to declare war on the concept of representative democracy in order to achieve their exclusionary ends.

The job of democracy advocates gets harder by the day. When every challenge requires force and every struggle is a war, it is easier to divide the electorate and take an absolutist view of rights, freedoms, and democratic benefits for the chosen people: every leader, every tribe, every nation for itself. When everyone is for themselves alone, no one is on the side of solidarity, of the public, of liberal democracy. And then we are mentally eclipsed by the shallow and impoverished vision of authoritarian populism.

We must return to our original question: Have the populists won? Has the fever claimed its victims? The short answer is, the authoritarian right has been emboldened and they've honed the big lie to a razor's edge. The populists have made big gains, normalized a paranoid style of politics, and put liberal democracy onto its back foot, fighting for its future. Now that they've tasted victory, they won't go quietly.

APPENDIX I

The Anti-System Vote in Thirty-Six Countries, Including Far-Right Opposition Parties, 2015–2021

Country	Party	Year	Gov't or opposition	Votes received (millions)	Popular vote (%)
US	Republican	2020	Opposition (president)	74.2	46.9
Canada	Conservative	2021	Opposition	5.74	33.7
Mexico	National Regeneration Movement	2018	Gov't (president)	30.1	53.2
UK	Conservative	2019	Gov't	13.9	43.6
France	National Rally	2022	Opposition	13.3	41.5
Netherlands	People's Party for Freedom and Democracy (VVD)	2021	Gov't	2.28	21.9
Germany	Alternative for Germany (AfD)	2021	Opposition	4.8	10.3
Denmark	Danish People's Party	2019	Opposition	0.310	8.7
Italy	Lega Nord	2018	Opposition	5.7	17.4
Finland	Finns Party (formerly True Finns)	2019	Opposition	0.54	17.5

Country	Party	Year	Gov't or opposition	Votes received (millions)	Popular vote (%)
Slovenia	Slovenian Democratic Party	2020	Gov't	0.222	24.92
Bulgaria	There Is Such a People Party	2021	Coalition partner	0.657	24.07
Estonia	EKRE	2018	Coalition partner	0.01	17.8
Poland	Law and Justice	2019	Gov't	8.05	43.6
Russia	United Russia	2018	Gov't (president)	56.4	76.7
Hungary	Fidesz	2022	Gov't	2.83	52.5
Austria	Austrian People's Party	2019	Gov't	1.79	37.5
Czech Republic	Action of Dissatisfied Citizens (ANO)	2021	Opposition	1.46	27.1
Greece	Syriza	2019	Opposition	1.78	31.5
Ukraine	Servant of the People	2019	Gov't (president)	13.5	73.2
Turkey	Justice and Development	2018	Gov't (president)	26.3	52.59
Israel	Likud	2021	Opposition	1.07	24.2
Philippines	Partido Federal ng Pilipinas	2022	Gov't (president)	31.63	58.8
South Korea	People Power Party	2022	Gov't (president)	16.39	48.6
India	BJP	2019	Gov't	270	45
South Africa	Economic Freedom Fighters	2019	Opposition	1.9	10.8
Nicaragua	Sandanista National Liberation Front (FSLN)	2021	Gov't	2.09	75.87
El Salvador	Nuevos Ideas	2019	Gov't (president)	1.4	53
Argentina	Justicialist Party	2019	Gov't	12.9	48.2

Country	Party	Year	Gov't or opposition	Votes received (millions)	Popular vote (%)
Chile	Christian Social Front	2021	Runoff for president	1.96	27.9
Bolivia	Movement for Socialism	2019	Gov't	2.9 (disputed)	47.1
Peru	Popular Force	2021	Opposition	8.79	49.87
Venezuela	PSUV	2018	Gov't	6.2	67.8
Brazil	PSL	2018	Gov't (president)	57.8	55.1

Source: Authors' original dataset, 2022

APPENDIX II

The Reelection Prospects of a Cross-Section of Populist Governments and Far-Right Opposition Parties

North America

United States

Running on a Republican ticket, Donald Trump won the presidency in 2016 and then lost in November 2020. In the congressional elections that same year the Democrats lost seats in the House and gained only a single seat in the Senate. It is expected that the Democrats will lose control of the House and Senate in the midterm congressional elections in November 2022. Trump still controls the Republican Party and is amassing a war chest to challenge Joe Biden. Biden's approval ratings have been hammered by the pandemic and fears of persistently high inflation. Every indication is that Trump will run for president in 2024.

Mexico

Angel Manuel López Obrador, former mayor of Mexico City, won the presidency for the first time in 2018. His party, the National

Regeneration Movement (MORENA), was founded in 2011 and went from winning 35 seats in the Chamber of Deputies in 2015 to winning 189 of the 500 seats in 2018. He remains stubbornly popular with his base due to his pro-poor policies (he raised the minimum wage multiple times) and his promise to reverse the privatization of Pemex. He is building a billion-dollar refinery to make Mexico less dependent on the export of oil and gas products and more self-reliant. Mexico has one of the worst environment, social, and governance (ESG) rankings, placing Pemex 253 out of 261 countries in an index of how well oil and gas producers are managing risks. AMLO tried and failed to increase governmental control over Mexico's electricty markets but succeeded in nationalizing Mexican mining and extraction of lithium deposits that are necessary for building next generation batteries for electric vehicles. López Obrador cannot run again because of constitutional term limits, but he will influence Mexican politics for many years to come.

Europe

United Kingdom

Prime Minister Boris Johnson won his first election in 2019, which was the fourth consecutive victory for the Conservative Party. The Tories handed Labour its single largest defeat in the postwar era and have a very large majority in the House of Commons. Johnson's popularity is quite volatile according to public opinion polls. Since 2020 Johnson has weathered several scandals, the most important of which involves garden parties at 10 Downing Street while the UK was under "lockdown" public health orders. Furthermore, Brexit has been a drag on the British economy and the Labour Party has a new leader. Keir Starmer is less controversial than the previous leader and polls suggest he is well-liked by the electorate. Johnson is unlikely to repeat his smashing victory of 2019 and was forced to resign in 2022.

Poland

Andrzej Duda won the presidential election as a Law and Justice (PiS) party candidate in 2015 and 2020. In that period the party experienced a minor dip as popular vote fell from 51.5 percent to 51 percent. The conservative ruling coalition has been able to unite Poles behind them in their battle with the EU. There is a strong opposition from women voters, but so far the opposition has not been able to challenge Polish populists electorally. Law and Justice faces increasing opposition in the EU for its attacks on the rule of law and independence of judges. But following the invasion of Ukraine and Poland's frontline support, including the movement of American weapons across its borders, it is likely that Law and Justice will hold onto power. The party has become more popular as it has positioned itself as a strong defender of sovereignty in Europe.

Russia

Vladimir Putin won the presidency for the fourth time in 2018. In this most recent election, he received a greater percentage of the popular vote (77 percent) than he had in the previous election in 2012, but that number is challenged by independent observers due to suspicion of widespread election fraud. Thousands of the opposition are in jail and face legal and other threats. Following constitutional amendments in 2019, it is likely that Putin will seek a fifth term, and he could govern unopposed up to 2036. But following the brutal attack on Urkaine, Putin's future is in the balance. Cascading Western sanctions will continue to corrode the Russian economy until it is brought lower than it was in 1990, and they will not let up until Putin is gone.

Putin in Russia is the only populist leader to face worldwide repudiation of his fascistic violence and cruelty, and even here, it ought to be noted that at the time of writing this book his invasion of Ukraine was still broadly supported in his own country, although thousands of Russian have been arrested for demonstrating against the war. Putin maintains support through a vast misinformation network and authoritarian security state so it is always difficult to know what Russians think when civil society faces so much repression.

Hungary

As leader of Fidesz, Victor Orbán is the longest serving of the populist strongmen inside the European Union. He won his fourth election in 2018 and increased his share of the popular vote from 45 percent to 49 percent due largely to a disorganized opposition. Opposition parties have recently agreed to a new primary system and unified list that combines the support of multiple parties behind a single candidate. But even a unified front was not enough to dislodge Orban who went on to increase his share of the popular vote yet again, in April 2022. Hungarian elections have been characterized as free but not fair, because of the way that Orban's party controls the levers of democracy and the mass media. He will hold onto power for another five years.

Netherlands

As a centrist populist, Mark Rutte leads the People's Party for Freedom and Democracy. He has been prime minister of the Netherlands since 2010. He has formed cabinets in 2010, 2012,

2017 and was reconfirmed in 2021. In 2017 his party won 33 of the 150 seats; increased their seats to 35 in 2021 despite the entire cabinet resigning over a scandal involving child welfare payments. The further right populists also increased their vote share alongside Rutte's centrist populists, and together they have an outsized influence in the parliament and the political life of the country. For the time being, Rutte seems secure.

Austria

Sebastian Kurz and the ÖVP won their second electoral victory in 2019. While technically not a populist party, the ÖVP leaned towards populist messaging when in coalition with the FPO, who are explicitly authoritarian and populist. They went from 62 seats in 2017 to 71 seats in 2019, increasing their share of the popular vote from 31.5 to 37.5 percent despite a corruption scandal. Eventually that scandal brought down Kurz and he left politics in 2021 to work for American tech billionaire Peter Thiel, an early supporter of Donald Trump. Kurz's party remains a powerful force in Austrian politics.

Slovenia

Janez Janša served as prime minister of Slovenia three times. He was also defense minister from 1990 to 1994, a period that included the Slovenian War of Independence. He has led the right-wing Slovenian Democratic Party since 1993. Janša was convicted of corruption but not jailed in 2013. The SDP won a plurality in the 2018 elections, but Janša was passed over as PM because of his extremism. He became PM in March 2020 following the resignation of Marjan Šarec. But he and his party were trounced in parliamentary elections in 2022, when the newly formed left leaning Freedom Movement won forty seats in the Slovenian legislature. They show no sign of losing influence.

Czech Republic

Andrej Babiš founded ANO 2011, a centrist populist party in 2011, and went on to form two governments as prime minister. He joined a coalition government in 2013, was deputy prime minister by 2015, and became prime minister in 2017 when ANO 2011 won 29 percent of the popular vote and 78 of 200 seats. Babiš subsequently lost a confidence vote but formed a second coalition. He served as prime minister from 2018 to 2021, when his party was defeated following the publication the Pandora Papers, a cache of financial documents. It included evidence that Babiš, a billionaire, used offshore companies to buy a luxury estate in France. Babiš will remain a force in Czech politics.

Greece

Alexis Tsipras, a left-of-center populist, entered the Greek national scene in 2012 during the Greek-EU debt crisis. He won national elections, in January and September 2015, as leader of Syriza with 36.3 percent of the popular vote. Tsipras was voted out of office in July 2019. Populism on the left and right remain a visible power in Greek politics and Tsipras has served as leader of the official opposition since 2019. Left populism is a potent force in Greek politics.

Ukraine

Like Trump, centrist populist Volodymyr Zelensky was known for his television roles before entering politics and was a well-known cultural figure in both Russia and Ukraine. In 2019 Zelensky soundly defeated Petro Poroshenko, the incumbent candidate, in the second round of voting, winning 73 percent of the popular vote and forming a majority government—a first in Ukraine's fragmented political system. And although Zelensky was a third-way candidate, running between the pro-Moscow right and the old left, he is now a national hero, immortalized as a wartime leader embodying Ukrainian courage in the face of Russian aggression.

The Ultra-Right European Opposition

Germany

Throughout Europe the far right has won the support of the electorate, sending elected officials to its many bodies from the national to the local. In Germany it is expected that the AfD will continue to be a commanding populist voice in the German parliament. It received 12 percent of the popular vote in the 2017 election and became the biggest opposition party in the Bundestag. Since then it has become more nationalistic and xenophobic, and the 2021 election saw their share of the vote decline to 10 percent. The ultra-right faction forced the resignation of the current leader at which time he said, "The heart of the party beats very far to the right these days," and he added, "Parts of the AfD rejected Germany's constitutional order." He said, "I see clear echoes there of totalitarianism" (*Washington Post*, January 30, 2022). Outside of parliament AfD's influence has grown and the party has been a major supporter of Germany's anti-vaccine movement, drawing over 400,000 people to its massive street protests in January 2022, according to a security official. Support for anti-vaccine movements has hardened after the government brought in new restrictions. AfD has positioned itself as a major force in German politics.

Italy

In Italy, the League, Forza Italia, and Fratelli d'Italia received 35 percent of the popular vote despite the personal popularity of prime minister Draghi, the former head of ECB. The Italian ultra-right are a significant presence in parliament and civil society but are deeply divided by their leadership rivalries and ideological differences. So far they are unable to work together to create a common front of the extreme right. The extreme right is well connected to the anti-vax movement and could make significant gains in the next election. With Draghi's popular decision to continue as prime minister, the ultra-right parties will face new obstacles to growing politically. So for the moment the far right will remain deeply divided although capable of capturing more than 30 percent of the popular vote in the next election.

France

In France the political spectrum has been pulled to the right by the conservative Macron presidency, the growing influence of Marine Le Pen and her party and her new challenger Éric Zemmour, a hard right, "big lie" anti-immigrant TV celebrity. Public polling shows that one-third of the French are supporters of far-right parties. At the present time France's left parties have fallen to historic lows. The right today receives almost half the vote nationally. In April 2022 Macron won a second presidential term with 58.5 percent of the vote, but Le Pen's 41.5 percent was the highest she has ever polled in a presidential election. The populists will remain a powerful force in French political life for the next decade, at least.

Portugal

Portugal's socialist government struggled to be reelected and faced a hard-right surge from Chega "Enough" challenging the Left Bloc, the communists, and the Liberal Initiative to become the third-largest party in the Portuguese parliament. Experts predicted that the election was too close to call and underestimated the appeal of the socialist government, which won a clear majority. Voter turnout was higher than the previous election. Both the socialist left and the far right increased their share of the vote. The socialists won close to 42 percent of the vote, five points more than in 2019. Chega increased its support from 1.3 to 7.2 percent of the vote and elected 12 MPs (up from one), becoming the third-largest force in parliament after the center-left PS. With a bigger presence than ever, the hard right is expected to play a larger role in the life of Portugal's fragmented political party system.

Middle East

Israel

Right-wing populist Benjamin Netanyahu won his fifth electoral victory in 2020. He was prime minister of Israel from 1996 to 1999, and then from 2009 to 2021. He was sworn in for a fifth term in a coalition with Benny Gantz as alternating prime minister following his indictment on corruption charges in 2019. Naftali Bennett dethroned Netanyahu, Israel's long-time prime minister, in June 2021 and formed an unwieldy coalition government including ultra-Zionists, moderates, secularists, independents, and Arabs who joined a governing alliance for the first time in Israel's history. Against all odds, Bennett survived and passed his first budget in November 2021. Netanyahu remains a powerful, if diminished force and has stated his desire to run again for another term. Bennett is not secure and Netanyahu may mount a comeback because at the time of writing the governing coalition failed to pass its budget. Israel has not yet entered a post-Netanyahu era.

Turkey

Recep Tayyip Erdoğan won his second presidential election as leader of the Justice and Development party in 2018. Erdoğan was prime minister of Turkey from 2003 to 2014 and was elected president in 2014. Constitutional changes in 2017 abolished the office of the prime minister and made the president the head of state as well as head of government. Erdoğan won the 2018 presidential election with 53 percent of the popular vote. With a deteriorating economy, high inflation, and falling incomes, Erdoğan's popularity has taken a hit and he faces a growing opposition. It is unclear whether his health will permit him to run for Turkey's highest office again, but there is no obvious successor to replace him.

Asia

Philippines

Rodrigo Duterte won his first national election in 2016. He was a long-time mayor of Davao City from 1988 to 1998, served in Congress from 1998 to 2001, then served three more mayoral terms from 2001 to 2010, after which his daughter succeeded him. He won the 2016 presidential election with 39 percent of the popular vote. In 2018, Duterte kept an election promise to move his country to a federal political system. The Consultative Committee subsequently ruled Duterte will serve as a transition president and that despite coming into power under the old system, he cannot stand for presidential election a second time. But he is still a force to be reckoned with because his daughter, who was also mayor of Davao City, is entering national politics. Philippine presidential politics are dominated by long-lived family dynasties. For example, Duterte's daughter is standing for the office of vice president in the 2022 elections and Ferdinand Marcos's son, Ferdinand Marcos Jr. is running for president. In 2022 the dynastic two families won the presidency and vice-presidency decisively despite evidence of wide-scale voting tampering.

India

Narendra Modi has worked in Indian politics since the 1970s and became chief minister of Gujarat in 2001. He resigned from regional politics upon his election as prime minister in 2014. He won reelection in 2019, increasing his majority by 21 more seats to 303 of 545 seats in the Lok Sabha. The Congress party of Nehru and the dynastic Gandhis is a shadow of its former self as the ultra-nationalist BJB consolidates power across India's sprawling federal system. Modi's popularity remains undiminished despite his attacks against Muslims and suffering a defeat at the hands of a year-long mass civil disobedience campaign by Sikh farmers angry at his neoliberal reform package. The pandemic has battered India's economy. Around 75 million people in India were pushed into extreme poverty in 2020, living on $2 or less a day, according to the Pew Research Center. A salaried worker in rural India earns an average of around 300 rupees ($4) a day and this compares with $6 a day for a similar job in urban areas, according to estimates by the International Labour Organization. By far the biggest threat is that agriculture's share of India's total employment rose for the first time in at least 15 years, by 3 percentage points to 45.6 percent

The government needs to create tens of millions of jobs that bring migrant workers out of farming and into India's urban, more productive economy or risk a lost decade of arrested growth. Even in the face of a looming economic slowdown and jobs crisis, the opposition parties are disorganized and lacking effective national leadership. Modi is such a powerful figure in Indian politics that he is likely to re-elected, barring a major crisis.

Central and South America

Argentina

Peronism has been a longstanding staple of Argentinian politics since the 1940s. Peronism's center-left politics became important again with the election of Nestor and Cristina Kirchner between 2003 and 2015. Following four years of center-right rule, Alberto Fernández won the presidency with an alliance of Peronist, Kirchnerist, left-wing, and communist parties who banded together to end the neoliberal Mauricio Macri presidency. With sky-high inflation and ongoing debt troubles with financial markets and the IMF, the political future of the Peronists is uncertain, but they hold on to power nevertheless.

Nicaragua

Daniel Ortega won his fifth national election in 2021. He was a member of the Junta of National Reconstruction in the 1979–90 Sandinista Revolution, served in the opposition between 1990 and 2007, and returned to the presidency in 2007. He won again in 2011. Term limits were abolished by constitutional amendment in an FSLN-dominated National Assembly in 2014. Ortega won a third consecutive term in 2016 following fraudulent elections and the arrest of many opposition leaders. He was sworn in for a fourth term in January 2022 after again jailing all potential challengers. His wife, Rosario Murillo, has served as vice-president since 2016. Ortega has given no sign of resigning from public life and when the Organization of American States criticized the unfair nature of Nicaraguan elections he withdrew from the organization, calling it "a diabolical instrument of evil."

Bolivia

Evo Morales and his Movement for Socialism party won three presidential elections and presided over a referendum to abolish presidential term limits, after which he ran a fourth time. After allegations of electoral fraud, he reluctantly resigned the presidency in November 2019. His handpicked successor, Luis Arce, won the presidential election in October 2020. Left populism remains a pivotal force in Bolivian domestic politics.

Venezuela

Nicolás Maduro won his first national election in 2013. He was elected to the National Assembly in 2000, rose to the post of foreign minister, and then the vice-presidency in 2011 under Hugo Chávez. Maduro became interim prime minister after Chávez's death in 2013. The election in 2017 was widely considered rigged, with many of the opposition jailed or exiled. In 2020, the main opposition parties boycotted legislative elections and Maduro's coalition claimed control of the National Assembly, which had previously backed its speaker and main Maduro opponent, Juan Guaidó, who had sworn himself in as interim president, with the backing of the US and the EU in 2019. Now Maduro governs without an effective opposition and will continue to do so for the foreseeable future.

Brazil

Bolsonaro became president of Brazil with 55 percent of the popular vote in 2018. Before that he had a 27-year career in Brazil's lower chamber of congress. He has been accused of recklessness and incompetence during the coronavirus pandemic. It has also been alleged that he masterminded a long-running embezzlement scheme to skim the salaries of his aides. He was served with articles of impeachment that went nowhere in the labyrinth of Brazilian politics. There have been mass demonstrations against his defense of the vaccine sceptics while Brazil experienced one of the highest death rates from the pandemic in the world. Bolsonaro is running for reelection in October 2022 and his main challenger is former president and left icon Luis Ignácio Lula da Silva. Like Trump, Bolsonaro has vowed to stay in office whatever the outcome of the next election saying, "Only God can remove me."

FURTHER READING
Our Top Recommendations

There is a rapidly growing academic and popular analysis of the populist spasm. A good place to begin is with the indispensable literature on the contemporary assault on liberal democracy. The best among them are Pippa Norris and Ronald Inglehart, *Cultural Backlash: Trump, Brexit, and Authoritarian Populism* (Cambridge, MA: Cambridge University Press, 2019) and Steven Levitsky and Daniel Ziblatt, *How Democracies Die* (New York: Crown, 2019). A powerful examination of the contemporary origins of authoritarianism is by Timothy Snyder: *On Tyranny: Twenty Lessons from the Twentieth Century* (New York: Penguin, 2017). A good general introduction to populism is Cas Mudde's *The Far Right Today* (London, UK: Polity, 2019).

We need to know more about the role of precarity and structurally embedded inequality in the rise of the populist insurgency. One of the best analyses of the socioeconomic roots of populism is Guy Standing's *The Precariat: The New Dangerous Class* (London, UK: Bloomsbury, 2011). Umberto Eco's prescient analysis of fascism as a legacy structure of modern society is indispensable reading: "Ur-Fascism," *New York Review of Books*, June 22, 1995, nybooks.com/articles/1995/06/22/ur-fascism. For a stimulating and contemporary study of the origins of fascism, see *From Fascism to Populism in History* by Federico Finchelstein (Berkeley: University of California Press, 2019). For the question of whether our political systems can recover, see *Reclaiming Populism* by Eric Protzer and Paul Summerville (London, UK: Polity, 2021).

If you're looking for lighter fare, Madeleine Albright's *Fascism: A Warning* (New York: HarperCollins, 2018) is a rewarding read. When it comes to case studies of far-right populism, authoritarianism, and the big lie, read Stephen Marche's *The Next Civil War: Dispatches from the American Future* (Toronto: Simon & Schuster, 2022), a compelling examination of what future populist civil strife might look like in the United States. Michael Wolff has written a trilogy on the Trump presidency, and the final volume, *Landslide: The Final Days of the Trump Presidency* (New York: Macmillan, 2021), is a gripping overview of the pivotal role of Trump in catalyzing the American insurgency.

In the populist narrative, the rise to power of the far right begets more chaos and insecurity in the international order. Ian Bremmer wrote *Us vs. Them: The Failure of Globalism* (New York: Penguin, 2018) to describe the forces creating a nationalist order for international relations. Anne Applebaum, *Twilight of Democracy: The Seductive Lure of Authoritarianism* (Toronto: Signal, 2020) documents the far right's rise to power in contemporary Europe. One of the best books on populist authoritarianism in Putin's Russia is by Masha Gessen, *The Future Is History: How Totalitarianism Reclaimed Russia* (New York: Riverhead Books, 2017). Finally, Adam Tooze has written a lucid and persuasive account of the impact of the coronavirus pandemic on the global economy, and he too has much to say about our populist moment in *Shutdown: How Covid Shook the World's Economy* (Viking, 2021).

ENDNOTES

Introduction

1   Many books have dissected the populist spasm in major econo-
mies. Among them are Pippa Norris and Ronald Inglehart, *Cultural
Backlash: Trump, Brexit, and Authoritarian Populism* (Cambridge,
MA: Cambridge University Press, 2019); Pankaj Mishra, *Age of Anger:
A History of the Present* (New York: Farrar, Straus and Giroux, 2017);
Jan-Werner Müller, *What Is Populism?* (Pennsylvania, PA: University
of Pennsylvania Press, 2016); Cas Mudde and Cristóbal Rovira
Kaltwasser, *Populism: A Very Short Introduction* (New York: Oxford
University Press, 2017); Ernesto Laclau, *On Populist Reason*, rev. ed.
(London, UK: Verso, 2018); Ian Bremmer, *Us vs. Them: The Failure of
Globalism* (New York: Penguin, 2018); Anne Applebaum, *Twilight of
Democracy: The Seductive Lure of Authoritarianism* (Toronto: Signal,
2020); Daron Acemoglu and James A. Robinson, *Why Nations Fail:
The Origins of Power, Prosperity, and Poverty* (New York: Crown, 2012).

2   It is important to say right at the outset that we don't define
populism as categorically separate from fascism. Populism does not
come only from the grassroots, and fascism does not come only

from elite contempt for democratic norms. We think that populism and fascism come from multiple directions at once. Some writers on populism are nervous about drawing a direct link between right-wing populism today and fascism of the twentieth century. Is it fair to call populists fascists? We don't think so, at least not in every instance, but we do think there is an important link between right-wing populism and fascism. And that link is authoritarian violence. The "Trumpism is not fascism" position has become fashionable in the past several years in American political science. We think this position's careful historical delineation of grassroots populist movements ignores the forest for the trees, with the predictable outcome that it avoids the question of whether the Republican Party, the party of Lincoln, is more than flirting with fascism.

3   A partial list of other notorious populists of recent vintage includes, in no particular order, Ian Paisley in the UK, Barry Goldwater in the US, Jean-Marie Le Pen in France, Lech Wałęsa in Poland, and Juan Perón in Argentina. These were big personalities who cast a long shadow over modern politics.

4   Wendy Brown, Peter E. Gordon, and Max Pensky, *Authoritarianism: Three Inquiries in Critical Theory* (Chicago: University of Chicago Press, 2018); Henry Rousso, *The Vichy Syndrome: History and Memory in France since 1944* (Harvard University Press, 1994). See also "Marine Le Pen's Denial of French Guilt," by the editorial board of the *New York Times*, April 12, 2017, nytimes.com/2017/04/12/opinion/marine-le-pens-denial-of-french-guilt.html.

5   Max Weber, 1910/2002, "Voluntary Associational Life (*Vereinswesen*)," ed./trans. Sung Ho Kim, *Max Weber Studies*, 2:2 (2002).

6   Jordan Kyle and Limor Gultchin, "Populists in Power around the World," Tony Blair Institute for Global Change, November 7, 2018, institute.global/policy/populists-power-around-world.

7   Ivan Krastev, *After Europe* (Philadelphia, PA: University of Pennsylvania Press, 2017).

8   Steven Levitsky and Daniel Ziblatt, *How Democracies Die* (New York: Crown, 2019).

9   Leila Abboud and Victor Mallet, "Vincent Bolloré, Éric Zemmour and the Rise of 'France's Fox News,'" *Financial Times*, October 4, 2021, ft.com/content/e794f9c5-4f1f-4206-8680 -f46f0fbaabbf.

10   Timothy Snyder, *On Tyranny: Twenty Lessons from the Twentieth Century* (New York: Penguin, 2017).

11   Norris and Inglehart, *Cultural Backlash*.

12   R. W. Davies, "Yeltsin Has Gone Mad," *London Review of Books* 23, no. 15 (2001), lrb.co.uk/the-paper/v23/n15/r.w.-davies/yeltsin-has -gone-mad.

13   Umberto Eco, "Ur-Fascism," *New York Review of Books*, June 22, 1995, nybooks.com/articles/1995/06/22/ur-fascism.

Chapter 1

1   Jordan Kyle and Yascha Mounk, "The Populist Harm to Democracy: An Empirical Assessment," Tony Blair Institute for Global Change, December 26, 2018, institute.global/policy /populist-harm-democracy-empirical-assessment.

2   Women who have played the populist card include Indira Gandhi, Golda Meir, and Sarah Palin.

3   Anthony Giddens, *Modernity and Self-Identity: Self and Society in the Late Modern Age* (Stanford, CA: Stanford University Press, 1991); Ernest Gellner, *Nations and Nationalism* (Ithaca, NY: Cornell University Press, 2009).

4   https://www.reddit.com/r/quotes/comments/9qzshg/patriotism_is _when_love_of_your_own_people_comes/'s.

5   Leila Abboud, "French Presidential Candidate Zemmour Convicted of Hate Speech," *Financial Times*, January 17, 2022, ft.com/content/a8674144-05c6-477f-9da8-0ccd810a9272.

6   Edward H. Miller, *A Conspiratorial Life: Robert Welch, the John Birch Society, and the Revolution of American Conservatism.* (Chicago: University of Chicago Press, 2022).

7   Casey Michel, "Meet White Nationalism's Newest Hero: Viktor Orbán," Think Progress, November 29, 2017, archive.thinkprogress .org/viktor-orban-klepcoratic-nationalism-c8e46a7080d6.

8   Vladimir Putin, "On the Historical Unity of Russians and Ukrainians," President of Russia (website), July 12, 2021, en.kremlin.ru/events/president/news/66181.

9   Timothy Snyder, *Bloodlands: Europe Between Hitler and Stalin* (New York: Basic Books, 2012).

10   Laclau, *On Populist Reason.*

11   Müller, *What Is Populism?*

12   For a review of recent political science findings on the unbridgeable domestic divide, see Thomas Edsall, "America Has Split and Is Now in Very Dangerous Territory," *New York Times*, January 26, 2022, nytimes.com/2022/01/26/opinion/covid-biden-trump-polarization .html.

13   Anton Jäger and Arthur Borriello, "Making Sense of Populism," *Catalyst* 3, no. 4 (2020), catalyst-journal.com/vol3/no4/making -sense-of-populism.

14   Mehreen Khan, "EU Grapples with Erdoğan Dilemma," *Financial Times*, March 3, 2020, ft.com/content/53c5ffba-5cfc-11ea-b0ab -339c2307bcd4.

15   Max Scheler, *Ressentiment*, ed. Lewis A. Coser (New York: Free Press, 1961).

16   Müller, *What Is Populism?*, 15–16.

17   Müller, *What Is Populism?*

18   Eco, "Ur-Fascism."

19   Eco, "Ur-Fascism."

20   Guy Standing, *The Precariat: The New Dangerous Class* (London, UK: Bloomsbury, 2011).

21 C. B. MacPherson, *Democracy in Alberta: Social Credit and the Party System* (Toronto: University of Toronto Press, republished 2013).

22 Wolfgang Streeck, *How Will Capitalism End?* (London, UK: Polity, 2016).

23 Yanis Varoufakis, *Adults in the Room: My Battle with Europe's Deep Establishment* (London, UK: Vintage, 2017).

24 Jack London, *The Iron Heel* (Orinda, CA: SeaWolf Press, 2017).

25 Edward Luce, "Lloyd Blankfein: 'I Might Find It Harder to Vote for Bernie Than for Trump,'" *Financial Times*, February 21, 2020, ft.com/content/b8961936-51a6-11ea-8841-482eed0038b1.

26 Giorgos Venizelos and Yannis Stavrakakis, "Left-Populism Is Down but Not Out," *Jacobin*, March 22, 2020, jacobinmag.com/2020/03/left-populism-political-strategy-class-power.

27 Levitsky and Ziblatt, *How Democracies Die*.

28 Megan Henney, "Warren Parts with Sanders on Whether Billionaires Should Exist," Fox Business, November 9, 2019, foxbusiness.com/money/warren-parts-with-sanders-on-whether-billionaires-should-exist.

29 Vladimir Putin, "'All This Fuss about Spies . . . It Is Not Worth Serious Interstate Relations,'" interview with Lionel Barber, *Financial Times*, June 27, 2019, ft.com/content/878d2344-98f0-11e9-9573-ee5cbb98ed36.

30 Richard Milne, "Swedish Prime Minister to Step Down in November," *Financial Times*, August 22, 2021, ft.com/content/cb3c2fd6-ab70-4db0-af71-48fb34c4667d.

31 On the critical role of the leader in right-wing nationalist movements, see Madeleine Albright, *Fascism: A Warning* (New York: HarperCollins, 2018).

32 Max Fisher, "When a Political Movement Is Populist, or Isn't," *New York Times*, May 10, 2017, nytimes.com/2017/05/10/world/asia/populism-france-south-korea.html.

33 Hyung-A Kim, "Moon's Populist Politics and its Effects," *East Asia*

Forum, December 26, 2019, eastasiaforum.org/2019/12/26/moons
-populist-politics-and-its-effects.

34 Michael Penn, "Why Is Populism so Unpopular in Japan?" *Al
Jazeera*, June 10, 2021, aljazeera.com/features/2021/6/10/why-is
-populism-so-unpopular-in-japan.

35 "China's 100 Richest," *Forbes*, accessed September 9, 2021, forbes
.com/china-billionaires/list/#tab:overall. This list is regularly
updated.

36 Chenchen Zhang, "Right-Wing Populism with Chinese
Characteristics? Identity, Otherness, and Global Imaginaries
in Debating Politics Online," *European Journal of International
Relations* 26, no. 1 (2020), doi.org/10.1177/1354066119850253.

37 Daniel Drache, David Clifton, and Marc D. Froese, "Che Guevara:
Modernity's Rock Star of Dissent," Counter-Publics Working
Group, York University, 2004, https://danieldrache.com/portfolio
/che-guevara-modernitys-rockstar-of-dissent/.

38 For the many iconic images of Che, see Drache, Clifton, and
Froese, "Che Guevara."

39 As a climate crisis resistance fighter, Swedish teenager Greta
Thunberg has replaced Guevara as a symbol of revolutionary
change in the twenty-first century.

40 Populism figured in the decolonization movement prominently.
Nassar, Nkrumah, Nehru, and Tito were all notably populist in
their messaging. See Pankaj Mishra, *From the Ruins of Empire: The
Revolt Against the West and the Remaking of Asia* (London, UK:
Picador, 2013).

41 Jorge Zepeda Patterson, "Despite It All, López Obrador Has My
Vote," *New York Times*, June 6, 2021, nytimes.com/2021/06/06
/opinion/amlo-López-obrador-election-mexico.html.

42 Reuters Staff, "Mexico to Raise Workers' Daily Minimum Wage by
15% in 2021," Reuters, December 16, 2020, reuters.com/article
/mexico-economy-wages-idUSL1N2IX053.

43 Amy Stillman, "Mexico Shuns International Oil Markets to Produce More Gasoline at Home," *Bloomberg Markets*, December 28, 2021, bloomberg.com/news/articles/2021-12-28/mexico-to-stop -exporting-oil-in-2023-in-self-sufficiency-quest.

44 Hannah Arendt, *The Origins of Totalitarianism* (1951; repr., New York: Mariner Books, 1991), 61.

45 Paolo Gerbaudo, *Tweets and the Streets: Social Media and Contemporary Activismci* (London, UK: Pluto Press, 2012).

46 Jesse Eisinger, Jeff Ernsthausen, and Paul Kiel, "The Secret IRS Files: Trove of Never-Before-Seen Records Reveal How the Wealthiest Avoid Income Tax," *ProPublica*, June 8, 2021, propublica.org/article /the-secret-irs-files-trove-of-never-before-seen-records-reveal-how-the -wealthiest-avoid-income-tax.

47 Armin Schäfer and Michael Zürn, *The Democratic Regression: The Political Causes of Authoritarian Populism* (Berlin: Suhrkamp, 2021).

48 Jan-Werner Müller, *Democracy Rules* (Farrar, Straus and Giroux, 2021); Francis Fukuyama, *Political Order and Political Decay: From the Industrial Revolution to the Globalization of Democracy* (New York: Farrar, Straus and Giroux, 2015).

Chapter 2

1 M.K. Venu and Maya Mirchandani, "Government Assault on Digital Media Reflects Modi's Paranoia," *The Wire*, May 29, 2021, thewire.in/government/attack-on-free-speech-reflects-modis -growing-paranoia. Bryan Harris and Michael Pooler, "Bolsonaro Tests Brazilian Democracy: 'Only God can take me from presidency,'" *Financial Times*, September 28, 2021, ft.com/content/1770b0f8 -3740-45db-a032-eedfdb0f8920.

2 Michael Wolff, *Landslide: The Final Days of the Trump Presidency* (New York: MacMillan, 2021).

3 Chris Giles, "The Real Price of Brexit Begins to Emerge," *Financial*

Times, December 17, 2017, ft.com/content/e3b29230-db5f-11e7-a039 -c64b1c09b482.

4   Alan Beattie, "Is Free Trading 'Global Britain' Just EU Mark II?" *Financial Times*, April 26, 2021, ft.com/content/3fe6e7f5-4d31-42c6 -b055-4b26f567ddee.

5   Benjamin Novak and Marc Santora, "Hungary's Independent Press Takes Another Blow and Reporters Quit," *New York Times*, July 24, 2020, nytimes.com/2020/07/24/world/europe/hungary-poland -media-freedom-index.html.

6   Reuters Staff, "PM Orban Vows to Preserve Hungary's Christian Culture," Reuters, May 7, 2018, reuters.com/article/us-hungary -orban-idUSKBN1I80NC.

7   Taking a "red pill" is a reference to opening your eyes to the conspiracies all around you. It comes from the 1999 film *The Matrix*, in which the protagonist takes a red pill to open his eyes to the true state of the world. The term has become a central metaphor in conspiracy communities on the internet, most recently in QAnon. Darlena Cunha, "Red Pills and Dog Whistles: It Is More Than 'Just the Internet,'" *Al Jazeera*, September 6, 2020, aljazeera.com/opinions/2020/9/6/red-pills-and-dog-whistles -it-is-more-than-just-the-internet.

8   Rachel Kleinfeld and John Dickas, "Resisting the Call of Nativism: What US Political Parties Can Learn from Other Democracies," Carnegie Endowment for International Peace, March 5, 2020, 41, carnegieendowment.org/2020/03/05/resisting-call-of-nativism-what -u.s.-political-parties-can-learn-from-other-democracies-pub-81204.

9   Peter F. Nardulli, "The Concept of Critical Realignment, Electoral Behavior, and Political Change," *American Political Science Review* 89, no. 1 (1995): 10–22.

10   Daniel Yergin and Joseph Stanislaw, *The Commanding Heights: The Battle for the World Economy* (New York: Simon & Schuster, 1998).

11   When banks and corporations in the allied nations of the United

States and the UK regained the reins of power, they rewrote the rules of the global system to benefit themselves. Financial stability, the top priority, turned out to be elusive when governments embraced market fundamentalism and weak financial oversight. Crisis struck Mexico in 1982 and 1994, again in 1997 with the Asian financial crisis, later in 2002 when crisis struck Argentina, again in 2008 with the global financial crisis, and once more in 2012 with the hydra-headed European crisis of Greece and other countries. Since 2020, the COVID-19 pandemic has brought about the mother of all financial crises, with exploding global debt, record levels of unemployment, and global trade collapsing. European, Japanese, and North American economies have shrunk more than 10 percent, the largest single drop in activity since the Great Depression in the 1930s. See Kevin P. Gallagher and Richard Kozul-Wright, *A New Multilateralism for Shared Prosperity: Geneva Principles for a Global Green New Deal* (Geneva: United Nations Conference on Trade and Development, 2019), 3.

12 Emilio Ocampo, "Commodity Price Booms and Populist Cycles: An Explanation of Argentina's Decline in the 20th Century," Universidad del CEMA, CEMA Working Papers 562, ideas.repec.org/p/cem /doctra/562.html.

13 Frances E. Lee, "Populism and the American Party System: Opportunities and Constraints," *Perspectives on Politics* 18, no. 2 (June 2020): 370–88, doi.org/10.1017/S1537592719002664.

14 Matthew Rosenberg, "Republican Voters Take a Radical Conspiracy Theory Mainstream," *New York Times*, October 19, 2020, nytimes .com/2020/10/19/us/politics/qanon-trump-republicans.html.

15 Trump wasn't even the biggest bird on Twitter. Former president Barack Obama has more than 130 million followers. See also "Indian PM Narendra Modi 'Scares' Millions of Social Followers," BBC World News, March 3, 2020, bbc.com/news /world-asia-india-51717786.

16   Evette Alexander, "Polarization in the Twittersphere: What 86 Million Tweets Reveal About the Political Makeup of American Twitter Users and How They Engage with News," Knight Foundation, December 17, 2019, knightfoundation.org/articles /polarization-in-the-twittersphere-what-86-million-tweets-reveal -about-the-political-makeup-of-american-twitter-users-and-how -they-engage-with-news.

17   Thomas Piketty, *Capitalism in the Twenty-First Century* (Cambridge, MA: Harvard University Press, 2018).

18   Branko Milanović, *Global Inequality: A New Approach for the Age of Globalization* (Cambridge, MA: Belknap Press, 2016).

19   Alan Feuer, "Fears of White People Losing Out Permeate Capitol Rioters' Towns, Study Finds," *New York Times*, April 6, 2021, nytimes.com/2021/04/06/us/politics/capitol-riot-study.html.

20   Roula Khalaf, Ben Hall, and Victor Mallet, "Emmanuel Macron: 'For me, the key is multilateralism that produces results,'" *Financial Times*, February 18, 2021, ft.com/content/d8b9629a-92b1-4e02-92b7 -41e9152d56ea.

21   Katherine Schaeffer, "6 Facts about Economic Inequality in the US," Pew Research Center, February 7, 2020, pewresearch.org/fact-tank /2020/02/07/6-facts-about-economic-inequality-in-the-u-s.

22   United Nations Department of Economic and Social Affairs, *World Social Report 2020*, un.org/development/desa/dspd/world-social-report /2020-2.html.

23   Nouriel Roubini, "The COVID Bubble," *Project Syndicate*, March 2, 2021, project-syndicate.org/commentary/us-economy-faces-risks -of-bubble-medium-term-stagflation-by-nouriel-roubini-2021-03.

24   "Global Populism Database," Harvard Dataverse, accessed September 29, 2020, doi.org/10.7910/DVN/LFTQEZ.

25   In the final years of the Cold War, there were many more socialist governments across Latin America, eastern Europe, and Eurasia. If such a study had been conducted back then, it would have registered

a much higher level of left populist speech. But today, conservative populism is ascendant.

26   Alessandro Nai, Ferran Martínez i Coma, and Jürgen Maier, "Donald Trump, Populism, and the Age of Extremes: Comparing the Personality Traits and Campaigning Styles of Trump and Other Leaders Worldwide," *Presidential Studies Quarterly* 49, no. 3 (2019): 609.

27   Franklin Foer, "Viktor Orbán's War on Intellect," *Atlantic Monthly*, June 2019, theatlantic.com/magazine/archive/2019/06/george-soros -viktor-orban-ceu/588070.

28   Foer, "Viktor Orbán's War on Intellect."

29   Mudde and Kaltwasser, *Populism*.

30   Zygmunt Bauman, *Community: Seeking Safety in an Insecure World* (London, UK: Polity, 2001), 74.

31   Sandra J. Sucher et al., "Layoffs: Effects on Key Stakeholders," Harvard Business School Background Note 611-028, pub. December 2010, rev. September 2014, store.hbr.org/product/layoffs-effects-on -key-stakeholders/611028?sku=611028-PDF-ENG.

32   Shoshana Zuboff, "You Are Now Remotely Controlled," *New York Times*, January 24, 2020, nytimes.com/2020/01/24/opinion/sunday /surveillance-capitalism.html.

33   An anonymous internet figure, Q, predicted that President Trump would battle the forces of evil in Washington and sweep them from power. Right up to the end of his single term in office, the true believers kept the faith: Trump would drain the swamp of Washington insiders and courtiers. When he failed to produce mass arrest warrants, they believed that if he won reelection, the gloves would come off and the Republicans would be emboldened to sweep the criminals from power. He lost, and the narrative adjusted accordingly. On January 6, 2021, before the vote was certified, Trump produced evidence against the enemies of the people. But the inauguration of a new president came and went, and nothing happened.

34 Mike Rothschild, *The Storm Is Upon Us: How QAnon Became A Movement, Cult and Conspiracy Theory of Everything* (Brooklyn, NY: Melville House, 2021).

35 Joseph E. Uscinski, Casey Klofstad, and Matthew D. Atkinson, "What Drives Conspiratorial Beliefs? The Role of Informational Cues and Predispositions," *Political Research Quarterly* 69, no. 1 (2016), doi.org/10.1177/1065912915621621.

36 Joseph E. Uscinski and Joseph M. Parent, *American Conspiracy Theories* (Oxford, UK: Oxford University Press, 2014). See chap. 6, "Conspiracy Theories Are for Losers."

37 Reuters Staff, "Philippines' Duterte Threatens Vaccine Decliners with Jail, Animal Drug," Reuters, June 22, 2021, reuters.com/world/asia -pacific/philippines-duterte-threatens-those-who-refuse-covid-19 -vaccine-with-jail-2021-06-21/.

38 Reuters Staff, "Philippines' Duterte Threatens Vaccine Decliners."

39 Zosia Wanat, "How Poland's Ruling Party Won the Internet," *Politico*, October 7, 2019, politico.eu/article/how-poland-ruling-party-pis-won -the-internet-kaczynski-law-and-justice-social-media.

40 Nicholas Vinocur, "Marine Le Pen's Internet Army," *Politico*, February 3, 2017, politico.eu/article/marine-le-pens-internet-army -far-right-trolls-social-media.

41 They received only 9.5 million votes.

42 Jason Horowitz, "Salvini Remains at the Eye of Italy's Political Storm," *New York Times*, January 22, 2020, nytimes.com/2020/01/22/world /europe/italy-salvini-elections-emilia-romagna-calabria.html.

43 Marzia Maccaferri and Andrea Mammone, "Can the Left Really Stop Salvini?" *Social Europe*, February 24, 2020, socialeurope.eu/can-the -left-really-stop-salvini.

44 Thomson Reuters, "Indian Farmers Storm Historic Red Fort in Republic Day Protests," CBC News, January 26, 2021, cbc.ca/news /world/farmers-tear-gas-protest-india-1.5887660.

45 Elizabeth Dias and Jack Healy. "For Many Who Marched, Jan. 6

Was Only the Beginning," *New York Times*, January 23, 2022, nytimes.com/2022/01/23/us/jan-6-attendees.html.

46 Valentina Romei and Chris Giles, "UK Suffers Biggest Drop in Economic Output in 300 Years," *Financial Times*, February 12, 2021, ft.com/content/96e19afd-88b3-4e8d-bc3e-a72bd1f60d3c.

47 Peter Campbell, "Investment in UK Car Industry Plummets Amid Brexit Uncertainty," *Financial Times*, July 2, 2021, ft.com/content /0c3427b2-5ce1-11e7-9bc8-8055f264aa8b.

48 Christophe Jaffrelot, *Modi's India: Hindu Nationalism and the Rise of Ethnic Democracy* (Princeton: Princeton University Press, 2021).

49 Jonathan Hopkin, *Anti-System Politics: The Crisis of Market Liberalism in Rich Democracies* (Oxford, UK: Oxford University Press, 2020).

50 Garry Kasparov, "Woke Is a Bad Word for a Real Threat to American Democracy," *Wall Street Journal*, November 17, 2021, wsj.com/articles /woke-is-a-bad-word-for-a-real-threat-to-american-democracy-cancel -culture-freedom-11637184284.

51 Noam Gidron and Peter A. Hall, "Populism as a Problem of Social Integration," *Comparative Political Studies* 53, no. 7 (2019): 1027–59, doi.org/10.1177/0010414019879947.

52 Thomas B. Edsall, "The Resentment That Never Sleeps," *New York Times*, December 9, 2020, nytimes.com/2020/12/09/opinion/trump -social-status-resentment.html.

53 Jason Stanley, *How Fascism Works: The Politics of Us and Them* (New York: Random House, 2020).

54 Sean Illing, "American Fascism Isn't Going Away: A Conversation with Yale's Jason Stanley about the Latent Pathologies in American Politics," *Vox*, January 29, 2021, vox.com/policy-and-politics/2021 /1/29/22250294/trump-american-fascism-jason-stanley.

55 Federico Finchelstein, *From Fascism to Populism in History* (Berkeley, CA: University of California Press, 2019).

56 For a superb historical literary analysis of the rise of interwar

German fascism, see *The Order of the Day* by Éric Vuillard (New York: Other Press, 2018).

57   Stanley, *How Fascism Works*. Eco, "Ur-Fascism"; Madeleine Albright, *Fascism: A Warning* (New York: HarperCollins, 2018).

58   Franck Bousquet, "Fragile and Conflict-Affected Economies Are Falling Further Behind," *IMF Blog*, January 21, 2022, blogs.imf.org /2022/01/21/fragile-and-conflict-affected-economies-are-falling-further -behind/.

59   Norberto Bobbio, *Left and Right: The Significance of a Political Distinction* (London, UK: Polity, 1996).

60   José Miguel Vivanco, "López Obrador Threatens Judicial Independence," Human Rights Watch, April 26, 2021, hrw.org /news/2021/04/26/lopez-obrador-threatens-judicial-independence.

61   "Covid Updates: Mexico Resists Vaccinating Children Despite Court Order," *New York Times*, October 26, 2021, nytimes.com /live/2021/10/26/world/covid-vaccine-boosters.

62   Stephanie Hegarty, "Covid: The Mexican Villages Refusing to Vaccinate," BBC News, July 21, 2021, bbc.com/news/world-latin -america-57893466.

63   In 2015, two babies died and twenty-nine became seriously ill in Chiapas. The cause of the extreme reaction remains undetermined, but six years later, the people of the villages of Southern Mexico remain unconvinced about vaccination.

64   Cynthia Blank, "BDS Fight to Move to Strategic Affairs Ministry," Israel National News, August 20, 2015, israelnationalnews.com /News/News.aspx/199687.

65   Uri Blau, "Inside the Clandestine World of Israel's 'BDS Busting' Ministry," *Haaretz*, March 26, 2017, haaretz.com/israel-news /MAGAZINE-inside-the-clandestine-world-of-israels-bds-busting -ministry-1.5453212.

Chapter 3

1 From Carl Sandburg, "I Am the People, the Mob," in Chicago Poems (New York: Henry Holt, 1916).

2 Read the entire poem at poetryfoundation.org/poems/45036/i-am -the-people-the-mob.

3 Partha Chatterjee, *I Am the People: Reflections on Popular Sovereignty Today* (New York: Columbia University Press, 2019).

4 Regine Cabato, "Philippine Leader Rodrigo Duterte Dreams of Holding Power for Years to Come," *Washington Post*, August 26, 2021, washingtonpost.com/world/asia_pacific/duterte-philippines-drugs -pandemic/2021/08/26/8eb6dcfe-0591-11ec-b3c4-c462b1edcfc8 _story.html.

5 CNN Philippines Staff, "Duterte Approval Rating Rises to 91% Amid Pandemic, Cayetano Suffers Drop—Survey," CNN Philippines, October 5, 2020, cnnphilippines.com/news/2020/10/5 /Duterte-approval-trust-rating-COVID-19-September-2020-Pulse -Asia-survey.html.

6 Chenchen Zhang, "Right-Wing Populism with Chinese Characteristics? Identity, Otherness and Global Imaginaries in Debating World Politics Online," *European Journal of International Relations* 26, no. 1 (2020), doi.org/10.1177/1354066119850253.

7 Katja Hoyer, "Germany Has a QAnon Problem, and It's Not Going Away Anytime Soon," *Washington Post*, November 1, 2021, washingtonpost.com/opinions/2021/11/01/germany-has-qanon -problem-its-not-going-away-any-time-soon.

8 Nancy L. Rosenblum and Russell Muirhead, *A Lot of People Are Saying: The New Conspiracism and the Assault on Democracy* (Princeton, NJ: Princeton University Press, 2020).

9 Holly Ellyatt, "UK Politicians 'Don't Do God' but Religion Matters in This Election," CNBC, Dec. 11, 2019, cnbc.com/2019/12/11/uk -politicians-dont-do-god-but-religion-matters-in-this-election.html.

10   Alain Minc, *Le nouveau Moyen Age* (Paris: Gallimard, 1993).

11   Nate Cohn, "How Educational Differences Are Widening America's Political Rift," *New York Times*, September 8, 2021, nytimes.com /2021/09/08/us/politics/how-college-graduates-vote.html.

12   Ellyatt, "UK Politicians 'Don't do God.'"

13   "Russia Labels Pussy Riot Members Foreign Agents," BBC News December 30, 2021, bbc.com/news/world-europe-59832838.

14   Masha Gessen, *The Future Is History: How Totalitarianism Reclaimed Russia* (New York: Riverhead Books, 2017), 249.

15   Editorial Board, "Putin Touts Christianity. So Why Is Russia Persecuting Christians?" *Washington Post*, June 6, 2019, washingtonpost.com/opinions/global-opinions/putin-touts -christianity-so-why-is-russia-persecuting-christians/2019/06 /06/9876523c-87d1-11e9-98c1-e945ae5db8fb_story.html.

16   Timo Soini, *Populism* (Helsinki: Pole-Kuntatieto Oy, 2020), 32.

17   Filipe Domingues, "Open Churches and Miracle Cures: The COVID-19 Response in Bolsonaro's Brazil," *Religion and Global Society* (blog), London School of Economics and Political Science (LSE), April 17, 2020, blogs.lse.ac.uk/religionglobalsociety/2020 /04/open-churches-and-miracle-cures-the-covid-19-response-in -bolsonaros-brazil.

18   Thomas Milz, "How Evangelicals in Brazil are Spinning COVID-19," *DW Akademie*, June 4, 2020, dw.com/en/brazil-evangelicals-preach -covid-19/a-53024007.

19   Bryan Harris and Andres Schipani, "Jair Bolsonaro's Radical Supporters: 'He Only Has Us, the People,'" *Financial Times*, May 19, 2020, ft.com/content/005dd722-b27d-4337-99ec-3b9a52a87f6d.

20   Timothy Steigenga, Kenneth M. Coleman, and Eduardo Marenco, "'En Dios Confiamos': Politics, Populism, and Protestantism in Daniel Ortega's Nicaragua," *International Journal of Latin American Religions* 1 (2017): 116–33, doi.org/10.1007/s41603-017-0005-6.

21   Norris and Inglehart, *Cultural Backlash*.

22 Ruth Igielnik, Scott Keeter, and Hannah Hartig, "Behind Biden's 2020 Victory: An Examination of the 2020 Electorate, Based on Validated Voters," Pew Research Center, June 30, 2021, pewresearch .org/politics/2021/06/30/behind-bidens-2020-victory.

23 Andrew Keen, "How the Internet Is Threatening Our Freedom," *Politico*, May 18, 2021, politico.com/magazine/story/2016/05/2016 -election-internet-campaign-facts-digital-new-media-213899.

24 Michael P. Lynch, *The Internet of Us: Knowing More and Understanding Less in the Age of Big Data* (New York: Liveright, 2016).

25 "France's Macron Responds to Yellow Vests with Promise of Reforms," BBC News, April 25, 2019, bbc.com/news/world-europe-48059063.

26 Paula Surridge, "Labour Lost Its Leavers While Tory Remainers Stayed Loyal," *Guardian*, December 13, 2019, theguardian.com/ commentisfree/2019/dec/13/conservatives-bridge-brexit-divide -tory-landslide.

27 Eduardo Porter, "How the G.O.P. Became the Party of the Left Behind," *New York Times*, January 27, 2020, nytimes.com/interactive /2020/01/27/business/economy/republican-party-voters-income.html.

28 Porter, "How the G.O.P."

29 Tom Lutey, "Trump: 'We're going to win so much, you're going to be so sick and tired of winning,'" *Billings Gazette*, May 26, 2016, billingsgazette.com/news/state-and-regional/govt-and-politics/ trump-we-re-going-to-win-so-much-you-re/article_2f346f38-37e7 -5711-ae07-d1fd000f4c38.html.

30 Rick Perlstein, *Reaganland: America's Right Turn, 1976–1980* (New York: Simon & Schuster, 2020).

31 Gidron and Hall, "Populism as a Problem of Social Integration."

32 Norris and Inglehart, *Cultural Backlash*.

33 Michael Lind, *The New Class War: Saving Democracy from the Managerial Elite* (New York: Penguin Random House, 2020).

34 Brendan Simms and Charlie Laderman, *Hitler's American Gamble:*

Pearl Harbor and Germany's March to Global War (New York: Basic Books, 2021.

35 Eric Lonergan and Mark Blyth, *Angrynomics* (Newcastle-upon-Tyne, UK: Agenda Publishing, 2020), 161.

36 Adam Taylor, "Ahead of Russian Elections, Putin Releases Official Details of Wealth and Income," *Washington Post*, February 7, 2018, washingtonpost.com/news/worldviews/wp/2018/02/07/ahead-of-russian-elections-putin-releases-official-details-of-wealth-and-income.

37 Amy Kazmin, "Narendra Modi Rode Wave of Money to Indian Victory," *Financial Times*, May 19, 2014, ft.com/content/ce68abf0-df3f-11e3-86a4-00144feabdc0.

38 Raksha Kumar, "India's Media Can't Speak Truth to Power," *Foreign Policy*, August 2, 2019, foreignpolicy.com/2019/08/02/indias-media-cant-speak-truth-to-power-modi-bjp-journalism.

39 Nikhil Inamdar, "How Narendra Modi Has Almost Killed the Indian Media," *Quartz India*, March 12, 2019, qz.com/india/1570899/how-narendra-modi-has-almost-killed-indian-media.

40 Rana Ayyub, "An Investigation Sheds Light into Modi's Machinery of Online Hate and Manipulation," *Washington Post*, January 18, 2022, washingtonpost.com/opinions/2022/01/18/the-wire-sheds-light-on-india-tek-fog-hate-online/.

41 Vindu Goel and Jeffrey Gettleman, "Under Modi, India's Press Is Not So Free Anymore," *New York Times*, nytimes.com/2020/04/02/world/asia/modi-india-press-media.html.

42 Goel and Gettleman, "Under Modi."

43 Michael Bueza, "Who's Who on Duterte's Poll Contributors List," Rappler, December 9, 2016, rappler.com/newsbreak/iq/duterte-contributors-list-2016-presidential-elections.

44 Aurora Almendral, "Crony Capital: How Duterte Embraced the Oligarchs," Nikkei Asia, December 4, 2019, asia.nikkei.com/Spotlight/The-Big-Story/Crony-capital-How-Duterte-embraced-the-oligarchs.

45 Ian C. Sayson, "Philippine Stocks Rebound as Duterte Makes
    Peace with Business Elite," Bloomberg Markets, May 5, 2020,
    bloomberg.com/news/articles/2020-05-05/philippine-stocks-up
    -as-duterte-makes-peace-with-business-elite-k9tnuh7x.

46 Lionel Laurent, "Viktor Orbán Profits from Friends and Funds
    from the European Union," Bloomberg Quint, April 7, 2020,
    bloombergquint.com/gadfly/hungary-s-viktor-orban-profits-from
    -eu-friends-and-funds.

47 Valerie Hopkins and Michael Peel, "But EU's Top Court Rules
    Against Hungary on NGO Funding," Financial Times, June 18,
    2020, ft.com/content/8bfbb02a-c144-4b75-a56a-9ee5c136e4cb.

48 Jennifer Rankin, "How Hungarian PM's Supporters Profit from
    EU-Backed Projects," Guardian, February 12, 2018, theguardian
    .com/world/2018/feb/12/how-hungarian-pms-supporters-profit
    -from-eu-backed-projects.

49 Emily Rauhala and Loveday Morris, "In the United States, QAnon
    Is Struggling. The Conspiracy Theory Is Thriving Abroad,"
    Washington Post, November 13, 2020, washingtonpost.com/world
    /qanon-conspiracy-global-reach/2020/11/12/ca312138-13a5-11eb-a258
    -614acf2b906d_story.html.

50 Sam Jones and Guy Chazan, "'Nein Danke': The Resistance to
    COVID-19 Vaccines in German-Speaking Europe," Financial
    Times, November 11, 2021, ft.com/content/f04ac67b-92e4-4bab
    -8c23-817cc0483df5.

51 Jovan Byford, "I've Been Talking to Conspiracy Theorists for
    Twenty Years: Here Are My Six Rules for Engagement," The
    Conversation, June 20, 2020, theconversation.com/ive-been
    -talking-to-conspiracy-theorists-for-20-years-here-are-my-six
    -rules-of-engagement-143132.

52 Ilya Yablokov, "Conspiracy Theories as a Russian Public Diplomacy
    Tool: The Case of Russia Today (RT)," Politics 35, no. 304 (2015),
    doi.org/10.1111/1467-9256.12097.

53 Vincent Bevins, "Where Conspiracy Reigns," *Atlantic Monthly*, September 16, 2020, theatlantic.com/ideas/archive/2020/09/how -anti-communist-conspiracies-haunt-brazil/614665.

54 The rise of hard-right populism to the extent we have seen in North America and Western Europe is troubling because extreme reactionary conservatism was discredited following World War II. The rhetoric of blood and soil has long been thought to be a gateway to fascist politics, and being too extreme in one's conservatism was thought to be political kryptonite, even for the most popular of big men, such as Joseph McCarthy. Even so, racialist messaging still dominated traditionalist social movements in the 1960s and '70s in northern Europe, Latin America, and the United States. George Wallace is the prime example of American populism in this period. A four-term governor of Alabama, he attempted to win the American presidency as a Democrat three times, and all three times, he failed. Wallace was an unabashed racist who stood for "segregation now, segregation tomorrow, segregation forever." Long before the Black Lives Matter movement, Martin Luther King Jr. denounced him as "perhaps the most dangerous racist in America today." See Howell Raines, "George Wallace, Segregation Symbol, Dies at 79," *New York Times*, September 14, 1998, nytimes.com/1998/09/14/us/george-wallace -segregation-symbol-dies-at-79.html. See also Alex Haley, "Alex Haley Interviews Martin Luther King Jr." [*Playboy*, January 1965], AlexHaley.com, alexhaley.com/2020/07/26/alex-haley-interviews -martin-luther-king-jr.

55 2020 Edelman Trust Barometer, edelman.com/trust/2020-trust -barometer.

56 Benjamin R. Barber, "Jihad vs. McWorld," *Atlantic Monthly*, March 1992, theatlantic.com/magazine/archive/1992/03/jihad-vs-mcworld /303882.

Chapter 4

1 Sun Yu, Qianer Liu, and Tom Mitchell, "China's Factories Pull in the Profits by Making Trump Merchandise," *Financial Times*, October 1, 2020, ft.com/content/9eb753d8-098a-4c05-af95 -0e11fb1607df.

2 Kevin Rudd, "Xi Jinping's Pivot to the State: An Address to the Asia Society," Asia Society Policy Institute, September 8, 2021, asiasociety.org/policy-institute/xi-jinpings-pivot-state.

3 Edward White and Mark Wembridge, "Xi Jinping Defends Crackdowns in 'Common Prosperity' Drive at Davos," *Financial Times*, January 7, 2022, ft.com/content/8963b1ee-9ffb-4f2e-8648 -472e641716ba.

4 Mark Penn and Andrew Stein, "Bill Clinton Saved His Presidency. Here's How Biden Can Too," *New York Times*, November 8, 2021, nytimes.com/2021/11/08/opinion/biden-democrats-2022-2024 .html.

5 Annie Linskey, "As Biden Heads to Europe, Trump's Potential Return Leaves Allies Skeptical," *Washington Post*, October 28, 2021, washingtonpost.com/politics/biden-trump-overseas-leaders-skeptical /2021/10/28/c328b258-3725-11ec-91dc-551d44733e2d_story.html.

6 Mark Blyth, *Austerity: The History of a Dangerous Idea* (Oxford, UK: Oxford University Press, 2014).

7 Steven Levitsky and Daniel Ziblatt, *How Democracies Die* (New York: Crown Publishing, 2018).

8 See Andrew Schonfield, *Modern Capitalism: The Changing Balance of Public and Private Power* (Oxford, UK: Oxford University Press, 1965) for a detailed account of the evolution of the modern state in the economy refuting the one-sided transactional narrative.

9 Helmut K. Anheier, "Germany's Modern Angst," *Project Syndicate*, December 3, 2021, project-syndicate.org/columnist/helmut-k-anheier.

10 Niall Ferguson and Fareed Zakaria, *Is This the End of the Liberal*

International Order? The Munk Debate on Geopolitics, ed. Rudyard Griffiths (Toronto: House of Anansi Press, 2017).

11   Raymond Vernon, *Sovereignty at Bay: The Multinational Spread of U.S. Enterprises* (Cambridge, MA: Harvard University Press, 1971).

12   Nick Aspinwall, "Duterte Turns Death Squads on Political Activists." *Foreign Policy*, June 10, 2019, https://foreignpolicy.com/2019 /06/10/duterte-turns-death-squads-on-political-activists/.

13   Joe Mayes, "Just a Year of Brexit Has Thumped U.K.'s Economy and Businesses," Bloomberg News, December 22, 2021, bloomberg.com/news/articles/2021-12-22/how-a-year-of-brexit -thumped-britain-s-economy-and-businesses.

14   Katrin Bennhold and Michael Schwirtz Navalny, "Awake and Alert, Plans to Return to Russia, German Official Says," *New York Times*, September 14, 2020, nytimes.com/2020/09/14/world/europe/navalny-novichok.html.

15   John Bolton, *The Room Where It Happened: A White House Memoir* (New York: Simon & Schuster, 2020).

16   Sherry Turkle, "Dynasty," *London Review of Books* 12, no. 23 (December 6, 1990), lrb.co.uk/the-paper/v12/n23/sherry-turkle /dynasty.

17   Stephen Krasner, *Sovereignty: Organized Hypocrisy* (Princeton: Princeton University Press, 1999).

18   Krasner, *Sovereignty.*

19   Jennifer Lind and William C. Wohlforth, "The Future of the Liberal Order Is Conservative," *Foreign Affairs*, March/April, 2019, foreignaffairs.com/articles/2019-02-12/future-liberal-order -conservative.

20   Robert Boyer and Daniel Drache, *States Against Markets: The Limits of Globalization* (London, UK: Routledge, 1996).

21   "Charter of the United Nations," United Nations, June 26, 1945, accessed December 10, 2020, un.org/en/charter-united-nations /index.html.

22 Fragile states index, en.wikipedia.org/wiki/Fragile_States_Index.
The IMF reports that 60 percent of low-income countries now face
debt distress—a number that has almost doubled since 2015. On the
list for potential defaults by LICs are Sri Lanka, Ghana, Tunisia, and
El Salvador as well as middle-income countries such as Lebanon,
Turkey, and Ukraine. Rising US interest rates presents a new danger.
IMF Blog, "The G20 Common Framework for Debt Treatments
Must Be Stepped Up," December 2, 2022, https://blogs.imf.
org/2021/12/02
/the-g20-common-framework-for-debt-treatments-must-be-
stepped-up/.

23 For a powerful account of colonialism's legacy and the attempt by
Washington to derail the course of history, see Susan Williams,
White Malice: The CIA and the Covert Recolonization of Africa (New
York: Public Affairs, 2021).

24 Michael Denning, "Impeachment as a Social Form," *New Left
Review* 122 (March–April 2020), newleftreview.org/issues/ii122
/articles/michael-denning-impeachment-as-a-social-form.

25 Laclau, *On Populist Reason*, 227–29.

26 Thomas B. Edsall, "The Trump Voters Whose 'Need for Chaos'
Obliterates Everything Else," *New York Times*, September 4, 2019,
nytimes.com/2019/09/04/opinion/trump-voters-chaos.html.

27 Marshall Berman, *All That Is Solid Melts into Air: The Experience of
Modernity* (New York: Penguin, 1988).

28 Christophe Jaffrelot, *Modi's India: Hindu Nationalism and the Rise
of Ethnic Democracy* (Princeton, NJ: Princeton University Press,
2021).

29 Daniel Drache, A. T. Kingsmith, Duan Qi, *One Road, Many
Dreams: China's Bold Plan to Remake the Global Economy* (London,
UK: Bloomsbury, 2019).

30 Chrystia Freeland, *Plutocrats: The Rise of the New Global Super-Rich
and the Fall of Everyone Else* (Toronto: Anchor Canada, 2014).

31 Masha Gessen, *The Man without a Face: The Unlikely Rise of Vladimir Putin* (London, UK: Granta Books, 2012).

32 Catherine Belton, *Putin's People: How the KGB Took Back Russia and Then Took on the West* (New York: Farrar, Straus and Giroux, 2020).

33 Michael Stott, "Why López Obrador's Mexico Is Stable in Protest-Prone Latin America," *Financial Times*, June 13, 2021, ft.com/content/55295ibe-7e8f-4fbc-a85d-7814cc519265.

34 Michael Stott and Jude Webber, "Biden Helps Mexico Enjoy Break from Economic Gloom," *Financial Times*, June 15, 2021, ft.com/content/87d90479-3151-4f82-b88a-33261db44fa3.

35 Denise Dresser, "Mexico's President is Spoiling for a Fight with Washington," *Foreign Affairs*, February 1, 2021, foreignaffairs.com/articles/mexico/2021-02-01/mexicos-president-spoiling-fight-washington.

36 Mary Beth Sheridan, "Mexico Fast-Tracks Law that Could Limit Anti-Drug Cooperation with U.S.," *Washington Post*, December 11, 2020, washingtonpost.com/world/the_americas/mexico-fast-tracks-law-that-could-limit-antidrug-cooperation-with-us/2020/12/11/aa2f90d4-3b43-11eb-98c4-25dc9f4987e8_story.html.

37 This rebranding exercise has not convinced markets and bond rating agencies that Pemex, with its $100 billion of debt, can be much help to state finances. But the symbolism is not lost on ordinary Mexicans who have come to view privatization with deep suspicion. Nevertheless, AMLO has an instinct for state-building. But stopping the privatization of Pemex, Mexico's publicly owned oil company and the eleventh largest producer in the world, is not about national competition alone. It could be argued that AMLO has ulterior motives when it comes to Pemex. He uses the company as his administration's war chest to fund popular projects, like public housing, against the prevailing wisdom of financial markets.

38 Kenichi Ohmae, *The End of the Nation State: The Rise of Regional Economies* (New York: Simon & Schuster, 1995).

39 Gerbaudo, *Tweets and the Streets.*

Chapter 5

1   John J. Mearsheimer, "Bound to Fail: The Rise and Fall of the Liberal International Order," *International Security* 43, no. 4 (2019): 7–50, doi.org/10.1162/isec_a_00342.

2   Bolton, *The Room Where It Happened.*

3   Andrew Bacevich, *After the Apocalypse: America's Role in a World Transformed* (New York: Macmillan, 2021).

4   Robert Zoellick, "Are We Heading into Another Depression?" *Financial Times*, June 2, 2020, ft.com/content/f544bda2-a3fd-11ea -81ac-4854aed294e5.

5   John Gerard Ruggie, "International Regimes, Transactions, and Change: Embedded Liberalism in the Postwar Economic Order," *International Organization* 36, no. 2 (1982): 379–415, jstor.org/stable /2706527.

6   Bremmer, *Us vs. Them.*

7   Philip Georgiadis, Leslie Hook, and Jim Pickard, "Business Calls for More Action after COP26 Deal Is Watered Down," *Financial Times*, November 14, 2021, ft.com/content/a0c01a33-fda3-4918 -bead-dba61265ec48.

8   Mishra, *Age of Anger*; Quinn Slobodian, *Globalists: The End of Empire and the Birth of Neoliberalism* (Cambridge, MA: Harvard University Press, 2018).

9   It is very likely that the populists never think about the complex circuitry of invisible institutions that comprise international governance today. Take for example the postwar Convention on International Civil Aviation, which gave rise to airspace cooperation that allowed for the development of a modern international

aviation industry. Likewise, the Universal Postal Union, founded in 1874, coordinates policies among members of the UN that direct packages from sender to recipient. The International Bureau of Weights and Measures governs the standards for measuring everything from radiation to coordinated universal time.

10 Trump's use of presidential decrees pales in comparison with presidents of a hundred years ago. For example, Teddy Roosevelt signed an average of 145 executive orders per year. Franklin Roosevelt, whose presidency spanned the Great Depression and World War II, signed an average of 307 per year. See *The American Presidency Project*, "Statistics," presidency.ucsb.edu/statistics/data/executive-orders.

11 Demetri Sevastopulo and Aime Williams, "Why Trump No Longer Talks about the Trade Deficit with China," *Financial Times*, September 1, 2020, ft.com/content/081e6d25-8d67-4caa-918a-2765a66f0052.

12 James Politi, "US Trade Deficit in August Was Widest in 14 Years," *Financial Times*, October 6, 2020, ft.com/content/9ee10f23-067b-47b9-88ab-246a82d74647.

13 Christian Davies and Jennifer Rankin, "'Declaration of War': Polish Row over Judicial Independence Escalates," *Guardian*, January 24, 2020, theguardian.com/world/2020/jan/24/declaration-of-war-polish-row-over-judicial-independence-escalates.

14 Barry Gewen, *The Inevitability of Tragedy: Henry Kissinger and His World* (New York: Norton, 2020).

15 What mattered to Kissinger first and foremost was American control of the political process. Outcomes are often affected by fate and fortune, but maintaining a tight grip on the process was everything, even with such a difficult president as Nixon. Kissinger accepted swapping coexistence by turning a blind eye on human rights in Russia. He abandoned Ngo Dinh Diem in

Vietnam in order to end the war and recognize the communist north. He betrayed the South Vietnamese, and yet hundreds of thousands came to make their home in America and became staunch patriots. In the conflict over Taiwan, Kissinger agreed to a "one China" policy in which the United States recognized China as the legitimate government of the territory claimed by Taiwan, a stinging defeat for the Taiwanese. In Latin America, there were plenty of compromises to be made with right-wing dictators, but none for socialist governments; thousands of socialist activists and social justice advocates were tortured and murdered. In a terrible and literalistic way, Kissinger took no prisoners, supporting extreme military dictatorships in the name of American security.

16 Peter Navarro and Greg Autry, *Death by China: Confronting the Dragon—A Global Call to Action* (Upper Saddle River, NJ: Prentice Hall, 2011); Peter Navarro, *The Coming China Wars: Where They Will Be Fought, How They Can Be Won* (Upper Saddle River, NJ: FT Press, 2006).

17 Kishore Mahbubani, *Has China Won? The Chinese Challenge to American Primacy* (New York: Public Affairs, 2020), 125.

18 Alexi Drew, "The Rise of Twitter Diplomacy Is Making the World More Dangerous," *World Politics Review*, August 10, 2020, world-politicsreview.com/articles/28976/the-rise-of-twitter-diplomacy-is-making-the-world-more-dangerous.

19 Graham Allison, *Destined for War: Can America and China Escape Thucydides's Trap?* (Boston, MA: Mariner Books, 2018).

20 Shi Jiangtao, "Destined for Conflict? Xi Jinping, Donald Trump and the Thucydides Trap," *South China Morning Post*, May 21, 2020, scmp.com/news/china/diplomacy/article/3085321/destined-conflict-xi-jinping-donald-trump-and-thucydides-trap.

21 Amitai Etzioni, "The Rising (More) Nation-Centered System," *Fletcher Forum of World Affairs* 42, no. 2 (2018): 30, static1.squarespace

.com/static/579fc2ad725e253a86230610/t/5b81095d562fa70992dccda6=
/1535183213973/Pages+29-53+-+Etzioni_42-2.pdf.

22 Sean Sullivan and Robert Costa, "Trump and Sanders Lead
Competing Populist Movements, Reshaping American Politics,"
Washington Post, March 2, 2020, washingtonpost.com/politics
/2020/03/02/two-populist-movements-sanders-trump.

23 Robert Kagan, "Our Constitutional Crisis Is Already Here,"
Washington Post, September 23, 2021, washingtonpost.com
/opinions/2021/09/23/robert-kagan-constitutional-crisis.

24 Sullivan and Costa, "Trump and Sanders."

25 Levitsky and Ziblatt, *How Democracies Die.*

26 Steve Hendricks, "'Hate Crime' Attacks by Israeli Settlers on
Palestinians Spike in the West Bank," *Washington Post*, November
29, 2021, washingtonpost.com/world/middle_east/west-bank
-settlers-violence-attacks/2021/11/28/7de2f9d2-4bb7-11ec-a7b8
-9ed28bf23929_story.html.

27 Islamophobia in Europe, *Open Society Foundations*, May 2019,
opensocietyfoundations.org/explainers/islamophobia-europe.

28 Mitra Taj and Julie Turkewitz, "Left and Right Clash in Peru
Election, With an Economic Model at Stake," *New York Times*,
June 6, 2021, nytimes.com/2021/06/06/world/americas/peru
-election.html.

29 The Risks of a Rigged Election in Nicaragua, The Crisis Group, May
20, 2021, crisisgroup.org/latin-america-caribbean/central-america
/nicaragua/088-risks-rigged-election-nicaragua.

30 Chile Events of 2020, *Human Rights Watch*, hrw.org/world-report
/2021/country-chapters/chile.

31 Richard Hofstadter, *Anti-Intellectualism in American Life* (New York:
Knopf, 1963).

32 Roger Cohen, "France and U.S. Agree on the Perils of a Rising
China, Blinken Says," *New York Times*, June 25, 2021, nytimes.com
/2021/06/25/world/europe/blinken-france-china-macron.html.

Chapter 6

1   Kelly Mena, "White House Rips Fauci after Criticism of Atlas and Trump's Pandemic Response," Cable News Network, November 1, 2020, cnn.com/2020/10/31/politics/white-house-fauci-trump-atlas-pandemic-response/index.html.

2   Jane Spencer and Christina Jewett, "Twelve Months of Trauma: More Than 3,600 US Health Workers Died in Covid's First Year," *Guardian*, April 8, 2021, theguardian.com/us-news/2021/apr/08/us-health-workers-deaths-covid-lost-on-the-frontline. The Canadian Institute for Health Information (CIHI) reports that nearly 100,000 people working in the health care sector were diagnosed with COVID-19 in the first five and a half months of 2021. Sharon Lindores, CTV News, August 19, 2020, ctvnews.ca/health/coronavirus/nearly-100-000-canadian-health-care-workers-have-contracted-covid-19-this-year-alone-report-finds-1.5553834.

3   "James K. Galbraith Says More . . ." *Project Syndicate*, November 17, 2020, project-syndicate.org/say-more/an-interview-with-james-k-galbraith-2020-11.

4   Rick Bell, "Kenney Goes on Offence for His Best Summer Ever Plan," *Calgary Sun*, May 28, 2021, calgarysun.com/opinion/columnists/bell-kenney-goes-on-offence-for-his-best-summer-ever-plan.

5   Sam Jones, James Shotter, and Guy Chazan, "COVID Backlash: Europe's Populists Eye Opportunity in Never-Ending Pandemic," *Financial Times*, November 30, 2021, ft.com/content/7ef50a97-c12d-4905-b6da-75c3c7bb4f16.

6   Jones, Shotter, and Chazan, "COVID Backlash."

7   Trip Gabriel, "Dr. Oz Says He's Running for Senate in Pennsylvania," *New York Times*, November 30, 2021, nytimes.com/2021/11/30/us/politics/dr-oz-senate-run-pennsylvania.html.

8   Donato Paolo Mancini, "Rich Countries Must Divert Covid Jabs to Developing World, Says Covax Executive," *Financial Times*,

December 1, 2021, ft.com/content/974b71d1-d196-46a5]-85d5
-d32d3aa7f106.

9 Adam Nagourney, "A Kennedy's Crusade Against Covid Vaccines
Anguishes Family and Friends," *New York Times*, February 26, 2022,
nytimes.com/2022/02/26/us/robert-kennedy-covid-vaccine.html.

10 Rich Barlow, "Vaccine Passports: COVID-19 Protection or
Discrimination against BIPOC and the Poor?" Boston University
Today, April 9, 2021, bu.edu/articles/2021/vaccine-passports-covid-19
-protection-or-discrimination.

11 "Former People's Party of Canada Riding President Charged after
Gravel Thrown at Trudeau," CBC News, September 11, 2021, cbc
.ca/news/canada/london/shane-marshall-people-s-party-gravel
-trudeau-1.6172690.

12 Tara Haelle, "This Is the Moment the Anti-Vaccine Movement Has
Been Waiting For," *New York Times*, August 31, 2021, nytimes.com
/2021/08/31/opinion/anti-vaccine-movement.html.

13 "In Florida, a Summer of Death and Resistance as the Coronavirus
Rampaged," *Washington Post*, September 5, 2021, washingtonpost
.com/health/2021/09/05/florida-coronavirus-delta-surge.

14 George Parker and Chris Giles, "Boris Johnson 'Deeply Sorry' as
UK's COVID Death Toll Passes 100,000," *Financial Times*, January
21, 2021, ft.com/content/675d737e-88a5-4d84-9222-013eb5fdf6e3.

15 Visual and Data Journalism Team, "Covid Map: Coronavirus
Cases, Deaths, Vaccinations by Country," BBC News, bbc.com
/news/world-51235105.

16 Antonia Noori Farzan and Miriam Berger, "Bolsonaro Says
Brazilians Must Not Be 'Sissies' about Coronavirus, as 'All of us
are going to die one day,'" *Washington Post*, November 11, 2020,
washingtonpost.com/world/2020/11/11/bolsonaro-coronavirus
-brazil-quotes.

17 Terrence McCoy and Heloisa Traiano, "The Amazonian City that
Hatched the Brazil Variant Has Been Crushed By It," *Washington Post*,

January 27, 2021, washingtonpost.com/world/2021/01/27/coronavirus
-brazil-variant-manaus.

18   McCoy and Traiano, "The Amazonian City."

19   "Bolsa Família, Brazil's Admired Anti-Poverty Programme, Is Flailing,"
     Economist, January 30, 2020, economist.com/the-americas/2020/01
     /30/bolsa-familia-brazils-admired-anti-poverty-programme-is-flailing.

20   But the tough-guy persona was an act. Behind the scenes, Trump
     was getting tested multiple times per day. He is a germophobe
     and the virus terrified him. But he was even more afraid of
     looking weak. In the first half of 2020, he reluctantly held off on
     political rallies, with the hope that the virus would be gone by the
     time he needed to campaign hard in the fall. But as his opponent,
     Joe Biden, gained in the polls, Trump returned to holding mass
     rallies by the end of June 2020, even though infections were
     stubbornly high and doctors were pleading with people to stay
     home. Winning was more important than the inevitable wave of
     infection and death that followed.

21   Philip Bump. "What's Amazing Is That Trump Didn't Contract
     the Coronavirus Even Earlier," *Washington Post*, December 1, 2021,
     washingtonpost.com/politics/2021/12/01/whats-amazing-is-that-trump
     -didnt-contract-coronavirus-even-earlier/.

22   "Estimating Mortality from COVID-19: Scientific Brief," World
     Health Organization, August 4, 2020, who.int/news-room
     /commentaries/detail/estimating-mortality-from-covid-19.

23   Adam Tooze, *Shutdown: How Covid Shook the World's Economy*
     (New York: Viking, 2021).

24   Keith Collins and Josh Holder, "How Rich Countries Got to
     the Front of the Vaccine Line," *New York Times*, March 31, 2021,
     nytimes.com/interactive/2021/03/31/world/global-vaccine-supply
     -inequity.html.

25   Ido Efrati, "Israel to Share Vaccination Data With Pfizer as Part of
     Secret Deal," *Haaretz*, January 10, 2021, haaretz.com/israel-news/

.premium-israel-to-share-covid-vaccine-data-with-pfizer-but
-agreement-remains-secret-1.9438504.

26 OECD, Access to COVID-19 vaccines: Global Approaches in a
Global Crisis, March 18, 2021, oecd.org/coronavirus/policy
-responses/access-to-covid-19-vaccines-global-approaches-in-a
-global-crisis-c6a18370/.

27 Jon Kamp, Robbie Whelan, and Anthony DeBarros, "U.S.
Covid-19 Deaths in 2021 Surpass 2020's," *Wall Street Journal*,
November 20, 2021, wsj.com/articles/u-s-covid-19-deaths-in-2021
-surpass-2020-11637426356.

28 Smriti Mallapaty, "China's COVID Vaccines Have Been Crucial—
Now Immunity Is Waning," *Nature*, October 14, 2021, nature.com
/articles/d41586-021-02796-w.

29 Jacob Mardell, "China's Coronavirus Vaccines: For Many
Countries, It's Not Political, It's the Only Choice," *South China
Morning Post*, The Coronavirus Pandemic, February 20, 2021,
scmp.com/comment/opinion/article/3122175/chinas-coronavirus
-vaccines-many-countries-its-not-political-its.

30 Bulbul Dhawan, "Pharma Sector Rose to Challenge during
COVID-19, Needs to Focus on Raw Materials, Traditional
Medicine: PM Narendra Modi," *Financial Express*, November 18,
2021, financialexpress.com/healthcare/pharma-healthcare/pharma
-sector-rose-to-challenge-during-covid-19-needs-to=-focus-on-raw
-materials-traditional-medicine-pm-narendra-modi/2372069.

31 Manoj Kumar, "India to Push for Patent Waiver for COVID-19
Vaccines at WTO," Reuters, November 26, 2021, reuters.com/world
/india/india-push-patent-waiver-covid-19-vaccines-wto-2021-11-26.

32 Joe Nocera, "There's a Precedent for Overriding Patents on Vital
Medications," Bloomberg Businessweek, May 11, 2021, bloomberg
.com/news/articles/2021-05-11/aids-drugs-in-south-africa-shows
-precedent-for-overriding-patents-on-medications.

33 Stephanie Nolan, "Here's Why Developing Countries Can Make

mRNA Covid Vaccines," *New York Times*, November 22, 2021, nytimes.com/interactive/2021/10/22/science/developing-country -covid-vaccines.html; Peter S. Goodman et al., "What Would It Take to Vaccinate the World Against Covid?" *New York Times*, May 17, 2021, nytimes.com/2021/05/15/world/americas/covid -vaccine-patent-biden.html.

34 Nolan, "Here's Why."

35 Elizabeth Merab, "Africa Seeks to Produce 60% of Its Vaccines by 2040," *The East African*, April 15, 2021, theeastafrican.co.ke/tea /science-health/africa-vaccine-manufacture-plan-3363628.

36 Goodman et al., "What Would It Take."

37 Hakobyan, "In the Race to Vaccinate."

38 Rebecca Robinns and Stephanie Nolen. "The Drive to Vaccinate the World Against Covid is Losing Steam." *New York Times*, April 23, 2022. nytimes.com/2022/04/23/health/covid-vaccines-world -africa.html.

39 "Pandemic of Greed," Oxfam International, March 3, 2022. oxfam.org/en/research/pandemic-greed.

40 Kristalina Georgieva, Gita Gopinath, and Ruchir Agarwal, "A Proposal to End the COVID-19 Pandemic," *IMFBlog*, May 21, 2021, blogs.imf.org/2021/05/21/a-proposal-to-end-the-covid-19-pandemic.

41 *IMF Blog*, "A New Trust to Help Countries Build Resilience and Sustainability," January 20, 2022, blogs.imf.org/2022/01/20/a-new -trust-to-help-countries-build-resilience-and-sustainability.

42 Tahsin Saadi Sedik and Rui Xu, "When Inequality Is High, Pandemics Can Fuel Social Unrest," *IMF Blog*, December 11, 2020, blogs.imf.org/2020/12/11/when-inequality-is-high-pandemics-can -fuel-social-unrest.

43 Stephen Marche, *The Next Civil War: Dispatches from the American Future* (Toronto: Simon & Schuster, 2022).

44 Jones, Shotter, and Chazan, "COVID Backlash."

45 Mark Landler, "Vaccine Mandates Rekindle Fears Debate over Civil

Liberties," *New York Times*, December 10, 2021, nytimes.com/2021
/12/10/world/europe/vaccine-mandates-civil-liberties.html. If the
number of vaccine sceptics include those in Russia and Turkey, we
are looking at over 200 million people hesitant or against vaccination. We can expect that the vaccine deficit will remain a structural
problem of public health in Africa without a massive international
effort to increase the supply of locally sourced medicine.

46 Isaac Stanley-Becker, "Steve Bannon Was Deplatformed. An
Obscure Media Mogul Keeps Him on the Air," *Washington Post*,
January 25, 2022, washingtonpost.com/politics/2022/01/24/steve
-bannon-war-room-real-americas-voice/.

47 Paul Mason, "Hard Labour," *Social Europe*, May 10, 2021,
https://socialeurope.eu/hard-labour.

48 Jan-Werner Müller, "Liberals Misunderstood Trump's Seductive
Appeal," *Financial Times*, November 10, 2020, ft.com/content
/56e1ea4b-1377-43b1-b956-c15590ae9a69.

Chapter 7

1 Arthur Koestler, *Darkness at Noon*, rev. ed. (1941; repr., New York:
Simon & Schuster, 2019).

2 Arendt, *The Origins of Totalitarianism*, 478.

3 Koestler, *Darkness at Noon*.

4 Pippa Norris, "Voters Against Democracy: The Roots of Autocratic
Resurgence," *Foreign Affairs* (May–June 2021), foreignaffairs.com
/reviews/review-essay/2021-04-20/voters-against-democracy.

5 Colby Itkowitz, "House MAGA Casting Squad Seeks to Expand
by Boosting Challengers to Fellow Republicans," *Washington Post*,
December 26, 2021, washingtonpost.com/politics/house-maga-squad
/2021/12/26/654f49ea-5448-11ec-8769-2f4ecdf7a2ad_story.html.

6 Philip Manow, "The Political Economy of Populism in
Europe: Hyperglobalization and the Heterogeneity of Protest

Movements," Europe Programme research paper, Chatham House, December 15, 2021, chathamhouse.org/2021/12/political-economy-populism-europe.

7   Gregory Korte, "U.S. Pollsters Mark Worst Performance in 40 Years in 2020 Campaign," *Bloomberg Politics*, July 18, 2021, bloomberg.com/news/articles/2021-07-19/pollsters-mark-worst-performance-in-40-years-in-2020-campaign.

8   Thomas Edsall, "Why Millions Think It Is Trump Who Cannot Tell a Lie," *New York Times*, January 20, 2022, nytimes.com/2022/01/19/opinion/trump-big-lie.html.

9   Ziblatt and Levitsky, *How Democracies Die*.

10 Wolff, *Landslide*.

11 Katherine Stewart, *The Power Worshippers: Inside the Dangerous Rise of Religious Nationalism* (London, UK: Bloomsbury, 2020).

12 Michael Stott, Brian Harris, and Michael Pooler, "Bolsonaro Embraces the Politics He Once Vowed to Abolish," *Financial Times*, December 23, 2021, ft.com/content/324df26b-eac0-468b-b738-9258f5d82aa5.

13 Gessen, *The Future is History*, 249.

14 Thomas Edsall, "The Moral Chasm That Has Opened Up Between Left and Right Is Widening," *New York Times*, October 27, 2021, nytimes.com/2021/10/27/opinion/left-right-moral-chasm.html.

15 David Leonhardt, "Our Broken Economy, in One Simple Chart," *New York Times*, August 7, 2017, nytimes.com/interactive/2017/08/07/opinion/leonhardt-income-inequality.html.

16 Igielnik, Keeter, and Hartig, "Behind Biden's Victory."

17 Hate in Elections How Racism and Bigotry Threaten Election Integrity in the United States, The Lawyers' Committee's James Byrd Jr. Center to Stop Hate, September 2020, https://lawyerscommittee.org/wp-content/uploads/2020/09/LC2_HATE-IN-ELECTIONS_RPT_E_HIGH-1.pdf.

18   At the time of writing it is likely that Lula, having his conviction overturned, will run for president against Bolsonaro in 2022.

19   James Shotter and Agata Majos, "Poland's Ruling Party Comes under Attack from Both Flanks," *Financial Times*, December 4, 2019, ft.com/content/95afcf30-0b91-11ea-b2d6-9bf4d1957a67.

20   Arendt, *The Origins of Totalitarianism*, 55.

21   Editorial Board of the *Financial Times*, "Lessons of Dominic Cummings' Testimony Are Still to Be Learnt," *Financial Times*, May 2, 2021, ft.com/content/9c2c7db1-6a28-4696-ae43-f62fc932147f.

22   Thomas Friedman, *The Lexus and the Olive Tree: Understanding Globalization* (London, UK: Picador, 1999).

23   Simon Archer, Daniel Drache, and Peer Zumbansen, eds., *The Daunting Enterprise of the Law* (Montreal: McGill-Queen's University Press, 2017).

24   Slobodian, *Globalists*.

25   Eric Hoffer, *The True Believer: Thoughts on the Nature of Mass Movements* (New York: HarperCollins, 2010).

26   Wilhelm Reich, *Listen, Little Man!* (New York: Farrar, Straus and Giroux, 1974).

27   Wilhelm Reich, *The Mass Psychology of Fascism* (New York: Farrar, Straus, and Giroux, 1933). See Chapter V, "The Sex-Economic Presuppositions of the Authoritarian Family."

28   In the 1940s and '50s, the Frankfurt School, led by Max Horkheimer and Theodor Adorno, attempted to locate the impulse to authoritarianism in the dialectic of enlightenment. The logic of capitalism gives rise to the instrumental rationality that can be used to create great monuments to humanity, or great crimes, like the pyramids or the ovens of Auschwitz. For an excellent overview of the conflicts between members of the school and their many achievements, see Stuart Jeffries, *Grand Hotel Abyss: The Lives of the Frankfurt School* (London, UK: Verso, 2017).

29   Hoffer, *The True Believer*, sec. 28.

30 Turkel, "Dynasty."

31 Political violence has reached new highs in Africa, where seven military coup d'états occurred in 2021 alone. See Remi Adekoya, "Why Are Coups Making a Comeback in Africa?" CNN, September 13, 2021, cnn.com/2021/09/12/africa/africa-coups-resurgence-intl-cmd /index.html.

32 José Ortega y Gasset, *La rebelión de las masas* [*The Revolt of the Masses*] (Madrid: Revista de Occidente, 1929). The English translation is available at pinkmonkey.com/dl/library1/revolt.pdf.

33 Roger Cohn, "Trump Bequeaths Biden an Upended World," *New York Times*, January 19, 2021, nytimes.com/2021/01/19/world/trump -legacy-biden.html.

34 Ortega y Gasset, *La rebelión.*

35 Ortega y Gasset, *La rebelión.*

36 Applebaum, *Twilight of Democracy*, 13.

37 R. B. J. Walker, *After the Globe, Before the World* (London, UK: Routledge, 2009).

38 Sam Jones, James Shotter and Guy Chazan, "Covid Backlash: Europe's Populists Eye Opportunity in Never-Ending Pandemic," *Financial Times*, December 1, 2021, ft.com/content/7ef50a97-c12d -4905-b6da-75c3c7bb4f16.

39 Richard Milne, "Sweden's Prime Minister Resigns Just Hours After Taking Office," *Financial Times*, November, 24 2021, ft.com/content /84eabd9c-fca9-4531-9434-3f927014e7e4.

40 "Global Survey Finds Widespread Broken-System Sentiment Accompanied with Populist, Anti-elites, and Nativist Views," *Ipsos*, July 28, 2021, ipsos.com/sites/default/files/ct/news/documents /2021-07/Broken-System%20Populism%20and%20Nativism%20 2021%20Global%20Survey%20-%20PR.pdf.

41 "Global Survey."

42 Neil MacFarquhar, "Jury Finds Rally Organizers Responsible for

Charlottesville Violence," *New York Times*, November 23, 2021, nytimes.com/2021/11/23/us/charlottesville-rally-verdict.html.

43 Michael Gorman, "Politicians, Academics Worry Where Extremist Behaviour in Canada Could Lead," CBC News, February 12, 2022, cbc.ca/news/canada/nova-scotia/covid-19-protests-politicians -extremism-threats-1.6349254.

44 "A New Blockade Snarls Traffic at U.S.-Canada Border," *New York Times*, February 9, 2022, nytimes.com/live/2022/02/09/world/canada -trucker-protest.

45 Tracey Lindeman, "Maple Leaf Flags, Conspiracy Theories and *The Matrix*: Inside the Ottawa Truckers' Protest," *Guardian*, February 11, 2022, theguardian.com/world/2022/feb/11/canada-ottawa-truckers -protest-covid-vaccine-mandates.

46 Lawrence Mishel and Julia Wolfe, "CEO Compensation Has Grown 940% Since 1978," Economic Policy Institute, August 14, 2019, epi.org/publication/ceo-compensation-2018.

47 Lawrence Mishel and Jori Kandra, "Preliminary Data Show CEO Pay Jumped Nearly 16% in 2020, While Average Worker Compensation Rose 1.8%," Working Economics Blog, Economic Policy Institute, May 27, 2021, epi.org/blog/preliminary-data -show-ceo-pay-jumped-nearly-16-in-2020-while-average-worker -compensation-rose-1-8.

48 Christoph Lakner et al., "Updated Estimates of the Impact of COVID-19 on Global Poverty: Looking Back at 2020 and the Outlook for 2021," *World Bank Blogs*, January 11, 2021, blogs .worldbank.org/opendata/updated-estimates-impact-covid-19 -global-poverty-looking-back-2020-and-outlook-2021.

49 Joseph Stiglitz, "Conquering the Great Divide," Finance and Development, International Monetary Fund, fall 2020, imf.org /external/pubs/ft/fandd/2020/09/COVID19-and-global-inequality -joseph-stiglitz.htm.

ACKNOWLEDGMENTS

Along the way we have received much encouragement and support from a network of friends and colleagues for which we are deeply appreciative. At different stages they read many drafts and made valuable suggestions to broaden our inquiry to address the many-sided dimensions of the global populist insurgency. We owe a debt of gratitude to the anonymous reviewers who made valuable suggestions that pushed our thinking particularly about sovereignty and populism. Special thanks to Bernie Frolic, Ed Dosman, Arthur Kroker, Gail Lord, Joyce Wayne, Marion Cohen, Lou Pauly, Phil Resnick for their critical reading of different drafts. Among our influencers we have to thank Roger Keil, Seth Klein, Harry Arthurs, Niraja Gopal Jayal, Irene Frolic, Carlos Pujalte, Alvin Yang, Bob Kellermann, Joel Bakin, Alan Hutchison, Simon Archer, Cesario Melo Franco, Geoffrey Hale for timely feedback over the life of this project. Special thanks to Shushanik Hakobyan and Jonathan Ostry for data assistance. Marjorie Cohen, Peer Zumbansen, Bruce Kidd, Michele Rioux, Isidro Morales, Amy Verhaeghe, Susan Aaronson, Isidro Morales, Duncan Cameron and Spencer Page gave extra timely support when needed. We are grateful to Emily Ferko, Pia Singhal, and Jessica Albert of ECW for their critical support. Susan Renouf, our editor at ECW, has been an enthusiastic advocate of our project from start to finish. We are in her debt. It goes without saying that our families' forbearance and support as always made a huge difference.

INDEX

activists, role in populism, 6
Africa, 21, 132, 134
Alberta, 45–46
Alternative für Deutschland (AfD),
    44, 136, 172–73
angry populist voter
    description, xviii, 5–6, 10, 23–24
    profile, 23–26, 68
    and "the system," 24–25
ANO (party), 171
Anonymous hacker collective, 16
antiestablishment populism, 16–17, 136
anti-liberalism, 114–16
anti-Semitism, in Hungary, 39–40
anti-system vote
    reelection prospects of far-right
        parties by country, 166–79
    in 2015–2021 by country, 163–65
anti-vaccine (anti-vaxx) movement
    and message, 123–25, 136–37
Applebaum, Anne, 155
Araud, Gérard, 85
Arce, Luis, 178
Arendt, Hannah, 24, 140, 148

Argentina, 164, 177
Austria, 164, 170
authoritarianism
    arrival and acceptance in Global
        North, 142–43
    danger in, 12–13
    definition and description, xiii
    end point, 144
    leftwing form, 21
    in post-truth politics, 49–50
    as threat, 141, 143–44, 162
    threat to, 141
    values, 151–52
authoritarian populist governments,
    ascendance worldwide, 18–21
    See also populist governments
authoritarians (authoritarian populist
    leaders)
    as global force, 54, 162
    and legal system, 52
    opposition to, 47
    and populism, xiv
    promises to people, xiv, 27, 149
    and sovereignty, 86, 92

tactics and playbook, xvii, 49
values, xvi
See also populist leaders; specific leaders

Babiš, Andrej, 157, 171
Bannon, Steve, xvi, 114, 137
Barber, Benjamin, 78
Bauman, Zygmunt, 40, 148
Bennett, Naftali, 174–75
Berlusconi, Silvio, xii
Bermuda Triangle, as metaphor, 49
Bharatiya Janata Party (BJP), 35, 46, 75
Biden, Joe
    continuation of policies, 117
    election of 2020, 136, 138
    executive orders, 108
    reelection chances, 166
    and sovereignty, 85
    stimulus packages, 145
big business, 73–76
big lie of populism, 28–31
Biroli, Flávia, 78
blame laying, as tactic, 17
Blankfein, Lloyd, 15
Blinken, Antony, 117
blue-collar voters, 69, 71
Blyth, Mark, 74
Bobbio, Norberto, 51
Bolivia, 165, 178
Bolsa Família system, 127
Bolsonaro, Jair
    and COVID-19, 126, 127, 131
    discontent with, 156
    as everyman, 5
    as populist leader, 66–67
    as president, 179
    social support withdrawal, 127
Bonaparte, Louis (Louis Napoleon), 91–92
Boric, Gabriel, 116
Bown, Chad, 109–10

Brazil
    anti-system vote, 165
    causes of populism, xiv
    conspiracy theories, 78
    COVID-19, 66, 126–27
    reelection prospects of far-right party, 179
Breaking Bad (TV show), 3
Bremmer, Ian, 105
Bretton Woods world, 104, 117
Brexit, xiv, 29–30, 47, 149
Britain, 29–30, 70, 93, 102, 126
    See also United Kingdom
Bulgaria, 164
bullying, 107, 110–12
business leaders, 15
Byford, Jovan, 77

Cable, Vince, 62–63
Cain, Herman, 124
Canada
    anti-system vote, 163
    elections and populism, 45–46
    freedom convoy, 159–60
Carlson, Tucker, 12
Castro, Fidel, 21
Central Europe, religion and identity, 64
Central European University, 76–77
Charlottesville riot, xv
Chávez, Hugo, 14, 22, 178
Chega (party), 174
Chile, 13, 116, 165
China
    COVID-19 vaccine, 129, 131
    inequalities, 37
    populism and authoritarianism in, 20–21
    and sovereignty, 84–85, 93
    Trump's strategy, 109–10, 112
Christianity, 31, 65
"the composed middle," 51–52

compromise and concessions, 111, 115
Concert of Europe, 91
Congress (party), 46, 176
Conservative Party (Canada), 45
Conservative Party (UK), 167–68
conservative populism
    ascendance and support, 17–19
    and existential threats, 60
    and sovereignty, 88–89
    in speeches, 38, 39
    See also right-wing populism
conservatives
    cultural narratives, 107
    and sovereignty, 83, 88–89, 91
conspiracy theories, xvi, 41, 60, 77–78
Conspirator-in-Chief, as archetype of
    populist leaders, 55, 56, 59–61
COP26, 105
COVID-19 pandemic
    as advantage for populism, 137–38
    and big lie of populism, 31
    deaths, 120, 124–25, 126–27, 128–29
    description as disease, 122
    and elites, 122, 123
    "every nation for itself," 129, 131,
        132, 134
    and nationalism, 129, 130, 134–36
    people's response, 121–23
    performance by country, 120–21
    and populist leaders, 118–19, 122–23,
        125–26, 128–29, 130, 134, 135–36
    response by populists, 119–21
    and sovereignty, 113
    unproven medicines, 124–25
    See also individual countries
COVID-19 vaccines and vaccination
    anti-vaxx movement and message,
        123–25, 136–37
    children in Mexico, 52–53
    divide in, 133–34
    formulas for, 131–32
    in Philippines, 42

    and populism, 122–23, 138
    as problem and lie, 31, 42
    production of vaccines, 129–31
    vaccine nationalism, 134–36
    vaccine passports, 123–24
cultural populism, 10–13, 16
Cummings, Dominic, xvi, 149
Czech Republic, 164, 171

Darkness at Noon (Koestler), 139
"darkness at noon" moment of popu-
    lism, 139–41
Death of a Salesman (Miller), 3
de Gaulle, Charles, 7
deindustrialization, 12–13
democracy
    loss of ground to populism, 114–15
    resetting to fix populism, 25–26
    revolt against, 154–55
    tipping point, xvi–xvii
    undermining and threat by populism,
        xix–xx, 51–52, 79, 141, 142, 162
Democratic Party (US), 166
Denmark, 163
deregulation, 33
DeSantis, Ron, 31
dictators, populist leaders as, 57
digital world, and sovereignty, 99
diplomacy, 111–12
distrust, 78
dog whistle, as puzzle, xv
Doria, João, 127
Draghi, Mario, 45, 173
"drain the swamp," 17, 102
Duda, Andrzej, 147, 168
Duterte, Rodrigo
    and big money, 75–76
    as Conspirator-in-Chief, 59–60
    as everyman, 5
    extreme language, 42–44
    as president, 175–76
    and sovereignty, 88

Eco, Umberto, xix, 12
economic establishment, blame on, 14–15
Economic Policy Institute, 160
economic resentment, 14, 37
Edelman Trust Barometer, 78
Ehrenreich, Barbara, 49
elections
    anti-system vote in 2015–2021 by country, 163–65
    ascendance of populism worldwide, 17–18, 117
    and COVID-19, 135
    election of 2020 in US, 43, 47, 71, 136, 138, 166
    and extreme speech, 38, 141–44
    hinge moments in politics, 33–34
    playbook of populist leaders, 146–47
    and radical views, 32
    reelection prospects of far-right parties by country, 158, 166–79
    and religion, 63
    repeat wins of populism, 144–48
    and sovereignty, 156
    and speech of populism, 43–44, 45–46
elite
    anti-elite sentiment, 158, 160–61
    in antiestablishment populism, 16–17
    in big lie of populism, 28–29
    and COVID-19, 122, 123
    definition, 16
    as enemies of Mexico, 97
    populist leaders as, 102
    as target of populism, xiv, xix, 9, 10, 16, 17, 161
    vs. true people, xiii, xix, 17
    use by populist leaders, 76, 146
El Salvador, 164
emotions, use in populism, 148

enemies of the people
    in antiestablishment populism, 16
    of authoritarians, xiv
    in cultural populism, 12
    in populism (generally), 10, 146
    and populist leaders, 58
    in socioeconomic populism, 14
Erdoğan, Recep Tayyip, 156–57, 175
establishment elite. See elite
Estonia, 164
Etzioni, Amitai, 113
Europe
    people's response to COVID-19, 121
    radical views in, 32
    refugee crisis, 11
    and sovereignty, 85–86
    See also specific countries
European Union (EU), 76–77, 110–11
everyman persona and narrative, 3, 4, 5
extreme speech, 38–40, 42–44, 141–44

facts, in populism, 50
failed states, 90–91
family, and values, 152
far-right parties
    anti-system vote in 2015–2021 by country, 163–65
    reelection prospects by country, 166–79
fascism
    as influence today, 50–51
    as mentality, 151–52
    modern version, 49–50
    "Ur-Fascism" (or "Eternal Fascism"), xix, 12, 158
Fauci, Anthony, 118
financial crisis of 2008, 71, 99, 161
Financial Times, and COVID-19, 126
Finchelstein, Federico, 50
Finland, 65–66, 163
First Citizen of the Empire, as archetype of populist leaders, 55, 56–57

Five Star Movement (Italian party),
44, 45
foreigners, as target of populism, xiv
foreign policy, 84, 85
France
anti-system vote, 163
reelection prospects of far-right, 173
sovereignty, 91–92
speech and elections, 44
support for populism, 157
voters, 69–70
fraud, in big lie, 28–29
freedom, 89, 152–53
freedom convoy, 159–60
Friedman, Thomas, 150

Galbraith, James, 120
Gantz, Benny, 174
Germany
anti-system vote, 163
populist parties, 136
QAnon in, 60
reelection prospects of far-right
party, 172–73
speech and elections, 44
gilets jaunes (yellow vests), 69–70
globalization
impact, 150
in lessons from populist leaders,
149–50
as source of populism, 11–12, 24–25,
37, 70–71
and sovereignty, 83–84, 99
Global North, and COVID-19 vaccination, 134
Global South, 131–32, 133
Greece, 11, 14, 164, 171
Guaidó, Juan, 178
Guevara, Che, 21–22

Hamas, 30
Hashimoto, Tōru, 19–20

hate speech to win elections, 141–44
herd, people as, 144
HIV medications, 131–32
Hoffer, Eric, 151, 152
Hofstadter, Richard, 116
Holy Crusader, as archetype of populist
leaders, 55, 56, 58–59
Hotez, Peter, 125
Hoyer, Katja, 60
Hungary
anti-system vote, 164
big lie of populism, 30–31
COVID-19, 120, 130
EU funding, 76–77
reelection prospects of far-right
party, 169
hyper-globalization. See globalization
hyper-individualism, xv–xvi, 107, 137,
160

"I Am the People, the Mob"
(Sandburg), 56–57
identity
archetypes of populist leaders, 55–62
national identity, 92–95
as weapon, 62–64
illiberalism, 114–16
immigrants, 8, 10–11, 29
income
and inequalities, 36–37, 160–61
in US, 145
and voters, 70–71, 161
India
anti-system vote, 164
COVID-19, 131–33, 135
income and employment, 176–77
media, 74–75
populism, xiv, 48
reelection prospects of far-right
party, 176–77
and sovereignty, 93
Indigenous people, and nativism, 8

industrial working class, 12–13
inequalities
    in income, 36–37, 160–61
    as source of populism, xviii, 36–38
Inglehart, Ronald, 68
international agreements, 105
International Criminal Court, 42–43
international order
    anti-liberalism, 114–16
    and COVID-19, 138
    replacement by nation-centered
        system, 103–4, 106–7, 113–14, 117
    revamp by populists, 86–87, 102–3,
        106–7, 117
    as target of populists, 93, 101, 102–5,
        143–44
    vulnerability, 115–16, 140
    See also system ("the system")
Israel
    anti-system vote, 164
    attacks on Palestinians, 30, 53
    big lie of populism, 30
    COVID-19, 120, 128, 130
    reelection prospects of far-right
        party, 174–75
Italy, 44–45, 163, 173
Ivermectin, 42

Janša, Janez, 170–71
Japan, 19–20
Johnson, Boris
    and Brexit, 7
    and COP26, 105
    COVID-19, 126
    discontent with, 156
    as National Defender, 58
    as prime minister, 167–68
    and sovereignty, 88

Kalil, Isabela, 67
Kazin, Michael, 115
Kennedy, Robert F., Jr., 123

Kenney, Jason, 46
Kent, Joe, 140
Keynesianism and Keynesian
    consensus, 33, 161
Kissinger, Henry, and diplomacy, 111
Knaus, Gerald, 11
Krastev, Ivan, 121
Kurz, Sebastian, 11, 170

Laclau, Ernesto, 9
land, and nativism, 8, 9
language
    expressions and terms for insiders,
        6, 60
    populism as, 153
    and violence, 42–43
    See also speech and speeches in
        populism
Latin America, 21, 77–78
Law and Justice Party (PiS), 43, 110,
    147–48, 168
law and legal system
    abuses in Poland, 110
    subversion by populist leaders,
        xv–xvi, 52, 103–4
Lee, Frances, 34–35
left/right binary, scrambling of, 148–49
left's response to populism, 137–38, 160
left-wing populism
    and capitalism, 14
    examples, 19
    iconic form, 21–23, 66
    and socioeconomic populism, 14
    in speeches, 38
Le Pen, Marine, xvii, 44, 157, 173
Levin, Brian, 159
liberal consensus of postwar, 14
liberal democracy. See democracy
liberal order or liberal internationalism.
    See international order
Liberal Party (Canada), 45
liberals, and sovereignty, 83–84, 99

libertarian form of populism, 121
Loman, Willy (character), 3
London, Jack, 14
Lonergan, Eric, 74
López Obrador, Andrés Manuel
  (AMLO)
  description as populist, 22–23, 67,
    96–97
  and legal system, 52
  as president, 166–67
  and sovereignty, 96–98
  vaccination of children, 52–53
  "low information voters," 69–71
  loyalty, 73
Lula da Silva, Luiz Inácio (Lula), 66, 179

Macri, Mauricio, 177
Macron, Emmanuel, 44, 173
Maduro, Nicolás, 178–79
Mahbubani, Kishore, 111–12
Marcos, Ferdinand, Jr., 176
Marx, Karl, 92
Mason, Paul, 138
Matczak, Marcin, 110
media, xii, 74–75
Mexico
  anti-system vote, 163
  COVID-19, 52–53, 97–98
  debt, 97
  legal system, 52
  populism in, 22–23
  reelection prospects of far-right
    party, 166–67
  religion, 67
  sovereignty narrative, 96–98
  vaccination of children, 52–53
middle-class, 36–37, 71, 160
Ministry of Strategic Affairs (Israel), 53
moderate voters (moderate middle),
  51–52
Modi, Narendra
  COVID-19, 131–32, 135

elections and populism, 46
  as everyman, 5
  financing and use of media, 74–75
  as prime minister, 176–77
  and social media, 36
  tactics, 46
Moon Jae-in, 19
Morales, Evo, 22, 178
Morawiecki, Mateusz, 106, 147
Morgan, Jennifer, 105
mRNA vaccine technology, 132
Mugabe, Robert, 21
Müller, Jan-Werner, 11, 25–26
Murillo, Rosario, 178

Napoleon, Louis (Louis Bonaparte or
  Napoleon III), 91–92
national community, 99
National Defender, as archetype of
  populist leaders, 55, 56, 58–59
national identity, 92–95
national interest, 101, 105
nationalism
  appeal, 152
  and COVID-19, 129, 130, 134–36
  definition, xiii
  as idea, lens, or ideology, 6–8
  and national interest, 105–6
  and sovereignty, 88, 91, 93, 104, 117
national security, 106–7
nation-centered system
  danger in, 129, 134–35, 138
  replacement of international order,
    103–4, 106–7, 113–14, 117
  return of, 105–7
  and sovereignty, 113
nativism
  definition, xiii
  examples, 8–9
  as idea, lens, or ideology, 6, 8, 9
  in the US, 145
  voters for, 68

Navalny, Alexei, 88
Navarro, Peter, 111
neoliberal era, 33, 99, 161–62
Netanyahu, Benjamin, 53, 130, 156,
	174–75
Netherlands, 163, 169–70
New York Times, 70, 75
Nicaragua, 67, 164, 177–78
Norris, Pippa, 68
Northern League (Italy), 44, 45

Occupy Wall Street, 16
Operation Warp Speed, 130
opposition parties (populist opposition)
	anti-system vote in 2015–2021 by
		country, 163–65
	reelection prospects of far-right
		parties by country, 166–79
	vote for in elections, 18
Orbán, Viktor
	COVID-19 vaccines, 130, 131
	as cultural populist, 11
	extreme speech, 39–40
	funding and tactics as populist
		leader, 76–77
	and nationalism, 106
	as nativist, 8
	as prime minister, 169
	vote for, 44
Ortega, Daniel, 67, 177–78
Ortega y Gasset, José, 154, 155
ÖVP (party), 170
Oz, Dr., 122

Palestine, 30, 53
pandemic. *See* COVID-19 pandemic
pandemics, impacts of, 135
Parent, Joseph, 41
Park Geun-hye, 19
patriotism, 7–8
Peace of Westphalia, 89
Pemex, 23, 98

People's Party of Canada (PPC), 45
Peronism, 177
Peru, 165
pharmaceutical companies, and
	vaccines, 131–32
Philippines, 42–43, 75–76, 164, 175–76
Piketty, Thomas, 36
Poland
	abortion laws, 148
	anti-system vote, 164
	big lie of populism, 30–31
	and EU system, 110–11
	promises of populism, 48
	reelection prospects of far-right
		party, 147–48, 168
	speech and elections, 43
polarization, as zero-sum game, 114
political institutions, decay of, 25
political parties, vulnerability to popu-
	lism, 34–35
politics
	"darkness at noon" moment of
		populism, 139–41
	extreme speech, 38–40
	lack of dominant ideology, 115
	paranoid style, 116–17
	radical views in, 32, 35
	realignment, 33–35, 161–62
	religion in, 62–64
	rise of populism, 23, 25, 33–35,
		158–59
	seismic shifts in, 33–35
populism
	achievements, 115–17
	appeal, xiii, 4, 35–36, 152–53, 154
	belief in movement, 50
	big lie, 28–31
	causes and reasons, xiv, xviii
	core players, xix
	as cycle, 33–34
	as "darkness at noon" moment,
		139–41

definition and description, xii–xiii,
    xix, 9–10, 27
ethos, 3–4
explanations for, xii, 35
and facts, 50
as force and language, 153
forms and types, xiii–xiv, 10–17, 121
future of, 156–59
as game-changer, 114–15
goals, 9, 27–28, 32, 48, 51, 78–79,
    143
influence worldwide (in the future),
    47–48, 54
libertarian form, 121
as malaise, 25–26
opposition to, 47
puzzles in, xv–xvii
and realignment in history, 33–35,
    161–62
and "red pill," 6
as revolt of the masses, 153–55
rise in politics, 23, 25, 33–35, 158–59
as self-inflicted problem, 140
support and mobilization for,
    157–60
tactics and paths, 50–51, 61, 148, 162
and true believers, 151–53
victory for, 159–62
warning on, xx, 140, 159
weaponization, 9–10, 62–64, 114
as worldwide phenomenon, xi
See also specific topics or countries
populist governments
    anti-system vote in 2015–2021 by
        country, 163–65
    ascendance of authoritarian govern-
        ments, 18–21
    reelection prospects of far-right
        parties by country, 158, 166–79
populist leaders
    archetypes, 55–62
    capture of mainstream, 25

common characteristics, 62
concessions by, 111
and COVID-19, 118–19, 122–23,
    125–26, 128–29, 130, 134, 135–36
discontent with, 156–57
earlier lives and roles, 62
electoral victories, 144–45
as elite, 102
everyman guise, 4, 5
and global governance, 102–4
goals, xiii, 27–28, 42, 55, 142–43
hate speech to win elections, 141–44
identification globally, 18–19
law and legal system subversion,
    xv–xvi, 52, 103–4
lessons and legacy from, 141–50
and loyalty, 73
motivation of voters, 55
as noise-makers, 42
as part of the problem, xviii
and people as herd, 144
personalization of authority, 109
power, 27–28, 57, 79, 102
and premodern social forms, 143
and religion, 64, 65–67
and sovereignty, xx, 83, 87, 92,
    94–95, 99, 102–3, 113
support for, 5–6, 157–58
as "system smashers," 48, 73
track record when elected, 147
as wealthy, 73–76
winning strategy, 146–47
See also authoritarians; specific
    leaders
populist movement
    as network globally, xvii–xviii
    sources and analysis, xviii
populist opposition. *See* opposition
    parties
populist post-truth insurgency,
    description, 10
Portugal, 174

post-truth activists, role in populism, 6
post-truth politics, xvi–xvii, 49–50
postwar order, dismantling of, xx
premodern social forms and view, 143
Presidential Studies Quarterly, 39
privatization, 33
Proud Boys, xv
public policy, and shifts in politics, 32
Putin, Vladimir
 as authoritarian, 64, 65, 95–96
 on elites, 17
 financial resources, 74
 invasion of Ukraine, 96, 168–69
 as nativist, 8–9
 as president and leader, 168–69
 and religion, 65
 Russia as power, 30
 and sovereignty, 88, 95–96
puzzles in populism, xv–xvii

QAnon, 41, 60, 77

racism, xv, 8, 10–11, 12, 72
radicalization in politics, 35
Reagan, Ronald, 33
"red pill," 6
refugees, 10, 11
Reich, Wilhelm, 151–52
religion
 in politics, 62–64
 populist leaders and use in
  populism, 64, 65–67
religious traditionalism, 64
Republican Party
 and COVID-19, 125
 nativism in, 145
 and populism, 35, 48, 145
 reelection prospects, 166
 and Trump, 47, 135
 voting for, 70, 71
resentment and resentment politics,
 11–12, 14, 37, 146–47

revolt of the masses, 153–55
Ribeiro Neto, Francisco Borba, 66
rich. *See* wealthy
right/left binary, scrambling of, 148–49
right-wing populism
 dismantling of administrative state,
  107–8
 fascism use, 49–50
 influence worldwide in the future,
  47–48
 in Latin America, 22
 modern version, 50–51
 as partners in government, 158
 rise in politics, 34–36
 and sovereignty, 102–3
Russia
 anti-system vote, 164
 autocrats, 64–65
 big lie of populism, 30
 big money in populism, 74
 COVID-19 vaccine, 129
 invasion of Ukraine, xiii, 9, 96,
  168–69
 and liberal ideas, 103
 reelection prospects of far-right
  party, 168–69
 religion and history, 65
 security state apparatus, 96–98
 sovereignty narrative, 95–96
Rutte, Mark, 169–70

Salvini, Matteo, 44–45
Sandburg, Carl, 56–57
Sanders, Bernie, 14, 15, 17
Schäfer, Armin, 25
Schama, Simon, 155
Scheler, Max, 11
security (national), 106–7
Slovenia, 164, 170–71
social consensus, fracturing of, 158–59
social media, 35–36, 69, 74
social protection, 25

societal problems, 16–17, 40–41
socioeconomic populism, 13–15, 16–17
Soini, Timo, 65–66
Soros, George, 40
South Africa, 131, 132, 164
South Korea, 19, 164
sovereignty
    concept and definition, 89–91,
        98–99
    and digital world, 99
    and globalization, 83–84, 99
    in goals of populist leaders, xx, 83, 87,
        92, 94–95, 99, 102–3, 113
    loss of, 83, 94
    narrative examples, 95–98
    and national identity, 93–95
    and nationalism, 88, 91, 93, 104, 117
    as orthodoxy, 102–5
    populist form, 86–88
    power as narrative, 84, 88–89,
        99–100, 156
    reorientation examples, 84–86
    weaponization, 86–89, 93–94
speech and speeches in populism
    extreme speech, 38–40, 42–44
    goal, 43
    rise of, 38–39, 40
Springsteen, Bruce, 7
Stanley, Jason, 49–50
Starmer, Keir, 167–68
states
    and liberalism, 101
    and sovereignty, 88, 90–91, 99, 104
Swaminathan, Soumya, 122
Sweden, 18, 158
swing voters, 68–69
Syrian refugees, 11
"the system"
    and angry populist voters, 24–25
    and cultural populism, 10
    populist leaders as "system
        smashers," 48, 73

    victims of, 3–4
    See also anti-system vote

"taking the red pill," 6
technology, impact on populism,
    40–41
Thatcher, Margaret, 33
Thucydides Trap, 112
tolerance, as lost value, xvi
tribalism, 63, 72–73
Trudeau, Justin, 125
The True Believer (Hoffer), 151
true believers, and populism, 151–53
True Finns (now known as the Finns
    Party), 65–66
"true people"
    in antiestablishment populism, 16
    belief in populism, 50
    in big lie of populism, 30–31
    vs. elite, xiii, xix, 17
    in socioeconomic populism, 13
Trump, Donald
    China strategy, 109–10, 112
    and COVID-19, 118, 127–28, 130,
        135
    dog whistling, xv
    election of 2020, 43, 47, 71, 136, 166
    as everyman, 5
    executive orders, 108–9
    extreme speech, 39
    foreign policy, 109–10, 111–12
    identities as populist leader, 61–62
    impact on American life, 159
    influence on populism, xi, 46–47,
        107, 159
    and international order revamp,
        107–10
    methods and objectives, 107–8,
        109, 110
    and Mexico, 98
    reelection chances, 145–46, 166
    and Republican Party, 47, 135

and social media, 36
and sovereignty, 85, 88, 102
start in politics, 4–5
voters for, 70–71
trust, as value, 78
truth, in populism, 6
Tsipras, Alexis, 171
Tucker Carlson Tonight (TV show), 12
Turkey, 164, 175
Turkle, Sherry, 89
Twitter and tweets, 36

Ukraine
and allies, 85, 96
anti-system vote, 164
invasion by Russia, xiii, 9, 96,
168–69
reelection prospects of far-right
party, 171–72
"the undecided voters", 51–52
United Kingdom
anti-system vote, 163
big lie of populism, 29–30
populist policies, 47
promises of populism, 48
reelection prospects of far-right
party, 167–68
religion in elections, 63
seismic shifts in politics, 33
See also Britain
United Nations, 90, 106, 108
United States
anti-system vote, 163
big lie of populism, 29, 31
election of 2020, 43, 47, 71, 136,
138, 166
election of 2024, 145–46
executive orders of president, 108–9
and international order, 93
"low information voters," 70–71
nativism in, 145
promises of populism, 48

reelection prospects of far-right, 166
religion in elections, 63
rise of populism, 34
sovereignty, 85
trade deficit, 110
wealth gap and concentration, 37
"urbane tough guy" act, 66
"Ur-Fascism," xix, 12, 158
US Capitol invasion, 37, 43, 154–55
Uscinski, Joseph, 41

vaccines and vaccination. *See*
COVID-19 vaccines and
vaccination
Venezuela, 165, 178–79
violence
in fascism and populism, 51, 153–54
and language, 42–43
in populist nations, 116
vote (popular)
anti-system vote in 2015–2021
by country, 163–65
reelection prospects of far-right
parties by country, 158, 166–79
Vote Leave campaign (UK), 29–30,
149
voters (generally)
agency and preferences, 146
incentive to vote, 146
"low information voters," 69–71
moderate and undecided voters,
51–52
shift to populism, 161
swing voters, 68–69
voters for populism
and income, 70–71, 161
and populist leaders, 55, 72–73
portrait, 68–71
See also angry populist voter

Walker, Rob, 156
Wang Jisi, 112

wealth gap and wealth concentration,
37
wealthy, 36, 37, 73–76
Weathers, Charles, 20
"we the people," 61
White, Walter (character), 3
WHO, 134
workers, income and populism,
160–61
working class, 12–13, 14, 71
World Social Report 2020 (United
Nations), on inequalities, 37
WTO, 102, 108, 131

xenophobia and xenophobes, 12
Xi Jinping, 20, 112
Yakovlev, Alexander Nikolayevich,
64–65, 144

Zelensky, Volodymyr, 5, 171–72
Zemmour, Éric, xvii, 8, 173
Zoellick, Robert, 103–4
Zuma, Jacob, 21
Zürn, Michael, 25

MARILYN LAMBERT

DANIEL DRACHE is professor emeritus of political science and a senior research fellow at the Robarts Centre for Canadian Studies, York University, Toronto. His work and interests focus on understanding the changing character of the globalization narrative in its economic, social, and cultural dimensions. He has published widely on globalization, the public domain, WTO trade governance, and citizen activism, and many of his papers are available on his website. Among his books are *Defiant Publics: The Unprecedented Reach of the Global Citizen* (Polity, 2008); *Linking Global Trade and Human Rights: New Policy Space in Hard Economic Times*, edited with Leslie A. Jacobs (Cambridge University Press, 2014); *The Daunting Enterprise of the Law: Essays in Honour of Harry Arthurs*, edited with Simon Archer and Peer Zumbansen (McGill-Queen's University Press, 2017); and *Grey Zones in International Economic Law and Global Governance*, edited with Leslie A. Jacobs (UBC Press, 2018). His most recent book, co-written with A. T. Kingsmith and Duan Qi, is *One Road, Many Dreams: China's Bold Plan to Remake the Global Economy* (Bloomsbury Press, 2019).

danieldrache.com
drache@yorku.ca

ARABEL FROESE

MARC D. FROESE is Professor of Political Science and Founding Director of the International Studies Program at Burman University in Alberta, Canada. He writes about the politics of international economic law, with an emphasis on the interaction between international dispute settlement mechanisms, governmental legal strategies, and sub-national interests. Professor Froese has expertise in the integration dynamics of economic law, the relationship between regional and multilateral trade governance, and the political economy of Canadian trade policy formation. He is the author of books and articles on these and other issues, including *Canada at the WTO* (UTP, 2010) and *Sovereign Rules and the Politics of International Economic Law* (Routledge, 2018). He has published research in *The World Economy, World Trade Review, New Political Economy*, and other journals based in North America, Europe, and Asia. Research papers and some published work are available on the Social Science Research Network at http://ssrn.com/author=887299.

mfroese@burmanu.ca